CW00717912

Adventure Handbook Central Chile
1st Edition, 2002

ISBN 956-8144-00-5
Registro de Propiedad Intelectual N° 123.247

Published by
Viachile Editores
Europa 2081, Providencia, Santiago de Chile, CHILE
Ph. (+56-2) 378 37 63, Fax (+56-2) 378 37 64, e-mail: malte@contactchile.cl

Translated from German by Teresa Reinhardt, ChileHandbook@wordbridge.biz

Photography: As indicated in the margin of each photo
Cartoons: Peter Splett
Drawings: Mariano Bernal Morales (Birds), Fundación Gay (Flora), Defensores del Bosque Chileno (Fauna), Peter Splett (Fauna)
Geographic Maps: Julio Saavedra (Overview), Hugo Méndez (Detail)
Hiking Trail Sketches: Leonardo Cáceres
Design & Layout: Rafael Parada
Senior Producer: Malte Sieber

Publication deadline: November 2001

Printed by: Productora Gráfica Andros Ltda., Santiago de Chile

Orders: From the publisher's address

Website related to this book: www.trekkingchile.com

Disclaimer

Adventure Handbook
Central Chile

Franz Schubert • Malte Sieber

Cover Photo: El Morado National Park (Franz Schubert)

Table of Contents

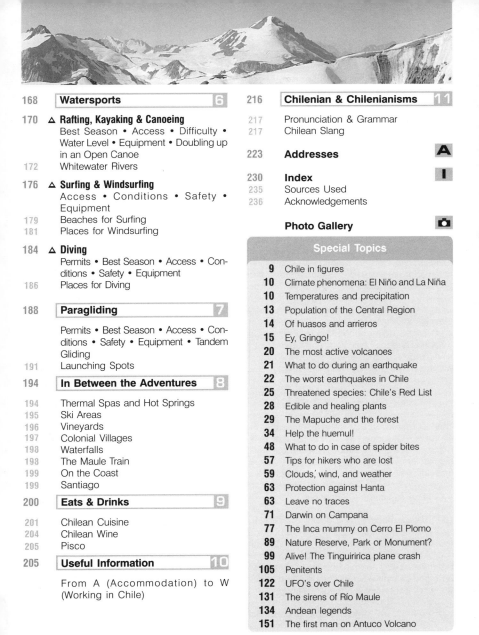

PREFACE

Those travelling to Chile will arrive by default in the center of this country that stretches over a length of 4,500 km, in its capital Santiago. But most visitors, seemingly afraid neither of the distances nor the discomforts involved, soon leave for the north or the south. By European standards, one might ask, Who would travel to northern Norway and to the Sahara, and all within three weeks?

What usually happens in this process is that the Central Region is overlooked. Which is a pity, in our opinion. While the Atacama Desert and Patagonia know how to impress the traveller, the attractions of Central Chile have nothing to be ashamed of by comparison. It is not only the political and economic heart that beats in this area between Río Aconcagua and Río Bío Bío. The fertile Central Valley between the High and the Coastal Cordilleras of the Andes is also orchard, vineyard, and breadbasket of the country all rolled in one. This is where the *huasos* and *arrieros* live, the Chilean versions of a cowboy. And only a few kilometers from the big city lights of Santiago is where nature lovers will be bowled over by a diverse fauna and flora, trekkers can climb lonely peaks, fans of whitewater kayaking find untamed rivers to explore, paragliders may admire the Andes from above, and surfers can tackle the tubes of the Pacific.

Chile is constantly being praised for the topographic and climatic contrasts that characterize the country. A closer look reveals that most of those contrasts are also to be found without leaving the Central Region. Cactus desert, savannas and the beginnings of the rainforest, active volcanoes, huge glaciers, and endless beaches – they are all available here, and they come with a sunny mediterranean climate and relatively good tourism facilities.

This book is intended exclusively as a description of this region, which is otherwise sorely neglected by guide books. We have intentionally emphasized trekking as an outdoor pursuit since 2002 is the International Year of Mountains. This is the first time that mountain tours in the central Andes are described in such detail that they should be easy to follow. Since we are ardent fans of trekking ourselves, we wanted to share our fascination with the rugged beauty of these mountains with those who feel likewise. Some of the routes described can handily hold their own when compared to the treks through the famous Torres del Paine National Park in southern Patagonia.

2002 has also been declared the International Year of Ecotourism. We wanted to do our share for this occasion by introducing the natural habitat that the traveller will find in Central Chile in detail. Promoting a conscious recognition of the species diversity and an environmentally sensitive type of tourism that respects and protects the habitats of threatened species has been an important motivation for compiling this book. It is with all that in mind that we would like to wish our readers unforgettable adventures in Central Chile.

Malte Sieber & Franz Schubert
Santiago/Talca, November 2001

Carrera a la Chilena

Malte Sieber

Nature & People
Discovering Central Chile

1

Topography
Chile in a Nutshell

The attempts at delimiting Central Chile geographically are almost as varied as the topography awaiting the traveller. For the purposes of this book, we have chosen the common definition that regards Río Aconcagua in the north and Río Bío Bío in the south as Central Chile's natural borders. According to this view, the Central Region then stretches from Los Andes to Los Angeles, or from 33° to 37.5° southern latitude, which corresponds to a length from north to south of about 500 km, with a width of 150 to 220 km from west to east, for a total of 115,000 square kilometers approx. That makes Chile's Central Region about the size of Pennsylvania, a little larger than Portugal, and a bit smaller than England. That's amazingly small, given the entire country's enormous length of 4,300 km!

But it's not size that matters! If you take a closer look, you will find that Central Chile abounds in topographic and climatic variety – from dry desert with cacti in the north, to the Mediterranean region around Santiago, to the beginnings of rainforests in the south, and from the icy High Andes to the foggy Coastal Cordillera. Due to the fact that the southern hemisphere has a smaller landmass, the climatic zones change more rapidly than on the northern hemisphere as you move south, and the seasons here are not comparable to those in Europe or North America. Glaciers and volcanoes, fertile valleys and basins, semi-desert and remnants of jungles together form the panorama of a region which in a compact area is home to the attractions of all of Chile.

In the north, Río Aconcagua has dug the last big valley running from west to east, south of which an interior basin stretching north-south called Central Valley starts. Reaching all the way to Puerto Montt between the Main and the Coastal Cordillera, it has been filled relatively level, and it is only occasionally crossed by a low chain of mountains. The big rivers running from the Andes to the Pacific have not carved distinct valleys. Their sediments fertilize the soil and provide irri-

gation water for the countless orchards, truck farms and vineyards of the Central Valley.

At the latitude of Río Aconcagua, the Cordillera de la Costa rises to over 2000 meters and remains visible as a coherent chain towards the south. It protects the Central Valley like a big screen from the influence of the ocean, reinforcing the dry continental climate of the country's center and catching the coastal fog so it drenches islands of natural vegetation on its western slope.

The Andean Cordillera reaches its greatest heights at the 33rd parallel, with Cerro Acon-cagua on the Argentinian side the highest mountain in the

Americas at 6,959 meters. The border between Argentina and Chile is dotted by several peaks (among them, Juncal, Tupungato, Piuquenes, and Marmolejo) more than 6,000 m high, before the Andes decrease in height the further south one goes. The border with Argentina runs, with a few exceptions, along the main ridge of the Andes, or the watershed between the Pacific and the Atlantic oceans.

See: Geology, page 16.

The Chilean Andes extend for 4,700 kilometers

Franz Schubert

Tongue Twisters and Bores

△ Cachapoal, Tinguiririca, Perquilauquén – many of the rivers in the Central Region do not only make formidable obstacles for hikers, but they can also be tricky tongue twisters. As is the case with many places, their names go back to the language of the aborigines, Mapudungun. While the Spanish referred to them as Araucanians, they called themselves Mapuche, people (che) of the earth (mapu). Their colorful place names indicate that they had settled the entire Central Valley when the Spanish arrived. These toponyms are usually combinations in the pattern of 'Antuco', Water of the Sun (antu = Sun, co = water, spring).

The Spanish did not get very creative; they either took over the designations of the Mapuche or they chose from a somewhat limited supply of their own, which is why there are oodles of Río Blancos, Cerro Negros or Laguna Verdes. Thus, the Rapel river is joined by three Río Claros on a stretch of only a few kilometers! Every waterfall that wants to be special is named Velo de la novia (Bridal Veil), and of course, the entire staff of the Catholic Church is present: Volcán San Pedro, Volcán San Pablo, etc.

* Estimates / ** adjusted for purchasing power parity (PPP) in international dollars
Sources used: INE, CIA Factbook, El Mercurio, UNDP

Chile in Figures (As of 2000)

Area	756,626 s q.km (w/o Antartica)
Population	15.211 million*
Population Density	20.1/s q.km*
Life Expectancy	75.7 y rs.*
Birth Rate	17.2 / 1000*
Death Rate	5.5 /1000*
Infant Mortality	9.6/1000 births *
Ethnic Groups	95% White & Mestizo, 3% Native Peoples, 2% Other
Literacy Rate	95,20%
Graoss Domestic Product (GDP)	US $ 70.0 billion (2000: +5.4%)
Per Capita GDP	US $ 4,603
Per Capita Income(PPP**, 1998)	US $ 8,787
Inflation (2000)	4,5%
Administrative Structure	Region Metropolitana (Greater Santiago) and 12 Regions, subdivided into provinces

Climate
Hot and Dry

One of the biggest plusses the Central Region has over the south of the country is a stable, sunny and dry climate for the major part of the year. While the temperatures near the Pacific Coast are moderated by the influence of the cool Humboldt current and the coastal fogs, in the Central Valley between Santiago and Chillán they can rise to close to the 40 degree (Celsius) mark in mid-summer. At night, however, it cools off pleasantly to 10 to 15 degrees. The average temperatures for the Central Region are 21 degrees in summer and 7 degrees in winter.

Within the Central Region, precipitation increases from north to south from 300 mm to over 1300 mm annually – in relationship to the distance, this is the strongest contrast in all of Chile. The precipitation chart is also impressive; the winter months of June to August are the wettest, while rain is very rare in the Central Valley and the Pre-Cordillera between November and mid-April.

See also Hiking Weather p. 58

El Niño and La Niña: The Moody Twins

△ Annual averages are one thing, but the reality of a certain season is quite another. Chile's climate has been shaken up considerably in recent years. This was caused by a phenomenon named 'El Niño' (The Kid), which appears in the Pacific area every two to nine years, with decreasing trade winds over the Pacific. These winds usually transport the warm surface waters from South America's west coast towards Australia and Indonesia, thus making room for the cool Humboldt current coming from the South Pacific. When El Niño interrupts this cycle, the ocean waters in the Eastern Pacific warm up by several degrees, and there is no precipitation in Southern Asia and Australia.

The last time the moody "Kid" appeared was 1997 causing severe storms and flooding in southern South America while huge forest fires were raging in Indonesia. In Chile, 30 people died during winter storms, and coastal fishermen suffered strong losses because the nutrient-rich (and thus fish-rich) cool current did not come.

The cusp of this phenomenon is always around Christmas, which is why Peruvian fishermen associated it with the Child Christ. El Niño was again followed by his equally moody sister, La Niña who causes the reverse effect: In 1998, there was no winter or spring precipitation, with severe consequences for agriculture as well as water and energy supplies.

Temperatures (ºC)

Location	Average Max. Temp	Average Min. Temp
	Hottest/Coldest Month	
Los Andes	Jan 31.6	Jan 12.4
	Jun 16.3	Jul 2.8
Santiago	Jan 29.4	Jan 12.4
	Jul 14.5	Jul 3.2
Valparaíso	Jan 22.5	Jan 13.3
	Aug 16.0	Aug 8.3
San Fernando	Jan 27.7	Jan 12.5
	Jul 12.2	Jul 3.7
Talca	Jan 30.8	Jan 12.7
	Jul 13.6	Jul 3.7
Concepción	Jan 18.8	Jan 11.5
	Aug 13.0	Aug 6.7

Precipitation (mm)

Location	Average Driest Month	Average Wettest Month	Hist. Annual Mean (rounded)
Los Andes	Jan 2.8	Jun 77.2	N/A.
Santiago	Jan 3.3	Jun 93.5	300
Valparaíso	Feb 2.6	Jun 134.1	N/A.
San Fernando	Dez 6.5	Jun 209	700
Talca	Jan 7.0	Jun 189.6	N/A
Concepción	Jan 10.6	Jun 182.7	1300

People
The Chilean "Race"

Latinos and Blond(e)s

For those who may hold the typical stereotype of the "Latino person", all it takes is a walk through the streets of a Chilean city to correct that image. Contrary to most South American countries, native ethnic heritage is not as strong here; more than 90% of Chile's population is fair-skinned mestizos who look more like southern Europeans. In addition to the Spanish who quickly blended with the native population, many other groups of immigrants, e.g., Italians, Germans, the French, Serbo-Croats, have left their marks in Chile in terms of hair color, facial features, and family names.

The descendants of the native population who still identify with their ethnic group only number about 500,000 today. The largest group among these by far, the Mapuche, are concentrated in the area around Temuco, and in the Central Region they are mostly found on the periphery of the big cities. Many try their luck here in the urban centers after they have been torn from their original surroundings.

Not much has remained of the rich culture and the way of life – in harmony with the earth - of the Mapuche. Over the centuries, they have been decimated by the European conquerors, exploited as cheap labor, cheated out of their land, and forced into social isolation. Unlike in other Latin American countries, being of native heritage is a disgrace in Chile – the beauty ideal is being blonde, easily confirmed by TV advertising as well as the countless artificial blondes.

Young and Catholic

At 1.2 percent annually, with a slightly falling trend, population growth is clearly below Latin American averages: Women had an average of 2.2 children in 2000; in 1982, that figure stood at 2.6. The population is very young: Three fifths of Chileans are younger than 34, with only one in ten older than 60. However, there is an aging trend caused by an increase in birth control and rising life expectancy (75.7 years).

Fernando Gómez

Three fifths of Chileans are under 34

Three quarters of the population claim they are Catholics, which is not to be confused with being a "practicing" Catholic. The Vatican cannot only boast many adherents in this former Spanish colony, but it also regards Chile as something of a last defense. The Catholic Church uses its unflagging influence in politics and society to encourage moral crusades against abortion, contraception, and divorce, with Chile being the last Christian country without divorce laws. On the other hand, Catholic congregations provide valuable social services, and during the military dictatorship, bishops and clergy had the courage to push for human rights.

In recent years, fundamentalist churches from the USA, as well as baptists and methodists, have gained ground in Chile. New Age groups have been building on the widespread belief in miracles, while protestants play only a very minor role. The few Lutheran churches were mostly founded by German immigrants.

Rich and Poor

While its adjusted per capita income of USD 8,800 places Chile among the top countries in Latin America, almost nowhere on the Continent is the "scissors" between rich and poor as wide as here. According to official statements, one out of five Chileans (3.17 million) lives in poverty, with as much as 5.7% of the population considered 'extremely poor' - and this with a poverty limit of a meagre USD 65.00 in urban, and USD 45.00 in rural areas. While corporate managers draw top salaries by international comparison, unskilled workers have to make do with the legal minimum wage of about USD 160.00/month. Professions important to society such as teachers and salaried employees, judges and policemen are chronically underpaid.

This social divide is reinforced by an educational system in which excellence can only be bought with money. While state-run schools are cheap or free, they cannot compare with the expensive schools of the middle and upper classes. Postsecondary education also comes at a stiff price to families with kids.

Life is the most difficult for those who cannot find permanent employment, or who work in the large shadow economy without a social "net". They often live in make-shift slum dwellings or in deficient public housing on the periphery of the cities, where they do not offend the eyes of the people living in the better neighborhoods. Despite these social inequities, the United Nations Human Development Index which evaluates, among other factors, life expectancy, education and income, ranks Chile among the 'highly developed' countries. In 2001, Chile ranked 39th, or third among South American countries behind Argentina (#34) and Uruguay (#37).

The Center and the Regions

Even though in theory there is lots of room in Chile, three quarters of the population – 11.3 million people – live in the Central Region which, at 115,000 square kilometers, makes up only 15% of the country's total area. This concentration is due to the favorable climate and conditions for agriculture, as well as the settlement history of the country. The Spanish pushed through the hostile desert of the north into the fertile Central Valley only to be stopped further south by the Mapuche. It was not until the end of the 19th century, when the Mapuche had been subdued, that the Chilean government started 'colonizing' the untamed regions of the south.

During the entire colonial period, Santiago formed the undisputed political and economic center of the country – a fact that has not changed to this day. Chile suffers from "centralitis". All important decisions are made in the capital; and this is where corporate headquarters, parties, associations, and the media reside. There is no getting around Santiago. The regions have but limited

Growing up in poverty: Children of the native population in the Cordillera

Malte Sieber

autonomy, and whatever timid attempts at decentralization may have been made, they soon got stuck in red tape. So it's not surprising either that 40% of all Chileans – more than 6 million people – are crammed into the Greater Santiago area.

There are major differences between urban and rural areas. While modern city dwellers wear European-style clothing, participate in the rat race, and vacation in Miami, time seems to be standing still in some of the dreamy villages of the Central Region. Here, life revolves around livestock and harvest, spurred *huasos* strut their stuff on horseback on Main Street, and now and then, you can still meet an ox cart with wooden disk wheels. However, this idyllic rural scene hides more difficult working conditions, a lack of educational opportunity, and shockingly low wage levels for the population. Small wonder then that many young people make their escape to the urban areas, where they hope to find economic opportunity. Roughly 86% of all Chileans are city dwellers at this point, and their numbers are rising.

José Pablo Jofré

La Moneda Presidential Palace in the center of Santiago

Source: Instituto Nacional de Estadísticas (2000)

Population of the Central Region (Year 2000, Estimates)

Region	Name	Capital	Area	Population	Pop.Density
V	Valparaíso	Valparaíso	16,396	1,561,400	95.2
R.M.	Metropolitana	Santiago	15,403	6,102,200	396.2
VI	Libertador Bernardo O'Higgins	Rancagua	16,387	788,800	48.1
VII	Maule	Talca	30,296	915,20	30.2
VIII	Bío-Bío	Concepción	37,063	1,936,300	52.2
Total			**115,545**	**11,303,90**	**97.8**
Chile Total			**756,096**	**15,211,300**	**20.1**

Of Huasos and Arrieros

Malte Sieber

△ Huasos – originally, sharecroppers on the peripheries of large haciendas – have over time become a Chilean character. Today, they stand for conservative traditional rural life, and a biting wit with few words wasted. While their Argentinian counterpart, the gaucho, constantly roams the Pampa, Chilean huasos represent the sedentary type of peasant who is loyal to his land owner. His typical outfit – wide-brimmed hat, a poncho with a short coat underneath, tight-fitting pants, and leather boots with huge silver spurs – is only worn on holidays or for rodeos, and his horse has been replaced by an offroad pick-up. The term 'huaso' was probably derived from the Quechua word for the back or the withers of animals. The native population was not familiar with animals for riding, so they called the Spanish on horseback 'huasu'.

The huaso's poor relation is the arriero, a herder on horseback who drives the animals to the high pastures of the Andes in the spring spending all summer with them. Because of his isolation, he is much closer to a gaucho than the huaso. *See p. 56*

See p. 56

Charles Darwin, who visited Chile in 1834, said the following about the difference between gauchos and huasos, "The Gaucho, although he may be a cutthroat, is a gentleman; the Guaso is in few respects better, but at the same time a vulgar, ordinary fellow. The Gaucho seems part of his horse, and scorns to exert himself except when on his back: the Guaso may be hired to work as a labourer in the fields. The former lives entirely on animal food; the latter almost wholly on vegetables. The chief pride of the Guaso lies in his spurs, which are absurdly large."

Patriotic and Hospitable

As varied as Chile's topography are its people. But what unites them all, from the copper miner in the north to the coastal fisherman from Chiloé, to the office worker in Santiago, to the sheep rancher on Tierra del Fuego, is a strong feeling of patriotism which reaches its most obvious pinnacle while discussing neighboring countries, or watching the national soccer team play. If, despite all the regional and social differences, there is anything like a Chilean national character, it is characterized by two extremes. On the one hand, there exists a strong inferiority complex stemming from the isolation, the traditional insignificance of the "country at the end of the world" in international terms, and the pessimistic outlook on one's own options. On the other hand, there is the pride in Chile and everything that Chileans have achieved and are achieving despite these adverse conditions, thus nurturing the extreme cult with which the (few) Chilean stars in soccer or tennis, TV or literature are celebrated.

Having to compete in a market economy has so far not been able to destroy a basic trait of Chilean mentality: their pronounced support among each other, which is not only limited to the immediate family clan, but reaches beyond that, too. One proof of that is the success of the numerous charitable campaigns of foundations or aid organizations in the social arena. This 'solidarity' is contrary to an apparent insouciance when it comes to planning and saving for the future. Chileans have learned to live with disasters (earthquakes, tsunamis, droughts, etc.) and to pick themselves up, dust themselves off, and keep going.

And finally, one absolutely has to mention the cordial hospitality of the people. Especially travelers from Europe or North America can count on being welcomed cordially and politely. *Si vas para Chile,* if you go to Chile, is how a sad folksong starts in which an exiled singer asks a traveller to take his greetings to his loved one at home. And then it goes, *Y verás como quieren en Chile/ al amigo cuando es forastero.* And you will see that in Chile they love a stranger like a friend.

Santiago street

On the Internet

www.ine.cl
Instituto Nacional de Estadísticas; statistical data on population, territory, industries, etc.; in Spanish only

www.gobiernodechile.cl
Official government information, news, links for important agencies; in Spanish, very little in English

www.odci.gov/cia/publications/factbook/geos/ci.html
CIA-Factbook: Comprehensive and relatively current information about Chile: Population, politics, economy, telecommunications, transportation, etc.; in English

www.localaccess.com/chappell/chile/
Private site of a Spanish teacher in Washington State; information about history, politics, society, culture; not very current; in English

Ey, Gringo!

△ If your hair is only half-way light-colored and you speak Spanish with a foreign accent, you will have to get used to being called **gringo** or **gringa** by the locals. It does not make any difference that this designation was originally reserved for North Americans; it is also used for the British, Germans, and Russians. Depending on the context, it can have approving, friendly or disrespectful connotations.

There are several versions of how the word 'gringo' originated. One of the more credible ones goes back to the Mexican-American War (1846-1848). The Americans' uniforms were green, and the Mexicans are supposed to have yelled, "Green, go!". Others say 'gringo' goes back to the Greek word 'griego' – since English was as difficult to learn as Greek. When Chileans cannot identify a foreign language, they say, 'Habló en gringo' (He was speaking Gringian.)

Other informal names for people from other countries, some of them pejorative:

- US-Americans: **yanqui**
- Germans: **Otto** (figure in a popular comic strip spoofing German immigrants)
- French: **franchute**
- Italians: **bachicha**
- Arabs: **turco** (also used for Lebanese, Syrians, Palestinians, etc.); **paisano**
- Peruvians, Bolivians: **cholo**

Chileans usually welcome foreign tourists; however, they dislike strong body odor and unshaved legs and underarm hair in women

Geology
Of the Forces of the Earth

What would be dearer to hikers than the earth they walk on! As in a huge open air museum, our route is bordered by craters and hardened lava flows, granite peaks and hot springs – on each tour, you will witness the explosive force of volcanism and the equally effective, but more long-term effects of erosion. Where does the energy come from that moves continents and forms mountains? Why is Chile a country of volcanoes and earthquakes? For hikers asking themselves questions like this, we have collected a few answers on the following pages – enough to while away the time on a rainy day.

Mountains
In the Minority

The world of the mountains – we seem magically attracted to it. Is that maybe because mountains present such a small minority? Less than 5% of the earth's surface are above 3000 meters. The lion's share consists of the ocean floor at a depth of 4500 meters and the continental plates with about 600 meters. It could be said that these two altitudes dominate the entire surface of the earth; the rest is all exceptions.

This phenomenon can even be simulated in a bath tub. If you float a few wooden boards on the water, you get two altitude levels, the surface of the boards and the bottom of the bath tub. Our earth consists of heavy basalt rock – the bottom of the bath tub -, with the lighter continents - the boards - floating above.

Even time is affected by the mountains. If you feel that time flies while you are vacationing in the mountains, there is now a scientific explanation for that impression. The physicist Stephen Hawking found out that time runs faster in the mountains because gravity is lower there than at sea level. This hypothesis was tested by attaching precise clocks at the bottom and the top of a tower. It was indeed found that the upper clock ran faster.

Photo: At the crater of Peteroa volcano (trekking tour 11)

The Andes
The Longest Massif

From the Caribbean to the Antarctic, the Andes rise for a length of over 10,000 km along the west coast of South America. Out of that, 4,700 km lie on Chilean soil – by comparison, the Himalayas are about 3,000 km long.

The Andes folded up about 60 million years ago in a process that continues to this day. In Chile, a lower chain formed along the coast, the Cordillera de la Costa, before the main massif, the Cordillera de los Andes. The Coastal Cordillera stretches from the Peruvian border to Chiloé Island, and then peters out in the midst of the many islands in the Pacific. It consists mainly of bedrock, while the peaks of the main massif are volcanic in origin, and the Pre-Cordillera and the longitudinal valley were predominantly formed from sediments. An interesting detail: Where the Cordillera de los Andes runs today, there used to be a basin partially filled by sea water, which is why geologists keep finding sea shells in the High Andes.

Geothermal Energy
The Everlasting Oven

The residual heat from the big bang has been used up long ago, and the friction energy created by the tides gets used up by the rotation of the earth. And yet, there are tremendous forces raging deep below us. The increase in energy inside the earth, called the geothermal gradient, averages about 0,3 °C per 10 meters. Where does this energy come from that melts rock, makes volcanoes spit fire, and moves entire continents?

Scientist have been wracking their brains to find an answer, and presently it is assumed that geothermal energy is created, at least partially, by the decay of radio-active isotopes with Uranium-238, Thorium-232 or Potassium-40 providing the necessary fuel for this giant nuclear power plant. Radioactive elements deposit easily in granitic rocks, i.e., the earth's crust. This theory is supported by the fact that the temperature in the upper layers of the earth increases faster than at great depths.

Continents
Huge Plates

At the beginning of the 20th century, the German scientist Alfred Wegener developed the theory of continental drift, according to which the original continent Pangaea broke into several parts that drifted off like ice floats thus forming our continents. However, since no one knew how to explain the forces necessary for shifting entire continents, Wegener's theory was virtually forgotten. It was not until the mid-sixties that it made its mark in a modified form. Today many areas in the theory of plate tectonics are well-understood and accepted.

Which are the forces behind this continuous movement of plates? A starting point is the decay of the radio-active isotopes mentioned above, setting free energy that melts rock. The hotter, the lower the density of the resulting magma that rises, cools, and then sinks again. This 'convection flow' is – like a big dynamo - probably also the cause of the earth's magnetism.

Rising magma usually penetrates the earth's

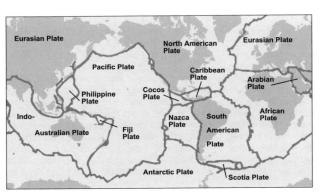

Eurasian Plate
North American Plate
Eurasian Plate
Pacific Plate
Caribbean Plate
Arabian Plate
Philippine Plate
Cocos Plate
African Plate
Indo-
Nazca Plate
South American Plate
Australian Plate
Fiji Plate
Antarctic Plate
Scotia Plate

crust at the bottom of the oceans forming long drawn-out mountain chains. Starting from those rift zones, the earth's surface is pushed apart in a process called seafloor spreading, which leads to collisions in other places. There is a total of 12 major plates moving against each other. The continents stick out of the oceans like big islands, but they are part of the plates and are thus moved with them.

Gondwana
The Continent That Broke into Pieces

It was a small province in Central India that gave its name to a landmass existing on the Southern hemisphere 500 million years ago, which consisted of what was later to become the continents of South America, Africa, Southern Asia, Austra-

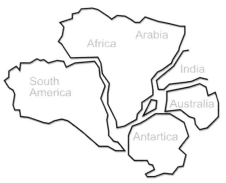

lia and Antarctica. A huge Mediterranean ocean called Thethys separated Gondwana from its northern counterpart, Laurasia.

Due to the process of plate tectonics, Gondwana fell apart into the parts we know today. First Antarctica detached itself from the original continent and, floating on liquid magma in the earth's interior, drifted towards the South Pole. During the heighday of marsupials, Australia detached itself, followed by Madagascar during the time of the first insectivores, predators, and prosimiae. When South America separated from India, which was still united with Africa, it took on its journey guinea pigs, sloths, opossums, aardvarks, and capuchin monkeys like a giant Noah's Ark. To this day, South America is drifting from Africa by about a centimeter a day.

△ The Friends of the Chilean Forest are not dreaming of the original continent, but of a future Gondwana. Their ambitious plan is having virgin forests south of the 40th parallel placed under protection worldwide. Defensores del Bosque Chileno, an environmental organization, in concert with activists in Argentina, Australia, New Zealand and South Africa, has been trying since 1994 to establish an international protected area for the preservation of the oldest forest type in the world. These Gondwana forests can be found on the southern tip of South America, on the southern island of New Zealand, in Tasmania, in some Australian provinces, in New Guinea and New Caledonia, as well as on other islands in the South Pacific. They are homes to various types of nothofagus, as well as the unique fitzroya (alerce), araucaria and dozens of other plant and animal species endemic to this area.

Volcanism
At the Ring of Fire

According to Roman mythology, a small island near Sicily was the seat of the fire god, Volcan (Vulcano). The mountains named after him form a group unto themselves which keeps reminding us of the earth's lively activity. In doing so, they reverse all the rules – they form valleys without erosion, and their lava flows dam small streams into big reservoirs. Their unpredictability has been proved time and again by the catastrophic consequences of eruptions bidding us to respect them. Chile has formed about 2,000 volcanoes during its geological history, 50 of which are still active. But why here of all places? The explanation is provided by plate tectonics.

Basically, there are two types of plate borders. While the 'rift zones' are the edges of plates that drift away from each other, and as such consist of submarine ridges made of basalt, the 'subduction zones' are edges pushing against, and either sliding above or below, each other. This is where chains of explosive volcanoes form, moving ashes and lava upwards. Only about 5% of all active volcanoes are not located on the edge of plates, but created by 'hot spots' instead.

Chile stretches along a subduction zone and is thus the perfect place for volcanoes. The Nazca plate is pushing away from the East Pacific ridge and under the South American plate at a speed of about 9 centimeters per year. As a matter of fact, the entire Pacific Ocean is surrounded by subductions and their volcanic fireworks – the famous 'Ring of Fire'.

Roughly 400 of the world's most active 500 volcanoes are bubbling along subduction zones. Contrary to rift volcanoes, here the magma is not rising from great depths, but it is generated where the subducted plate reaches a depth of 100 to 200 kilometers. The assumption used to be that the friction between both plates created enough heat to melt magma. As a matter of fact, the subducted plate has a cooling effect. What's really going on is that the melting point of the rock is lowered by water, carbondioxide, chloride and potassium minerals.

The shape of a volcano and the type of its eruption depend on the composition of the magma. In general, a high silicon dioxide content of 50 to 70% is typical for subduction volcanoes. The lower that percentage, the more fluid the magma,

so that it finally runs out like a glas of water that's too full, with far-reaching lava flows. More viscous magma, however, can be expelled in an explosive fashion, with lots of ashes. Lava and ashes will deposit in layers forming the conical shape of a stratovolcano so typical for Chile.

The Angry Patriarch

△ The Mapuche believed that the patriarch Pillán, who created the races and tribes, lived in volcanoes. Pillán was not feared, rather, he was venerated and respected. An eruption meant that he was angry at the improper behavior of one person or a group. People then would try to placate him with gifts and animal sacrifices. In the eyes of the Mapuche, Pillán was not only responsible for smoke, ashes and lava flows, but also for earthquakes, thunder, and lightning.

Other versions talk about several 'pillanes', describing them as evil spirits or devils living in the volcanoes. When a volcano rumbles, it is driving the pillanes from its depths.

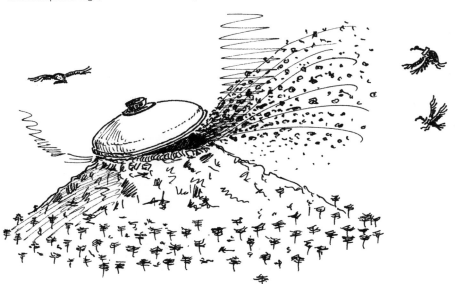

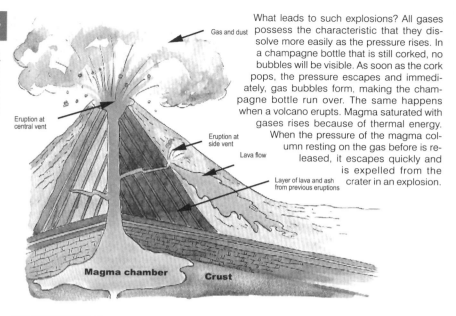

What leads to such explosions? All gases possess the characteristic that they dissolve more easily as the pressure rises. In a champagne bottle that is still corked, no bubbles will be visible. As soon as the cork pops, the pressure escapes and immediately, gas bubbles form, making the champagne bottle run over. The same happens when a volcano erupts. Magma saturated with gases rises because of thermal energy. When the pressure of the magma column resting on the gas before is released, it escapes quickly and is expelled from the crater in an explosion.

Gas and dust

Eruption at central vent

Eruption at side vent

Lava flow

Layer of lava and ash from previous eruptions

Magma chamber   **Crust**

The Most Active Firespitters in Chile

Volcano	Altitude	Region	Eruptions
Llaima	3,124 m	Araucanía	8
Villarrica	2,840 m	Los Lagos (X)	6
Antuco	2,985 m	Bío-Bío (VIII)	4
Peteroa	3,603 m	Maule (VII)	3
Lonquimay	2,822 m	Araucanía (IX)	3
Calbuco	2,015 m	Los Lagos (X)	3

(Note: The figures are stated as found in historical records. They can vary since some eruptions cannot be assigned with certainty.)

△ The earliest documented report about a volcanic eruption by the Jesuit historian Diego Rosales tells of an eight-day outbreak of Antuco volcano in 1624. Antuco (Trekking tour 23) was to be one of the top firespitters among Chilean volcanoes for the next few centuries.

The most violent among Chilean volcanoes is Villarrica. During its most recent major eruption in late December of 1971, a lavaflow 200 m wide raced down the mountain's south slope destroying villages and houses and killing more than 200. Earlier eruptions in 1948 and 1964 caused 100 and 22 casualties, respectively.

The biggest eruption of the 20th century was caused by Quizapu, a side crater of volcano Descabezado Grande (Trekking tour 14). In April of 1930, ashes were raining down so densely in the entire area from Rancagua to Chillán that the street lights had to be turned on during the day. The subterranean rumblings could be felt within a radius of 500 km, and ashes were blown all the way to Argentina, southern Brazil and South Africa.

Earthquakes
Land of Records

Sudden shaking is among the scariest phenomena on our planet. Chile is an especially popular target, due to its subduction zones mentioned above. So it's not surprising that Chileans have three words for 'earthquake': the neutral scientific term *sismo*; another word for 'harmless' tremors (that can well reach 5 or 6 on the Richter scale): *temblor*, and finally a terror-filled word for the big one: *terremoto*.

In 1960 at Valdivia, the strongest earthquake ever registered a 9.5 on the Richter scale (due to its magnitude, this value was not measured directly but instead simulated later on a computer.) This *terremoto* on the night of May 22 devastated large parts of southern Chile, and combined with the resulting tsunami which flooded large coastal areas, killed 5000.

90% of quakes are tectonic in nature caused by a relief of tension in the earth's crust. The epicenter lies above the focus of the earthquake, radiating the vibrations over the surface.

The American scientist Charles Francis Richter (1900-1985), after whom the Richter scale is named, once said that only fools, liars, and charlatans tried to predict earthquakes. However, scientists have kept searching for a way to know

when quakes are about to happen. Despite the fact that some progress has been made, none of the procedures developed so far can tell time, epicenter, or magnitude of a quake with any great accuracy. Chile is even missing some of the basic requirements; there is not even a network of sensor stations covering the entire country.

What to Do During an Earthquake

⚠ When hiking, you need to be prepared for mud slides and falling rocks, but any city might present more dangers. A few basic rules to follow:

- Stay calm, don't panic.
- Turn off electricity, water, and gas mains.
- Stay away from windows; open doors.
- As a rule, you will be safer inside a house than in front of it.
- Take cover under door frames or massive furniture.
- When evacuating, watch for falling debris.
- Follow instructions of emergency personnel.
- Do not use lighter or matches since there might be gas leaks. Have flashlights available.
- Have a portable radio ready.
- Do not use elevators.
- Outside, stay away from buildings and power lines.
- When driving, avoid bridges; don't leave your vehicle.

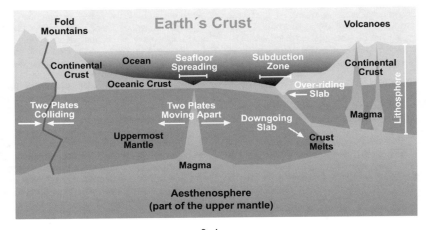

Earth's Crust

Fold Mountains · Volcanoes · Continental Crust · Ocean · Seafloor Spreading · Subduction Zone · Continental Crust · Oceanic Crust · Over-riding Slab · Two Plates Colliding · Two Plates Moving Apart · Downgoing Slab · Magma · Lithosphere · Uppermost Mantle · Crust Melts · Magma · Aesthenosphere (part of the upper mantle)

Earthquakes in Chile

△ Statistically, a very big earthquake "should" happen every 86 years in the Central Region of the country. After the last big ones in the Valparaíso – Santiago area (1971 – 1985), there should now be a long intermission... statistically.

The Worst Quakes of the 20th Century

Year	Epicenter	Magnitude	Deaths
1906	Valparaíso	8.6	20,000
1922	Vallenar	8.4	880
1928	Talca	8.4	300
1939	Chillán	8.3	28,000
1943	Illapel	8.3	12
1949	Punta Arenas	7.5	6
1960	Valdivia	9.5*	5,000
1965	La Ligua	7.5	280
1971	Valparaíso	7.5	85
1985	Valparaíso	7.9	177

* Computer calculation

Sources: ONEMI, National Earthquake Information Center, USA

Richter

The Richter or magnitude scale allows the force of an earthquake to be measured objectively with instruments. The Richter scale is open only in theory, since in practice, the deformation energy of the earth is limited thus making a quake above 9 next to impossible.

Mercalli

The 12-point Mercalli or intensity scale measures the amount of damage on the earth's surface. Step 1 describes quakes that only register on instruments. 4 means major shaking of buildings, and 8 generates major building damage. 12 is reserved for quakes resulting in total devastation and various damage to the land.

Erosion
One Bit at a Time

The 'constructive' force of volcanism is opposed by a 'deconstructive' one - erosion. On a river, you can hear all sorts of noises – besides the rushing of the water, there is also the rumbling of rocks colliding. Year in, year out, such a small mountain stream moves about 30 cubic meters of rock.

The following math problem can make us think about the finiteness of even the highest mountains. Given a height of 1500 m and a slope of 3 km length, a small mountain consists roughly of 3000 by 3000 by 1500, i.e., about 13.5 billion cubic meters of rock. A single small mountain stream would erode the entire mountain in about 500 million years. If you take into account that a mountain will be attacked by more than one stream, as well as rain, wind, slides and glaciers, our model mountain's lifespan is only a few million years.

Glaciers
Andean Coolers

The Central Andes are topped by about 1,000 square kilometers of eternal ice on Chilean territory. Some of these glaciers are covered by morain drift. At 12 km, the longest one of this kind is Cachapoal glacier near Rancagua. Where did those masses of ice come from?

When snow falls in the winter, you can often recognize the hexagonal shape of the snowflakes with your bare eyes. When freezing after a short rise in temperature, this powder snow turns into so-called 'firn'. By a process of repeated thawing and freezing, a hard snowcover forms, in which the spaces between the individual snowflakes have been filled with water or simply compressed. If this process goes on for years, this mass will become denser and denser, and finally turn into ice.

Real glacier ice – as opposed to the ice on bodies of water – is composed of ice in the form of spheres measuring from millimeters to centimeters. The air bubbles trapped during freezing initially make the ice look milky. Over time, these bubbles will dissolve from pressure which gives the ice its typical bluish cast.

La Paloma glacier in the Yerba Loca valley

The snowline in Central Chile is around 1,000 meters in the winter, depending on the region. In most places, the snow melts completely during the summer, but there is eternal snow in the highest altitudes and on the shaded side, in this case the south-facing slopes, of mountains. This area is called the feeding zone, as opposed to the melting zone below where during the course of the year, more snow melts than accumulates. At extreme altitudes, there is no formation of glaciers, either. The snow crystals are simply blown about since the sun cannot make them stick together.

With its crystalline structure, ice is nothing other than supercooled liquid, and so it can flow. Using a marker, it is easy to measure the speed of a glacier. While some, e.g. in the Arctic or in the Patagonian icefield, move several meters a day, most glaciers move a lot more slowly.

But flow speed does not equal growth. Ice can move fast, but it can melt even faster at the bottom. Due to its lack of flexibility, the ice can break when travelling over ground that is not level, creating dangerous crevasses. On its way downhill, the ice 'scrapes' the rock around it and deposits the material in the valley. That's where the iceflow creates a dam over time, the so-called terminal moraine. When the glacier recedes, this natural dam fills with melting water and forms a glacier lake. Fine silt flows into the lake as glacier milk, settling on the bottom as light-colored mud. Together with sunlight, these sediments amplify the natural color of the water thus creating the gorgeous turquoise color of the lake.

Receding glaciers leave U-shaped valleys, while rivers carve out V-shaped ones.

Despite the inhospitable conditions on the ice, some organisms manage to survive there. One of them is a worm filled with 'antifreeze', which gnaws through the ice in search of encapsulated edibles. Fleas congregate in small lentil-shaped groups in icemelt puddles. In Chile, you can also frequently observe a species of black earwigs on glaciers.

On the Internet

www.geo.cornell.edu/geology/cap/CAP_WWW.html
Cornell University research projects on the geology of the Andes; in English

http://geothermal.marin.org/geomap_1.html
Detailed information from the Geothermal Education Office, California; in English

www.extremescience.com/PlateTectonicsmap.htm
Easy-to-understand scientific introduction to plate tectonics; in English

http://vulcan.wr.usgs.gov/Volcanoes/Chile/framework.html
Descriptions of a few Chilean volcanoes, with links; in English

www.geo.mtu.edu/~boris/Chilehome.html
Two Chilean volcanologists about a number of southern Chilean volcanoes; in English

www.neic.cr.usgs.gov/neis/eqlists/10maps_world.html
List of the world's worst earthquakes since 1900; in English

www.nativeforest.org/campaigns/gondwana/
The Gondwana Network; in English

http://pubs.usgs.gov/prof/p1386i/chile-arg/contents.html
Scientific articles on glaciers in Chile and Argentina; in English

www.glacier.rice.edu
All you need to know about glaciers and ice, from Rice University; in English

Environmental and Species Protection
Preserving Diversity

The word 'eco' goes back to a Greek word signifying as much as 'house'. Ecology is the science of the interdependence of all living beings and their environment. Meanwhile, the term 'ecological', when used in one sentence with environmental and species protection, has changed its once valuefree meaning. For even in a monoculture of pine trees, which has replaced the natural forest with its abundance of species, a few species will live in their own ecological equilibrium. The 'value' of nature is much better described using the term biodiversity which states the number of species in an ecological system.

Species preservation is not an invention of the Greens; it can already be found in Genesis 6 and 8, *You are to bring into the ark two of all living creatures, male and female, to keep them alive with you.* Noah's Ark had neither First nor Business Class, and as far as life after flood was concerned, the plan was, *Bring out every kind of living creature that is with you – the birds, the animals, and all the creatures that move along the ground – so they can multiply on the earth and be fruitful and increase in number upon it.*

Many species had survived the boat trip and were able to propagate quite happily until just recently. But meanwhile, humans can boast of being able to eradicate species which took nature thousands of years to create, at a rate of over 70 a day.

Chile's natural landscape has not escaped this practice unscathed. Large parts of formerly virgin forests have been clearcut, and even the proud national beasts of the country, the condor and the huemul, are threatened in their existence. The mentality of the conquerors, who held that

Virgin forests have become rare

nature existed to be dominated and exploited by man, is still dominant in many heads today. Consequently, logging companies and fishing fleets are able to proceed without regard for nature. Even though cutting protected tree species is against the law and punishable, there are not enough effective controls in many sparsely populated and difficult to access areas of the country.

A number of environmental organizations, under among them the NGO Comité Nacional Pro Defensa de la Fauna y la Flora (CODEFF), have been trying for years to raise the consciousness of Chileans for the preservation of their natural environment – a difficult task in a country where social problems not only abound, but where their solution seems all too often in direct opposition to environmental protection. How do you explain to a small forest owner that he should look at his property as capital and practice sustainable methods, if he is used to just going in and clearcutting by the cubic meter every time he has financial problems?

1

On the Internet

www.chiper.cl/reports/index.asp?r=5
On the diversity of species, how they are threatened and protected in Chile; in English

www.codeff.cl
Site of the Chilean environmental NGO Codeff; in Spanish only

Threatened Species: Chile's Red List

Malte Sieber

Guanaco

△ Chile's Red List distinguishes between quasi extinct species *(extinto)*, those threatened by extinction *(en peligro de extinción)*, vulnerable *(vulnerable)* and rare species *(raro)*. In the Central Region, among the mammals that are threatened by extinction are:

- **Huemul** *(Hipocamelus bisulcus)*; Andean deer, *see p. 33*
- **Guanaco** *(Lama guanicoe)*: Llama species, *see p. 32*
- **Gato Colocolo** *(Felis colocola)*: Small feral cat
- **Cururo** *(Spalacopus cyanus maulinos)*: Rat species, *see p. 36*
- **Chinchilla Chilena** *(Chinchilla lanigera)*: Rodent, quasi extinct
- **Vizcacha** *(Lagidium viscacia)*: Rodent, *see p. 36*
- **Huillín** *(Lutra provocax[1])*: Nutria, an endemic river dweller, almost extinct because of its fur

As for birds, the Red List is headed by, among others:

- **Pingüino de Humboldt** *(Spheniscus humboldti)*: Penguin, *see p. 46*
- **Halcón peregrino** *(Falcus peregrinus)*: Peregrine falcon, *see p. 44*
- **Loro tricahue** *(Cyanolyseus patagonus byroni)*: Parrot species, *see p. 43*
- **Carpintero negro** *(Campephilus magellanicus)*: Black woodpecker, *see p. 43*

Among the most endangered trees and shrubs of the Central Region are:

- **Ciprés de la cordillera** *(Austrocedrus chilensis)*: Chile cedar; heavily used for its extremely hard wood.
- **Palma chilena** *(Jubaea chilensis)*: Chilean palm tree, *see p. 70*
- **Ruil** *(Nothofagus alessandrii)*: Nothofagus species of the Coastal Cordillera; extremely rare now. Its water resistant wood was popular for boat building.
- **Belloto del Norte / del Sur** *(Beilschmiedia miersii / berteroana)*: Evergreen rugged sclerophyll *(see page 132)*.
- **Queule** *(Gomortega keule)*: Evergreen endemic deciduous tree with yellow fruit; a victim of clearcutting in the Coastal Cordillera, like ruil.
- **Pitao** *(Pitavia punctata)*: Evergreen deciduous tree of the Coastal Region similar to canelo.
- **Michay Rojo** *(Berberidopsis corallina)*: Almost extinct brush with coral-colored blossoms.

[1] Listed sometimes also as Lontra provocax

25

Malte Sieber

Flora
False Friends

Almost half of the area of present-day Chile is supposed to have been covered by forests before the Spanish arrived. The Spanish historian Alonso de Ercilla still thought that the densely forested areas of the home of the Mapuche would never be discovered and conquered – but he was wrong. After less than 500 years, the major part of the original vegetation has disappeared, being made into timber for construction, fences or charcoal, or it was simply burnt as firewood. As the result of such rape, the riparian forests are almost entirely gone, and virgin forest is only to be found in remote areas of the Pre-Cordillera as well as in some National Parks and preserves.

Since the conquistadores were not familiar with the endemic tree and plant species, they used European or other colonies' examples in naming them. 'Hazelnut' (Avellano) or 'cinnamon tree' (Canelo) have, like many other plant species, the same names as European cousins because of superficial similarities but botanically speaking, they have little in common. Many of the names that the Mapuche used for plants have been preserved, too.

Because of the great differences in climates in Central Chile, an unusually diverse fauna has developed here. The individual vegetation zones overlap like tongues from north to south. For example, the Quisco cactus has its southernmost habitat in the Cordillera between Río Tinguiririca and Río Teno; in the Central Valley, however, it occurs south of Talca. And the sclerophylls typical for the Santiago area coexist from Río Tinguiririca for a considerable distance with the beginnings of the nothofagus forests, which in turn slowly transit into the Valdivian rainforest further south. We have adopted the distinction between coast, longitudinal (Central) valley, and Cordillera as made by the Chilean botanist Adriana Hoffmann.

On the Internet

http://misdb.bpa.arizona.edu/~guoxiang/chile/biod/webdesc.html
Data bank 'Flora of Chile', with photos and info about endemic species; in English

The Coast

Ruil

In the coastal area, the virgin forests have been almost completely replaced by monotonous plantations of Monterey pine (*Pinus radiata*) and the fast-growing Australian eucalyptus. These tree species are not only extremely sterile and quick to burn, but they also leave the soil depleted after few generations. On top of all that, Chilean forestry companies still prefer clear-cutting for harvesting wood, thus scarring the landscape over and over.

Peumo

Remnants of the original vegetation have survived in hard to access gorges and in some nature preserves, such as **ruil** *(Nothofagus alessandrii)*, **peumo** *(Cryptocarya alba)* or **belloto del norte** *(Beilschmiedia miersii)*. On the slopes of the rocky coast, one can find **yelmo** *(Griselinia scandens)*, various **bromelia** species (e.g., **chagual**, *Puya chilensis*), **bellflower** *(lobelia tupa)* and **francoa appendiculata**.

Belloto del Norte

In very few places in the Coastal Cordillera, small stands of the **Chilean palm tree** (*Yubaea chilensis*, *see p. 70*) are left. Out of the roughly 170 cactus species occuring in Chile, only few grow on the coast of Central Chile, such as the spherical *Neoporteria subgibbosa* with its pink blooms, and *Echinopsis litoralis*.

Longitudinal (Central) Valley

Due to the same climatic conditions, the sclerophyll vegetation originally found here resembles the fauna of the Mediterranean. Thanks to the mild winters, trees and bushes need not shed their leaves which are protected against the long dry summers by being hard and resistant. Since many species have adapted to the climatic conditions in the same way, they look alike superficially and are hard to tell apart by the layperson. The sclerophyll vegetation is especially endangered by the fact that it shares its habitat with two thirds of the Chilean population and consequently, there are only occasional remnants of those species to be found.

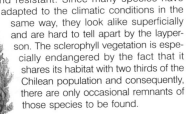
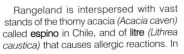

Litre

Rangeland is interspersed with vast stands of the thorny acacia *(Acacia caven)* called **espino** in Chile, and of **litre** *(Lithrea caustica)* that causes allergic reactions. In

Chagual

Quillay

Neoporteria curvispina

Crucero

Roble

Ñirre

Avellano

some places, the relatively frequent espino gives the Central Valley the character of a savanna. Protected by this tree, other native plants such as buckthorn (**crucero**, *Colletia spinosa*), the long-leafed brush **huañil** *(Proustia ilicifolia)* and the vine **voqui negro** *(Mühlenbeckia hastulata)* will grow. Also quite frequent is the soapbark tree (**quillay**, *Quillaja saponaria*), whose bark is made into soaps and shampoos, as well as **boldo** *(Peumus boldus)* with its considerable healing powers.

As for **cacti**, you will find *Echinopsis chilensis*, the barbed-wire *Neoporteria curvispina* and **colla** *(Opuntia berteri)*.

Pre-Cordillera

The steepness with which the Central Valley rises up to the Andes causes a quick succession of different plant societies. Above the sclerophyll zone of the Central Valley follows the summer forest area, which spreads towards the south characterized by several varieties of Southern beech. The designation **Southern beech** is used for the nothofagus family with 36 known varieties in Argentina, Chile, New Zealand, New

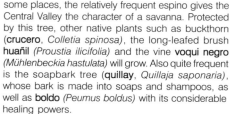

Boldo

Coihue

Tasty and Healing

Canelo

△ For the Mapuche, the diverse vegetation of their home served as grocery store and pharmacy alike. The fruits of the trees formed an important basis of their nutrition, especially the 'piñones' of the **araucarias**, which don't start until south of Los Angeles. Among the edible fruits of the Central Region are the berries of **arrayán, luma**, and **maqui**, which ripen towards the end of the Summer and make a delicious snack for hikers. These berries are also turned into a good-tasting liqueur. With some luck, you will also find the yummy small wild **strawberries**. A refreshing salad can be made from the stems of the large coltsfoot leaves of the southern rainforest, called **nalca** or **pangue** in Chile, as well as from the young tips of the bamboo-like **colihue**. In late summer, the blackish-brown nuts of the **avellano** tree can be cracked. The forests also harbor many edible mushroooms; the locals especially like the light-colored spheres of **digüeñe** *(Cyttaria espinosae)*, which grows as a parasite on nothofagus trees in the spring.

The Machis (wise women) knew about the healing powers of all plants, and in many cases, those were later proven scientifically. Thus, the important ritual function of the **canelo** tree for the Mapuche is related to its diverse therapeutic powers – the leaves are turned into a stomach tea, the boiled bark is taken against scurvy and for healing wounds, and the juice helps against arthritis. In most cases, specific fatty acids, tannins or vitamins in the plant are responsible for its healing power, such as in **arrayán, laurel**, and **radal**, with whose leaves and bark a number of ailments are treated. Especially popular among the locals are stomach teas with leaves from the **boldo** and **matico** trees, as well as the small plants **ruda, paico**, and **llantén**.

△ The 'People of the Earth', the Mapuche, have an intimate relationship with the natural forest. Trees are not only regarded as sources of food and healing and therefore protected, but they are also respected as living beings on the same level as humans. While the Valley Mapuche make a carved tree trunk with seven magical steps *(rehue)* the center of their ceremonies, the Pehuenche, the aboriginal inhabitants of the Andes, place a living araucaria *(pehuen)* on their meeting place for the celebration.

In the cosmic vision of the Mapuche, not only living things but also rocks, soil, and water possess a soul. All elements are connected among each other and with humans according to a pre-determined order; whatever happens in nature will also happen to humans. Nature is revered like a loving mother, called Pachamama among the tribes in the High Andes, or Ñukemapu by the Mapuche. Love and respect are shown to her, among other ways, by giving a small portion of every drink or meal to the earth.

For the Mapuche, trees are like antennae which receive messages 'from above' and pass them on through their trunk to people. The old wise people were able to read or recognize in the bark of foiye (canelo) – the sacred tree of the Mapuche – or of trihue (laurel) the wishes of the gods every morning, and they would know how the day would turn out.

Ciprés de la cordillera

Caledonia, New Guinea, and Tasmania. The 10 varieties occuring in Chile – three of them evergreens – are all endemic. Among the evergreen ones is **coihue** or **coigüe** *(Nothofagus dombeyi)*, which grows up to 40 m tall, with small dark-green leaves arranged in layers. The stately **roble** *(Nothofagus obliqua)*, however, will turn yellow to red in the fall just like the elfinwood-like **ñirre** *(Nothofagus antarctica)*, which grows along the treeline.

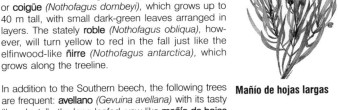

Mañío de hojas largas

Copihue

In addition to the Southern beech, the following trees are frequent: **avellano** *(Gevuina avellana)* with its tasty "hazelnuts" , the long-leafed, yew-like **mañío de hojas largas** *(Podocarpus saligna)*, the myrtle tree **arrayán** *(Luma apiculata)* with its typical reddish bark, **maqui** *(Aristotelia chilensis)* with its yummy fruit resembling blueberries, **maitén** *(Maytenus boaria)* and the Chilean cedar (**ciprés de la cordillera**, *Austrocedrus chilensis)*. Along the water thrives the "cinnamon tree" **canelo** *(Drimys winteri)* which carries its lancet-shaped, dark-green leaves on reddish branches.

Chilco

In the shade of the forest, several flowers hide, among them the **lily of the Incas** *(Alstroemeria)*, the (red or white) Chilean bellflower (**copihue**, *Lapageria rosea)* which is the national flower, the edible *gunnera*, various ferns, and the red-flowering hardy fuchsia **chilco** *(Fuchsia magellanica)*. As for cacti, you will occasionally find the prickly spheres of *Eriosyce sandillon*.

Arrayán

High Andes

Alstroemeria

Siete Camisas

Above the treeline, which runs at max. 2,000 m depending on the orientation of the slope, lies the area of the High Andes. In the transition area you will find the following: the bamboo species **colihue** *(Chusquea cumingii)*, which can form dense thickets further south, the flaming red flowers of "Crimson Spire" (**siete camisas**, *Escallonia rubra)* and various **barberries** *(Berberis)*. The dry lava and scree areas support only sparse growth, but along the streams the vegetation flourishes.

The most frequently found flowers in the High Andes are: **orchid** *(Chlorea)*, **slipper flowers** *(Oxalis)*, **lily of the Incas** *(Alstroemeria pulchra)*, stinging **nettles** *(Loasa tricolor)*, the brightly colored **butterfly flowers** *(Schizanthus)*, the climbing vine **clavel del campo** *(Mutisia)* with red or yellow blossoms, the spiky shrub **hierba negra** *(Mulinum spinosum)*, **azorella**, which forms cushions, and various compositae. At even higher altitudes, you might spot the rosettes of **viola volcánica**, cushions of white-blooming *nassauvia revoluta*, **añañuca de la cordillera** *(Rhodophiala rhodoliorion)* from the amaryllis family, another **lily of the Incas** *(Alstroemeria spathulata)* and various lichens.

In some areas above the treeline, the cactus species *Neoporteria curvispina* and *Neoporteria castanea* can be found. In the highest mountains, the rare *Austrocactus hibernus,* and on volcanic rock, the groundcover-like cactus species *Maihuenia poeppigii* and *Maihuenia philippi* make their home.

Chlorea

Schizanthus

Viola volcánica

Clavel del Campo

Colihue **Añañuca de la Cordillera** **Maihuenia poeppigii**

Franz Schubert

Fauna
Unique and Threatened

Squeezed out by civilization and decimated by poachers, the originally diverse and often endemic fauna has sought shelter in protected areas and inaccessible mountain regions. If you are traveling on foot or horseback through the Andes, you might occasionally be rewarded with a glimpse of it.

In the vicinity of Chillán volcano, there is still a herd of the skittish deer, the Chilean national animal, the **huemul**. With much luck, you will come across the **vizcacha**, a hare. Every now and then, small herds of **guanacos** will cross the Andes from Argentina. Even **foxes** are hard to see. Even rarer is the big cat **puma**, which catches small mammals, and occasionally also a sheep or two. The dwarf deer **pudu** is at home only in forests with dense bamboo thickets. On rivers, you might observe **nutria**, Chile's largest rodent. On the coast, **sea lions** are found in a number of places, and sometimes even **penguins**.

The avian world is especially well-represented in Chile with 439 species. When hiking, one can often observe the majestic **condor** or flocks of **burrowing parrots**. Even a short walk on a beach will yield **oystercatchers, pelicans, sandpipers** and many other shorebirds. Everywhere in Chile you will find the noisy **lapwing,** the soaring **vulture,** the raptor **chimango,** as well as a number of **egrets** by the rivers. Around human habitations, you can often see **colibris** flitting around in search of nectar, the long-tailed **meadowlark,** and the Chilean **house-wren,** which will nest even in the smallest crack in a wall.

Photo: Flamingos are a rare sight in Central Chile

Mammals

Of the 91 species of mammals in Chile, 16 are endemic, i.e. they only occur here. Most also live in the Central Region. We have selected the most unusual and interesting ones.

Guanaco • Lama guanicoe
The Elegant Mountain Camel

A long time ago, not only the South American aboriginal population came to America across the Bering Strait, but also a number of animals. With camels, it was the other way round. They migrated from America to Asia, where they adapted to the climatic conditions, became bigger, and formed humps.

There are altogether four kinds of camels or llamas living in the Andes: the wild vicuñas and guanacos, as well as llamas and alpacas, which were domesticated about 5000 years ago. While vicuña, llama and alpaca are limited to the Peruvian-Bolivian-Chilean Highlands, guanacos have their range all the way down to Tierra del Fuego. In Central Chile, these elegant animals can only be observed – and only with lots of luck – while hiking in the high valleys of Azufre and Los Cipreses rivers; usually, they only cross the border occasionally from the neighboring, more sparsely populated Argentinian area.

Chile's largest wild mammal on land can also survive at above 4,000 m altitude. What makes that possible is above all, its larger-than-average size heart and its thick brown fur. It feeds on grasses, leaves, and buds, can survive for a long time without water, and even drinks saltwater.

These alert animals warn each other with piercing cries when they sense danger. Guanacos usually live in 'families' with one male, several females and young. The male uses his scat to mark his territory, and he chases away rival males. The females with their calves are free to leave and join another group. Occasionally, groups consisting of male loners only have been observed.

The female will lie down on the ground on her belly during coitus, and after a gestation period of up to 360 days, she will bear one calf with a birth weight of 8 to 15 kg. It is weaned at 8 months, and driven away by the male leader at about one year of age.

From a Goose to a Penguin

△ South America was conquered at a time when the Catholic Church in the conquerors' home countries was not only the deciding instance in matters of faith and politics, but also in science – however, a very limited version thereof which was mainly based on the interpretation of the Holy Scriptures. The never-before-seen animals encountered in the New World were not easily reconciled with the legend of Noah's Ark. Thus, the life forms in America were simply declared to be emigrated descendants of survivors of the Great Flood. Even Sir Walter Raleigh called them 'climatically caused variations' of Old World species.

For simplicity's sake, the Spanish often named the endemic animals of Chile (the ones only occuring here) after ones they knew from their home country, and with similar looks. In many cases, these misnomers were later corrected. Thus, the South American hippopotamus became the tapir, and the Magellan goose turned into the penguin. Despite that, many Old World names remain for the fauna of Chile.

Pudu • Pudu pudu
The Little Shy One

The two Chilean deer species can be distinguished easily by their size alone: the stately huemul and the pudu, at 80 cm max. the smallest deer in the world.

Of the two existing pudu species, only the *pudu pudu* occurs in Chile. Because of their isolated lifestyle in dense forests, little is known about them. They live in areas from the coast to about an altitude of 3,000 m, and they prefer humid regions with dense bamboo growth where it is easy for them to hide. Ideal conditions are provided by the Chilean lowland forests; however, those have mostly been destroyed. No successful count has been done so far, but it is assumed that the pudu is not immediately threatened by extinction.

If you will see a pudu at all, it will be as a solitary animal. Ruminants like all deer, they feed on fruit, ferns, brush, and sprouts. In doing so, they roam slowly, nibbling on everything and checking their surroundings carefully all the time. The males have a small set of antlers, like all deer, which

they use as a weapon against rivaling males in the fall. It will be dropped later in order to form again the next spring. After a gestation period of about six months, the female gives birth to usually one calf only.

Among the pudu's enemies are not only pumas and foxes, but increasingly also feral dogs.

Huemul • Hippocamelus bisulcus
The Threatened National Animal

The huemul's name is derived from the Mapuche term *huemin*, which means as much as "follow each other". Supposedly, these light brown animals with the long ears are in the habit of walking single file. The first reports from the Spanish emphasized repeatedly how trusting the huemul were. They approached humans with hardly any shyness and could be caught by hand. This was also their downfall, since they competed for food with the sheep driven further up into the mountains all the time. So the "pests" were shot and killed unscrupulously and, in addition, they were decimated by the parasites introduced, until they were considered extinct – also in Central Chile.

Originally, huemuls were living all over Chile in two species, the Northern and the

Southern huemul. They live in varied terrain with steep slopes and brush vegetation. Contrary to the legend of the single-file march, the huemul leads a fairly unsociable life; it usually occurs alone or in nuclear families with a male, a female and a calf. The male carries a simple pair of antlers with only one branch-off. Just as with pudus, the female gives birth to one calf after a gestation period of six to seven months.

Help the Huemul

△ Larger herds of huemul have only survived in some areas of Patagonia. With money donated by the Zoologische Gesellschaft Frankfurt and The Nature Conservancy, the Chilean Organization for Environmental Protection CODEFF has been trying to preserve the national animal in Central Chile, too. So a protected area was established on the northern side of Nevados de Chillán volcano (Trekking tour 22) providing a refuge for the last 20 huemuls. This 10,000 hectare preserve named "Huemules de Niblinto" is considered a 'high biodiversity area' with an unusually high number of species.

The biggest hurdle for a lasting protection of the huemul is presented by the distances existing between the isolated populations; small groups are not able to procreate any longer. The preservationists would like to establish a 'biological corridor' in Central Chile in order to facilitate genetic exchange. They want to buy up additional areas or persuade the owners to join the initiative.

Zorro • Fox • Canis
The Loner

The big zorro culpeo (*Pseudalopex culpaeus*), as well as the somewhat smaller grey fox, zorro chilla (*Canis griseus*) both live in Central and Southern Chile. They prefer to feed on rodents, birds, birds' eggs and snakes. In comparison with other canids (e.g., wolves), the culpeo does not live in packs. Next to its anus, it has a sack that can be emptied with precision for the purpose of marking its territory.

Foxes bear young once a year. For that purpose, the female digs a cave or takes over an existing one. After a gestation period of 60 days, she gives birth to up to six pups who will also have six teats at their disposal.

Foxes can generally transmit rabies.

Puma • Felis concolor
An Encounter of the Scary Kind

Your chance of seeing a puma on a hike is very slim, but if you should 'be so lucky', you might also be sorry. A puma can easily tip the scale at 100 kg. However, this big feline will only attack humans when pushed into a corner. Never turn and run! First of all, any puma is definitely faster than you, and secondly, you will trigger its prey instinct. Theoretically, you are supposed to make yourself as tall as possible; maybe it would help to put one's backpack on one's head...

Originally, the puma lived all over America, from the north of Canada to Tierra del Fuego, from the rainforest to the semi-desert, but it has always avoided human settlements. On young

pumas, the pattern on the head is all black dots. All that's left over from the youthful markings are a black dot on the upper lip, black backsides of the ears, and a black tail tip.

One of the puma's most important preys is the pudu. Pumas hunt alone, and they can easily control an area of 50 square kilometers. Fights with other pumas are rare, and they are usually about a female, who can bear two to four young.

Chingue • Skunk • Conepatus chinga
Full Blast Against the Enemy

Skunks, which occur exclusively on the American continent, are easily recognized by their black fur with white stripes, small head with pointed snout and the long claws. If you are still not quite sure whether it really is one, you will find out when you make acquaintance with its spraying powers. Skunks have perfected their anal glands to such an extent that they can deliver a vile-smelling load of fluid to an adversary over a distance of several meters. When a skunk approaches on stiff legs and with its tail raised, it is high time to beat a retreat. Especially photographer's clothes are at risk if they try to get a close-up: After making contact with what the Guinness Book lists as the fluid that smells the worst you might as well toss your fancy outdoor coat or pants.

Enemies such as pumas or foxes are easily discouraged by that kind of defense. Birds, however, do not have a sense of smell that is as well-developed as that of predators; thus eagles and owls present a much greater danger to skunks. If they get hit in the eye, however, they can temporarily go blind.

This night-active animal is a carnivore that hunts insects, small mammals, birds and reptiles, but also eats fruit and eggs. You are most likely to see them as roadkill in the Central Region; otherwise you need a considerable portion of luck (or not?) to see one. Beware: Aggressive skunks can be carriers of rabies.

Liebre, Conejo • Hares • Lepus europaeus, Oryctolagus cuniculus
Like Rabbits

While endemic animals are often hard to find, the cute little rabbits introduced from Europe can be seen hopping around all over the place. Nothing special, you will think, but do you know how to tell a rabbit from a hare?

Hares occur practically throughout the world. Other than rodents, they have a second pair of incisors, and they are divided into two families: hares and rabbits. They feed on seeds, grass and bark, but also on small animals, insects and snails.

Most rabbits dig caves which they furnish with a soft lining for their numerous offspring, while most hares are content to use small depressions in the ground or dense vegetation. These animals make up for their high mortality rate in the wild (90%) by an equally high fertility. Most species are ready to procreate at only a few months' age, and their gestation period is only 30 to 40 days. Their ovulation is not determined by a cycle, but it rather happens in response to copulation thus reducing the times between births. Some can even carry embryos at different stages concurrently in the two branches of their uterus.

Young hares have a fur from birth, and their eyes are open. Rabbit babies, however, are naked and less developed; their eyes only open after several days. Hares, by the way, don't make any sounds, but they communicate by their typical drumming with their legs, and especially through scent signals.

Coipo • Nutria • Myocastor coipus
The River Swimmer

The world of rodents can be a bit confusing to the layperson. Among them is also the nutria which is endemic to South America and was not introduced in Europe until after WWI to be bred for its fur. Nutrias used to be plentiful on the rivers of the Central Region all the way up to Coquimbo. Their valuable furs made them a coveted hunting target, and so they are rarely seen anymore.

This nocturnal dark brown herbivore measures almost a meter from head to tail, and it has webs on its hind feet. A 1-2 m tunnel whose entrance is partially under water, leads to a 1 m cave. The female bears 5-12 young twice a year; her six teats are sitting on the side so that the young can nurse better in the water.

Cururo • Coruro • Spalacopus cyanus
The Wannabe Mole

The coipo's colleague, the coruro, a brownish-grey animal 30 cm long, likes it drier and darker. This social rodent that lives in colonies loves to

tunnel through sandy mountain slopes with its short, strong legs, much to the chagrin of hikers. If you get caught on one of these vast dwellings, every other step will make you break through their dining or bedroom ceiling. Their small eyes and their acute senses of hearing and smell make them well suited to a life underground. They feed on tubers and roots. When digging, they can close their nose, eyes, and ears to keep the dirt out. At night, they cover the entrance to their cave with loose sand to keep the temperature inside stable. When they hear a noise, they stick their little black heads out, and in case of danger, they call "Cururu".

Vizcacha • Mountain Viscacha • Lagidium viscacia
The Rock Climber

This rodent in the chinchilla family is also related to guinea pigs. In the north of Chile, viscachas live in areas up to an altitude of 5,000 m, in the south they are found down to an altitude of 600 m. After the chinchilla was almost extinct, the hunt turned to viscachas because of their soft fur and their meat. While they are not considered a threatened species, they can now only be found in the most remote spots in Central Chile.

This cute, rabbit-size animal is characterized by long ears, whiskers, a long bushy tail, and a solid body with long hind legs. Thanks to fleshy pads on their soles, viscachas can climb even steep rock walls easily, with their hopping moves reminiscent of a kangaroo. In the sparse areas of the Andes, they feed on a variety of plants, and even lichens.

Mountain viscachas form colonies of up to 60 animals living together peacefully in caves and cracks of remote rocky areas. The only quarreling occurs during mating season. When it's cold, they can occasionally be seen sitting by sunny rocks. They issue a warning call when they spot danger, whereupon everybody hides. Their varied repertory of sounds covers a wide range of situations such as disturbances or disagreements.

On the Internet

www.fauna-australis.puc.cl
Research and animal protection project by scientists from Universidad Católica de Chile; in English and Spanish

http://animales.esfera.cl/clasificacion/CONTENTS.html
Large photo gallery of Chilean fauna; in English and Spanish

Monito del Monte • Dromiciops gliroides
The "Little Monkey"

This one is one of the rarities among the marsupials of the world. It is totally nocturnal, light brown in color, about the size of a hamster, and quite rare already – a combination that makes it unlikely that you will spot it often. A max. of 13 cm

long, with a tail of the same length, and with remarkably big eyes, this 'little monkey' stores the fat for hibernation in its tail. Since the monito can use its thumb and its tail for gripping, it moves swiftly on trees, which represent its habitat.

It feeds mostly on insects and larvae. When still at an almost fetal stage, the young – usually 3 to 5 – climb into their mother's pouch and are raised there with four teats. When they are bigger, they move to small nests on trees or in the bamboo thickets. Marsupials have the advantage that mothers are more independent during bad times – they don't have to carry their young to term in times of food shortages or danger.

Lobo del Mar • South American Fur Seal • Arctocephalus australis
Standing Guard

The fur seal belongs in the family of eared seals; they are very different from the seals of the Northern hemisphere. The ear has not "disappeared" completely yet, and they are very mobile on land. In the water, they move around by paddling fiercely with their front fins. Next to whales and manatees, this water predator has been best able to adapt to its wet environment. This seal can reach speeds of up to 30 km/h when swimming, it's resistant to very low temperatures, and it can stay underwater for up to 30 minutes. Its blubber keeps its body

temperature at a constant range of 36.5 to 37.5 °C. Even more important insulation is provided by the dense, dark brown fur with a hair density of up to 50,000 per square centimeter. In earlier times, hunters were especially interested in the furs of these seals so that entire colonies were brutally slaughtered.

Their most important sense is their hearing, which also serves for orientation purposes; the ear has a closing mechanism for diving. Their sense of smell is used especially for identifying their own young. They feed primarily on clams, crabs, and fish but they will not turn down seabirds such as penguins, either.

Even though these seals are very well adapted to life in the water, for the purposes of procreation and shedding their fur, they do have to move onland, where they gather in large colonies on rocks close to the shore. The bulls jealously defend their territories and their vast harems. The bachelors are forced to keep their distance, but they will keep trying to abduct a female.

Males can reach the impressive height of up to 2.5 meters and a weight of 300 kilograms, while females are typically much smaller and top out at about 150 kg.

Birds

More than 400 different species of birds – about 5% of birds occuring worldwide – nest in Chile, about 300 of those in Central Region, thus representing the majority of the fauna that can be observed during a vacation in the natural areas of this region.

For birdwatchers, visiting the nature preserve of Laguna Torca near Vichuquén, with its thousands of black-necked swans and about 100 species of birds, would be especially worth their time. Laguna Reloca near Chanco is also known for its numerous waterfowl. There are several coastal lagoons like that in Central Chile; in some places, flamingos can be observed, too. More detailed information from the Chilean Ornithologists' Association UNORCH *(see Addresses)*.

Obviously, the following list does not attempt to be complete; it simply mentions some especially interesting or easily observed bird species.

On the Internet

www.ccpo.odu.edu/~andres/aves/
Comprehensive list of Chilean bird species, with descriptions and photos; in Spanish

http://camacdonald.com/birding/sachile.htm
Info on birdwatching in Chile, with lots of links; in English

WATERFOWL

Garza grande • Great Egret • Casmerodius albus

Reaches a height of over 80 cm, with all white feathers, a yellow beak, and black legs. Like other egrets, mostly found around bodies of water where it feeds on small fish, amphibians, larvae, and insects.

Garza chica • Snowy Egret • Egretta thula

Reaches a height of up to 60 cm, smaller than the great egret, and is easily distinguished from it by its black beak and yellow legs. During the breeding season the male grows long ornamental feathers on his head and chest.

Huairavo • Night Heron • Nycticorax nicticorax

The night heron, with a height of up to 56 cm, is easily identified by its long yellow beak, short, yellow legs, and its short neck. It is black on its shoulders, with grey wings, and a chest that is light grey to whitish. If you can get a little closer, you will see two or three very long feathers on its head.

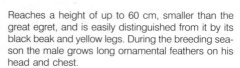

Huairavillo • Stripe-backed Bittern • Ixobrychus involucris

The stripe-backed bittern, especially small at 33 cm height, usually hides in dense reeds on river banks. It has brown-and-tan stripes, and its beak is a yellowish green.

Tagua • Red-gartered Coot • Fulica armillata

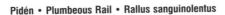

This bird belonging to the rallidae is up to 50 cm tall and handily identified by its black feathers, yellow beak, and yellow forehead that can have a red outline in some. It prefers still, reedy bodies of water and feeds mostly on aquatic plants, which it will also dive for.

Pidén • Plumbeous Rail • Rallus sanguinolentus

Wings and shoulders are dark brown to olive green, its belly and chest are grey. This rail that can be up to 39 cm tall, is usually hiding in dense riparian vegetation and is hard to observe. Right before sundown, it starts a beautiful concert somewhat reminiscent of a European thrush.

Yeco • Olivaceous or Neotropic Cormorant • Phalacrocorax olivaceus

This cormorant can get up to 73 cm tall; it is completely black with black legs and a brown beak. Contrary to most other waterfowl, cormorants do not possess a gland that allows them to make their feathers impermeable to water. The resulting buoyancy would hinder their diving. That's why you will often see cormorants sitting at the bank with their wings spread out – they have to dry them.

Gaviota dominicana • Kelp Gull • Larus dominicanus

This biggest Chilean gull can measure up to 58 cm. With the exception of the black wings and a black back, they are all white. In some, the yellow beak has red spots in the jaw area; the legs are yellow to green.

Pato Jergón Grande • Brown Pintail • Anas niceforoi

Only one of many ducks that are especially difficult to distinguish for the layperson.

Huala • Great Grebe • Podiceps major

This is by far Chile's largest diving bird (78 cm), with an especially long, pointed beak. Rivers, lakes and sometimes even the ocean harbor this swift underwater hunter.

Cisne de cuello negro • Black necked Swan • Cygnus melancoryphus

This one is easy to tell, all white with a black neck and a red beak! This swan, which can reach 122 cm, is found mostly in lagoons close to the coast.

Flamingos: Elegance on Stilts

△ Elegant is the word – that's how they strut around in shallow lagoons and take to the air spreading their colorful plumage. Without any doubt, flamingos are among the great attractions in Chile's fauna.

According to fossil finds, flamingos already existed ten million years ago. Their pedigree is unclear; possible relatives that have been mentioned are egrets, geese and shorebirds. Specifically for the purpose of scooping up its unusual diet – microscopically small algae (hapalosiphon and diatomeae) as well as invertebrates – is why this bird developed its characteristic long legs, a long neck with 19 vertebrae, and above all, an unusual beak. It is bent down from the middle for filtering out its food with comb-like lamellae while the tongue is pumping water in and out of the mouth three to four times a second. In order to be able to immerse the upper jaw of the beak into the water, flamingos have developed an unusually flexible upper jaw that is unique in the animal world.

Out of the four flamingo species occuring in Chile, only the Chilean Flamingo is found in the Central Region and further south to Tierra del Fuego; especially in salty lagoons close to the coast. The other species are only seen on the northern Chilean Altiplano. The whitish-pink plumage of Flamenco chileno has red borders and black areas only visible in flight. During breeding season, which is dependent on the food supply, the female will lay one egg, occasionally also a "back-up" one on a 30 cm high nesting pile made from mud and reed pieces that she builds herself. Both parents take turns sitting on the egg(s) until one hatches; the second one is usually left behind.

When the chicks are born, they are covered in fluffy grey down, and their beak is not curved yet. After several weeks, they can already feed by themselves, and after they have left the nest, they band together in "kindergardens". They learn to fly at eleven weeks. They don't breed until their grey coloring has turned completely into pink when they are two or three years old.

The flamingo's habitat is impacted severely by the mining of salt on the salt lakes. In addition, their eggs are a favorite delicacy for the native population.

Chercán • House Wren • Troglodytes aedon

This 12 cm bird with its reddish-brown back and yellowish-white front likes to nest close to humans, and in the most unusual locations.

Loica • Long-tailed Meadowlark • Sturnella loyca

This brown, blackbird-size bird is frequent in the Central Valley and the Pre-Cordillera.

Zorzal • Austral (Falkland) Thrush • Turdus falklandii

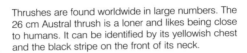

Thrushes are found worldwide in large numbers. The 26 cm Austral thrush is a loner and likes being close to humans. It can be identified by its yellowish chest and the black stripe on the front of its neck.

Chincol • Rufous-collared Sparrow • Zonotrichia capensis

This 15 cm bird prefers living close to human habitations, and the male is easily recognized by his crest.

Picaflor • Chile Hummingbird • Sephanoides galeritus

These tiny birds with their shimmering green plumage seem to constantly be flying around and "kissing" all yellow and red blossoms such as fuchsias or quintral *(see following page)*.

Tordo • Austral Blackbird • Curaeus curaeus

The easily identifiable Austral blackbird occurs in flocks, is completely black and measures up to 28 cm.

Churrete • Dark-bellied Cinclodes • Cinclodes patagonicus

This 20 cm bird with brownish-grey plumage is given away by its light-colored, pronounced "eyebrows". It is usually spotted on the banks of rivers.

Cometocino • Sierra Finch • Phrygilus gayi

Frequent guests at mountain camps. Only 16 cm, with a dark head and yellow chest, they will hop around fearlessly in front of your tent looking for crumbs.

Hummingbird: The Macho Kisser

△ The hummingbird, whose Chilean name **picaflor** means 'flowerpicker', is often associated with the tropics or subtropics. But originally, it occurred from Alaska to Cape Hoorn, and it is widely found throughout Chile. The cute 'buzzer' with its high wing frequency has been posing difficult riddles to scientists for a long time. They even believed once the little guy was a feathered butterfly. And they couldn't understand why a bird that seems to drink nectar dies in captivity despite having enough syrup. The famous ornithologist John James Audubon found the answer to this enigma in the 19th century: hummingbirds also eat small insects they find in the blossoms; nectar provides mostly 'propulsion fuel'.

The tiny bird does need a lot of fuel since it uses an enormous amount of energy relative to its small stature. When watching a hummingbird, you can barely see its wings when they are moving with a frequency of up to 70 beats a minute. And in order to keep its body temperature at a constant temperature of 41 degrees, the little guy has to eat more than half its bodyweight a day. When the ambient temperature falls a lot or the bird cannot find enough food, it enters a catatonic state.

Hummingbirds are among the few machos in the avian world. The males are only in contact with the females during mating season, after which she is on her own when it comes to building a nest, sitting on the eggs, and raising the young. The latter are often fed from a flying position with regurgitated food.

Queltehue • Chile Lapwing • Vanellus chilensis

One of the most typical birds for Central and South Chile – they walk around in pairs looking for morsels in pastures and fields, breaking into their characteristic screeching at the slightest sign of danger. They grow to 36 cm, and their plumage has beautiful markings in their grey, black, and white feathers. When they fly low and screech, it's said to rain for sure.

Chucao • Chucao Tapaculo • Scelorchilus rubecula

This small brownish bird lives in humid forests or brush, has big toes, a reddish chest and is usually seen walking around on the ground. With its low, varied tune you can often hear it without necessarily being able to see it, too. According to the native population, it can predict luck or death.

Bandurria • Buff necked Ibis • Theristicus caudatus

Without doubt, this is one of the most spectacular birds of these latitudes – for one, for its multi-colored appearance (tan, brown, black, and red), its size of more than 70 cm and its long, arching beak, and on the other hand for its piercing, rhythmical cries that will make sure you don't sleep in.

Codorniz • California Quail • Callipepla californica

This bird was introduced in Chile; it is easily identified by the striking feather on its head. It prefers dry areas and always occurs in flocks.

Perdiz chilena • Chilean Tinamou • Nothoprocta perdicaria

This 29 cm bird is camouflaged by its brown plumage with black spots. You often won't notice it until you have flushed it from its hiding place after getting as close as a meter, and it flies away with loud cries. This relative of the grey partridge is very coveted by hunters and poachers.

Tórtola • Eared Dove • Zenaida auriculata

The most-hunted bird species in Chile grows to 26 cm, is grey with black spots on the head and wings, a black beak and reddish legs. They forage for food on the ground in small flocks.

Piuquén • Andean Goose • Chloephaga melanoptera

Up to 75 cm in size, this goose is white with black wingtips, black tail, red beak and red feet. They are found – in pairs – on lakes and swampy grasslands in the Andes.

Carpintero negro • Magellanic Woodpecker • Campephilus magellanicus

The male is especially easy to tell by his red head. This 45 cm bird can be heard from afar pecking on the bark of trees in search of larvae and insects. On the Red List.

Tricahue • Burrowing Parrot • Cyanoliseus patagonus

The tricahue with its green and blue wings and its yellow chest is Chile's biggest species of parrots. For the night, large flocks of these birds head for their nests on steep slopes and rocks, screeching noisily.

Tiuque • Chimango Caracara • Milvago chimango

This 40 cm falcon species has a brown and yellow plumage with a lighter-colored chest. At sundown, you can often see them in noisy flocks.

Peuco • Bay winged Hawk • Parabuteo unicinctus

With its 53 cm a little bigger than the chimango, it usually flies alone. You can easily spot the white stripe at the end of the tail. This hawk is heavily hunted since it occasionally helps itself to a chicken.

Halcón peregrino • Peregrine Falcon • Falco peregrinus

The swiftest and most agile among Chilean raptors, black and white, up to 47 cm. At 320 km/h it holds the diving world record. It kills smaller birds in flight with its impact and its sharp claws. Threatened by extinction.

Jote de cabeza negra • Black Vulture • Coragyps atratus

You will often see this excellent soarer circle above while hardly moving its wings. Together with its colleague, the condor, this completely black vulture, which can reach a size of up to 65 cm, carries out one of the most important tasks in the cycle of nature: getting rid of dead animals. That's why its head is naked; feathers would only hinder its foraging.

Cóndor • Andean Condor • Vultur gryphus

With a wing span of more than 3 m, the mythical condor is among the largest birds in the world. In the air, it is distinguished from a vulture by the long feathered wingtips and the almost motionless flight. Interestingly enough, it's descended from the stork family (see sidebar).

△ Next to the huemul, the condor is the second national animal of Chile, and it is far more likely that you will observe one of those rather than the Andean deer threatened by extinction. While the habitat of the 'King of the Andes' has also been severely curtailed by humans, the bird still nests in almost all of Chile in the upper reaches of the Andes.

Contrary to a wide-spread misbelief, the condor only eats dead animals. It circles high above valleys and slopes, constantly looking for carrion, while it hardly needs to beat its wings due to its wingspan of up to 3.5 m. As with vultures, not having feathers on its head helps keep the bird from getting soiled when feeding. Similar to roosters, male condors have a pronounced crest, visible in flight, just like the white neckband.

Since finding food can be a lengthy affair, the condor's elastic stomach walls enable the bird to eat as much as 2 kg of food at a time, which is an impressive amount for someone who weighs 13 to 15 kg. But a full belly doesn't soar well, and taking off is even harder. So, in case of danger, the condor will regurgitate its prey to lighten the load.

The pairs nest by themselves in rocks in remote areas, and incubate a single egg for 55 days. The young are not sexually mature until they are about six years old. Because of their highly involved raising practices, condors only breed every two or three years.

SEA BIRDS

Pilpilén • American Oystercatcher • Haematopus palliatus

With their black heads and red beaks, oystercatchers can often be seen looking for clams on the beach in small groups. They nest in small indentations that they like to line with mollusk shells.

Piquero • Peruvian Booby • Sula variegata

Boobies dive from great heights with their wings folded into the water to catch fish. Protection from the impact is provided by an air cushion. They breed in colonies on rocks leaving guano droppings, which were long mined as a fertilizer.

Flamenco chileno • Chilean Flamingo • Phoenicopterus chilensis

The Chilean Flamingo, which can reach up to 1 m height, is distinguished from other species by its yellow beak with a black tip, and its light blue legs (see p. 40).

Fauna: Birds

Pelícano • Chilean Pelican • Pelecanus thagus

Unmistakable because of their huge beaks, pelicans can be found on the entire Central Chilean coast. They fly single file in elegant formation close to the waves while using the thermals rising from the water. They feed on fish exclusively.

Pingüino • Penguin • Spheniscus

The habitats of two penguin species overlap in Central Chile; that of the Humboldt *(Spheniscus humboldti)* and of the Magellanic penguin *(Spheniscus magellanicus)*. Both can be up to 70 cm tall, and they are mostly distinguished by the fact that the Humboldt has one black stripe in the neck area, while its southern cousin has two *(see below)*.

Penguin: Dance with the Polar Bear

△ Why doesn't the polar bear eat penguins? The answer to this riddle lies in the history of their name. The bird, which was discovered in the 16th century and later called Magellanic penguin, was thought to be one and the same as the great auk, called 'pingouin' by the French, that occured in the Northern hemisphere. When the last great auks were slaughtered in the 19th century, only the penguins on the Southern hemisphere were left, and so the polar bear has not been able to eat "penguins" anymore.

Just like sea lions among mammals, among the birds, penguins adapted to the water. The fact that their habitat stretches from the Antarctic to the Galapagos Islands proves their adaption to various climatic zones. The tropical species, especially Humboldt penguins, have a much thinner fat layer, a thinner feather coat, and even bare spots in their faces providing additional cooling.

Penguins have to go onland for mating, raising their young, and the molt. They breed in groups or colonies, usually in small caves. As a rule, they lay two eggs which – with northern penguins - hatch simultaneously after 39 days of incubation. The young are fed by their parents who take turns hunting for plankton, fish and small crab for days, which they then regurgitate.

On the coast of the Central Region, penguins can only be observed rarely, e.g., on the rocky islands off Cachagua and Algarrobo.

Reptiles and Amphibians

Among the most 'visible' reptiles of the Central Region are the various kinds of lizards (Spanish: **lagartija**) of the genus *Liolaemus*. These skittish, agile greenish animals like to sun themselves on tree trunks, walls or beams. Rarer is the big **iguana** *(Callopistes palluma)*, which is the biggest Chilean reptile at up to 40 cm.

Snakes do not make much of an appearance at all in Chile. If you should come across one anyway, you need not fear – they are largely harmless for humans. While all Chilean snakes do have venom sacks, their fangs are way in the back of their small mouths so that you would virtually have to stick your finger down there to be bitten. In Central Chile, the brownish-green **culebra de cola larga** *(Chilean groundsnake, Dromicus chamissonis),* which can measure up to 1.5 m, is much more numerous than its smaller relative with the shorter tail, **culebra de cola corta**.

Among the toads, **sapo de rulo** *(Bufo chilensis)* sticks out; it lives in wetlands, but not in the water. Near ponds and streams, you can hear the strange **sapito de cuatro ojos** ('Four-eyed toad', *Pleurodema thaul*) whistling at night, whose big hip glands look like another pair of eyes. Because of its tasty meat, the big **rana chilena** (Helmeted water toad, *Caudiverbera caudiverbera*) is hunted a lot, which is why this toad (zoologically speaking, a frog) is among the threatened species. In the Valdivian rainforests in the southern part of the Central Region you will find **ranita de Darwin** (Darwin Frog, *Rhinoderma darwinii*), also **sapito vaquero** (Cowboy frog). This amphibian, which was discovered by the British scientist, "eats" its own larvae in order to incubate them in special lateral sacks in its throat.

Spiders

There are few people who do not dislike spiders, where "big and ugly" need not be synonymous with "dangerous". Quite the contrary; most big spiders are relatively harmless, e.g. **araña pollito** *(Phrixotrichus rosea)*, which is frequent in Chile, a dark to coffee-brown species living in holes in the ground. Two smaller spiders, however, can really teach you to be afraid: **araña del rincón** (recluse, *Loxosceles laeta*) and **araña del trigo** (black widow, *Latrodectus mactans*).

The inconspicuous greyish-brown nocturnal **recluse** (araña del rincón) lives mostly in human homes where it builds its net in dark corners. Since its nature tends to be rather shy, it will bite only in self-defense, e.g., when a sleeping person rolls on it or if you put on a piece of clothing where it has made its nest. It then injects a toxin that leads to a necrotic process, which can have life-threatening consequences in a small percentage of cases *(see sidebar next page).*

The **black widow** (araña del trigo) is found more in rural areas (other Chilean common names are 'viuda negra' or 'araña de poto colorado'). Including legs, it measures about 4 cm, its spherical body is a smooth pitch black with red spots. It prefers living outside, in corn fields and haystacks, occasionally also in outhouses and sheds. Its bite transmits a potent neurotoxin leading to severe pain and convulsions within a short time, which can cause severe shock *(see sidebar next page).*

While painful for a while, the bite of a **scorpion** is not life-threatening. In Chile, there are four species, which live in rural areas and occasionally hide in shoes or pieces of clothing. The symptoms of the bite – swelling and pain - are best alleviated by cold compresses and painkillers.

△ A basic rule: Don't panic! First, observe the bite and the symptoms. The toxin from araña del trigo (widow) has more dramatic effects, but that of araña del rincón (recluse) is considered more dangerous. Never put a tourniquet on the bodypart that was bitten!

ARAÑA DEL RINCON (RECLUSE)

Symptoms: Localized pain; after about 6-8 hours, the area around the bite shows strong violet to black discoloration; after 36-48 hrs., a black scab will form.

Prognosis: Depending on the amount of venom, adjacent tissue can be affected. Especially at risk are people with health problems and a compromised immune system, children and old people. For this group, such a bite can have life-threatening consequences. Definitely see a doctor!

Treatment: Cold compresses on the extremity affected. A doctor can administer antibiotics and substances that stop the toxin from spreading. Anti-venoms are controversial, and they may not be available everywhere. If necrosis is severe, a tissue transplant can be necessary.

ARAÑA DEL TRIGO (WIDOW)

Symptoms: After 1 to 2 hrs. muscle spasms, severe pain, sweating, vomiting, heart arrhythmia and erection

Prognosis: While the symptoms usually abate after a few hours, they can become dangerous to children, old people, pregnant women and those with heart problems (risk of shock). See a doctor immediately!

Treatment: Strong analgesics, antispasmodic medication, hot baths. The anti-venom is not available in many parts of the country, and it is only recommended for persons at risk.

Insects

As in the rest of the world, insects also account for the largest part of the Chilean fauna as far as numbers go. There are 8,000 species; 70% of them endemic. We will just list a few especially conspicuous ones.

When hiking, you will 'meet' lots of beetles in all colors and shapes. The biggest one of them is the roughly 10 cm **madre de culebra** ('snake mother', *Acanthinodera cummingi*). The smaller, red male flies at night, while the female stays on the ground. It's leading position is challenged by the beauty of **ciervo volante** ('flying deer', *Chiasognatus grantii*). This big, dark brown beetle lives in nothofagus forests and is said to mean good weather. The characteristic 'pincers' of the male are actually its jaws.

South of Talca in the Valdivian rainforest is the home of the impressive, barely 5 cm long **coleóptero de la luma** (*Cheloderus childreni*), which is very colorful: reddish-black body, blue extremities, green head with red spots. Another beetle announces itself from several meters away, even before you might get to see it. The ground-dweller **chinchemoyo** (*Agathemera sp.*) likes to keep its enemies at bay with its bad smell.

Ciervo volante

Coleóptero de la luma

Chile's insect world offers many other beauties and rarities: buzzing dragonflies, bees and wasps, noisy crickets and cicadas, busy ants, locusts, and hungry termites. Roughly 170 butterfly species fly all over the country and there are also enough pesky **zancudos** (mosquitoes) and **tábanos** (horseflies) for everyone to go around. While their stings can hurt for a time and make you swell up, they are not carriers of dangerous diseases.

Especially annoying is the **colihuacho** *(Scaptia lata)*, a big horsefly, that can occur en masse between mid-December to the end of January. This fat, black insect with its violet wings that flies noisily is especially attracted to black clothing, moves slowly and can be shooed or swatted before it stings (painful). And yet, the sheer quantities of these nasty bloodsuckers can make any stay near bodies of water a pain, especially since commercial bug sprays don't impress them much.

Beware of the **vinchuca** bug *('kissing bug', Triatoma infestans)*. This bug, which occurs north of Talca, prefers to live in stables and adobe buildings that are not cleaned well, where they go on the hunt for mammalian blood at night. Their bites themselves are not dangerous; it's their excrement they leave on your skin that can be infected with the chagras disease. This chronic ailment which knows no cure causes the inner organs to enlarge. However, few cases of infections among tourists have become known. When bitten at night, do not scratch, and clean the bite.

Vinchuca

Nocturnal Skies
Of Red Giants and Black Holes

When the camp has been pitched, the dinner has been devoured, and the pots and pans have been washed, there is not much left that one can do. The first stars start twinkling, and for once, you will find some time to think about them. The clear nights in Central Chile, far from any smog or distracting sources of light which make it hard to discover any empty spaces between the glowing points, are an invitation to do just that. So, on the following pages we'll talk about the phenomena in the sky and the questions a layperson might ask about them.

The Moon
Man or Woman?

Hardly any celestial body has inspired human imagination the way the moon, this changeable sphere, has. Interestingly, personifications in various cultures have lead to different emotional associations. While the Sun is feminine and the Moon masculine in German, in Latin countries that is hard to imagine for people; there, it has always been *el sol* and *la luna*…

Aside from their 'mystification', Mr. or Ms. Moon also holds a number of interesting astrophysical

facts. Well-known is its period of revolution around the earth of 28, or to be more precise, 28.5 days. During that time, the moon revolves around her axis once, so that the same side always faces the earth, and so a moon day lasts two weeks. With the naked eye, one can see the dark spots known as oceans (mare) which are, however, completely dry. With a telescope, you can also spot the craters stemming from meteorites crashing into the surface. The altitude differentials of up to 10,000 m on the surface of the moon are huge, given its small size.

Photo: Nocturnal sky above the European Observatory at Paranal in northern Chile

The moon's best-known effects on earth are the tides. If her gravity were the only cause for high tide, it would have to occur every 24.5 hours according to the moon's position. The tides, however, have an actual rhythm of 12.5 hours. Why? Since the moon also possesses mass and thus, gravity – even though it is smaller than the earth's – our axis of rotation is shifting from the center of the earth towards the moon. Both our satellite as well as the earth rotate around this imaginary point. Due to the out-of-round momentum, the side of the earth facing away from the moon receives a higher centrifugal force, which also causes a high tide. That is why there is a high tide twice a day.

The light of the full moon saves us from walking with a flashlight, and it casts surreal shadows in the forests. If we were hiking on the moon with our backpacks and walking poles, we could enjoy the light of the full earth, which is 70 times brighter.

The Planets
The Big Carousel

The universe is one big carousel: Moons orbit planets, planets circle suns, suns form galaxies rotating around themselves - or, like planets, around other galaxies (Magellan's clouds) -, and galaxies form their own groups spinning around a center. It takes our moon 28.5 days to orbit the earth, which takes 365.25 days around the sun, which rotates around the galaxy's center in 230 million years...

Eight major planets orbit our sun, as well as thousands of small celestial bodies called planetoids. While they all circle in the same direction, their rotational senses differ.

The planets visible to the naked eye, Saturn, Jupiter, Venus, and Mars, were already known to the Sumerians around 3000 B.C. The last planet of our solar system – Pluto - was not discovered until 1930. Planets of other suns are not

SUN — MERCURY — VENUS — EARTH — MARS — JUPITER — SATURN — URANUS — NEPTUNE — PLUTO

Nature & People

ESO

An enigma for astronomers: a "black hole"

The energy of the suns is created by massive fusion of two hydrogen atoms into one helium atom. The surface temperature of our sun is about 6,000, the internal temperature is around 15 million degrees Celsius. The sun consists almost exclusively of hydrogen and helium. It is not until suns die that other elements are created, which in turn form the building blocks for planets and living beings. Thus, billions of years ago, the building blocks for our bodies were part of a sun…

When a sun's hydrogen starts running out, it inflates and becomes a red giant (e.g., Beteigeuze in Orion). Eventually, these red giants will explode and distribute the elements created in the process into space. In the center of the explosion, a weak kernel remains that continues to glow: a white dwarf. The star dust in turn will form the beginnings of a dark cloud which gathers until it has enough mass to glow as a star.

even visible through the best telescopes. Their existence can only be proved indirectly, such as by periodic obscurations of stars – a research task that astronomers in the large observatories in the north of Chile are focusing on.

Suns
An Eternal Cycle

With the naked eye, we can only see about 6,000 items in the starry sky. Most of those are distant suns, apart from the few visible planets. In our galaxy alone, there are billions of stars, and galaxies also number in the billions… If you take a closer look, you can discover differences in color and intensity. Their sizes vary, too; a sun like ours, though, would become unstable starting at the 60-fold mass.

The distances between the individual suns are far beyond imagination. Thus, the light (300,000 km/s) only takes 8 minutes to get from our sun to the earth, from the nearest sun (Alpha Centauri), however, it is already 4.5 years.

The black spots in our milky way called 'coal sacks' are created by diffused cold matter which swallows the light of the stars on its way to earth. When this matter is condensed, stars are born whose heat makes the left-over diffused matter glow (Orion nebula).

Galaxies
Starry Skies and Beyond

While the light only takes eight minutes from the sun to the earth, it takes about 100,000 years to cross our galaxy. About two thirds of our solar system are located outside the center of the galaxy, which in turn lies roughly in the sign of the zodiac of Sagittarius. That is also the reason why star nebulae are more frequent there since they form the 'birth place' of stars.

A rough estimate puts the 'big bang", the origin of the Universe, at 15 billion years ago. In the center of the galaxy, we can see younger stars in their various stages. The older stars are located on the opposite side, far from the center. The expansion of space causes all matter to move away from the center.

In between the older stars, we can see the open space and other galaxies. Two planet galaxies orbiting ours can be seen with the naked eye – Magellan's clouds. The milky way is nothing but a view of our galaxy with its roughly 200 billion stars, as seen from earth.

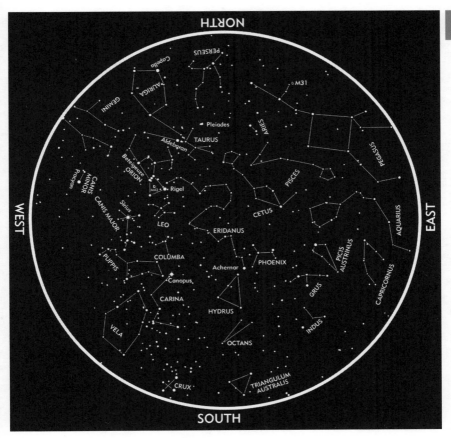

The starry skies of the southern hemisphere: Free range for the imagination

The Nocturnal Skies in Chile

When it comes to identifying planets or constellations, most people on the northern hemisphere are usually able to tell which is the Northern Star and the Big Dipper, whose southern equivalent is the famous **Southern Cross (Crux)**. Its four main stars serve to point travelers South (by extending the longitudinal axis of the cross four times towards its base.) The kite-shaped **Cruz del Sur** is easy to identify since it is always close to the 'coal sack', a dark nebula obscuring part of the milky way which otherwise shines brightly over Chile. The four stars of Crux are located between 88 and 490 light years from the earth. Also easy to discover is **Pegasus** showing up in the summer in the northern sky. It most resembles the Big Dipper of the northern hemisphere. A little west from there are the star nebulae of the **Pleiades** flickering like a pile of diamonds in the sky.

With a little patience, even a layperson should soon be able to distinguish Venus, Saturn, Jupiter and Mars. Since the planets of our solar system all move on one plane, it is relatively easy to tell them apart from stars. On the imaginary line on which the Sun and the Moon rise, moving across the sky and east (ecliptic), is where we also have to look for the planets. The brightest spot, **Venus**, is always close to the sun, and it is often the first or last "star" at sunrise and sunset. **Jupiter** also sticks out by its brightness, while **Saturn** is already quite a bit weaker. **Mars,** while not bright, is easily identified by its reddish cast. On the same line as the planets are also the twelve well-known signs of the zodiac. Especially well visible in the Chilean summer are **Taurus**, **Libra**, **Leo**, and **Virgo** in the evening sky, as well as the largest of all of them, **Scorpio**, towards dawn. Near the Milky Way close to the ecliptic, you will find the spectacular constellation **Orion**, interpreted by the Greeks as a great hunter with a sword and a dog. To the right below Orion, the brightest star in the sky, **Sirius**, the head of the big dog, is easily found.

The strikingly red outer star of Orion, **Beteigeuze**, is a red giant. Orion's belt is made up of three big stars in a line. Running outward diagonally from that, there are another three stars in a line, but closer together, forming the "sword". The center one, however, is not a star but star dust which has already formed new suns, the **Great Orion Nebula**.

In close proximity to the Crux, you can see two especially bright stars. The brighter one of the two, a double sun, is **Alpha Centauri**, the closest star system to our sun. You can recognize two galaxies, like two clouds with the same brightness as the milky part of the milky way and almost the size of our fist stretched out - the **Great** and the **Small Magellanic Clouds**. Right next to the small one there is the slightly washed-out looking dot of a star cluster in the constellation **Toucan**, one of the most exciting objects for hobby astronomers.

On the Internet

www.eso.org
Chile's big European observatories and their research; in English

www.ctio.noao.edu
Website of the Inter-American Observatory on Cerro Tololo, Chile; in English

www.astro.wisc.edu/~dolan/constellations/constellations.html
Everything about constellations and stars; in English

Trekking & Mountaineering
Happy Trails

2

Even though three quarters of Chile's population live in the central region of the country, they hardly seem to notice the mountains right in front of their doorsteps. They spend their vacations on the beach or in Miami, but hiking in the mountains is a foreign notion to many of them. At the most, Winter might find some of them – those who can afford it – skiing on the slopes of the few ski resorts. Only recently, the Santiago area has become the one place where you might find people with the same interests out and about in the Cordillera. Above all, the young have discovered the fascination of this wilderness close to the city. And yet, the Andes are still lightyears from the kind of tourist traffic that the European Alps or the Rocky Mountains are getting.

If you want to hike or climb in Chile you have to do without a lot of the creature comforts that have become standard in the mountain areas of Europe or North America – you won't find smooth roads delivering you right to the foot of the mountain, there are no kiosks selling refreshing drinks at the view points, and rarely will tired backpackers find a homey hut waiting for them at the end of the day. In exchange for that, you will find almost total solitude, breath-taking scenery, and refuges full of virgin natural treasures in the Andes. On top of that, the Central Cordillera of Chile boasts an excellent climate. From November to April, you are virtually guaranteed blue skies and sunshine, which makes for an extra long hiking season running from September to May.

The trekking tours and climbs described here are typical wilderness tours, conducted far from any signs of civilization, and mostly without any infrastructure: The roads are not sign-posted, a bridge is a rare sight, and rescue operations in case of an accident will be difficult accordingly. This makes thorough preparation and information, as well as observing basic safety rules, essential.

Photo: On the ascent to Peteroa – Azufre volcanoes (Tour 11)

Travelling in the Andes

Access to Hiking Tours

If you can't get there, the most beautiful hiking area is useless. As simple as that may sound, in Chile, accessing the trail can be more difficult than hiking the trail itself. For one, many areas in the Andes are hardly developed at all, even in the relatively densely populated central region. Gravel and dirt roads are the rule, usually requiring an offroad vehicle. Buses are few and far in between, and they usually only connect the major centers. So, do plan sufficient time for getting to the trailhead and back.

In addition, a major portion of central Chile, including many mountain areas, is fenced-in private property. While there is a law that guarantees all citizens free access to rivers, lakes and beaches, it is not valid for the mountains. If you go on a tour outside a National Park, you should always try and contact the owner or manager of the land to ask permission – especially if you want to camp there. In the Pre-Cordillera, access on gravel roads will sometimes be blocked by gates. In such cases, it is best to negotiate with those responsible if you want to take your car further.

When in doubt, we suggest you not insist but try elsewhere in order to avoid potential conflict. On the tours described in this book, you should not run into any problems of that kind.

Trails and Paths

With the exception of some National Parks, Chile has very few hiking trails, not to mention marked ones – unless you want to count cow pies and horse pucky. The trails and paths that do exist were mostly made by *arrieros* – as cowboys are called in Chile – and they also maintain them. This is where the *arrieros* drive the cattle entrusted to them to their summer pastures in the mountain valleys, where they spend several months in primitive conditions and total solitude. Right before the first snows, they bring the animals back down to the safer valley floor. They, of course, don't need any markers for orientation, except for the occa-

sional cairn. This makes them extremely valuable sources of information, not to mention that they also make very friendly and trustworthy conversation partners at your campfire.

The tours described here use trails that are well visible, but most of them do lead right through the wilderness; a good sense of direction is therefore indispensable.

Duration of Tours

During a hike, the only information to be had will usually come from an *arriero* – that is, if you can understand their broad dialect. They estimate distance from the point of view of a horseback rider. You should add about 30% to the times they give to account for yourself hiking with a pack weighing about 40 pounds.

The durations listed in our tour descriptions are only a general guideline, given the many factors that determine your speed such as fitness, weather, altitude or how you are feeling on that particular day. The times given are based on a pack weight of about 40 pounds.

Finding Your Way

As important as the information from the arrieros may be, they are usually only familiar with the few mountain ranges that they travel. While the routes described are mostly well-trodden obvious trails, there can, however, be many confusing and time-consuming opportunities for taking the wrong branch... And sometimes, there will

---

Five Golden Rules for Hiking

△ Do not overestimate your abilities

△ Get information ahead of time

△ Get maps for more difficult tours; take a compass, or better yet, a GPS receiver

△ Know how to converse in Spanish

△ Never tour alone; and best, go with a person who knows the area.

Franz Schubert

Sign posts are rare and not always clear

▲ Retrace your steps until you can see the trail clearly

▲ Look for the trail by walking outward from where you are in a spiral shape

▲ Once you succeed in finding your way, continue hiking with a smile

▲ If you don't succeed, sit down, take a break and do some thinking. Trails usually follow rivers, and they do it like a lazy cow – follow the easiest passage and only deviate when there is an impassable obstacle (like a drop-off at the bank). Just go uphill, around the obstacle, and then back along the river.

▲ If that doesn't help any, read the route description one more time, look at the map, target the nearest GPS waypoint, wait for someone who knows the way, and contemplate whether next time, you shouldn't hire a guide.

be no trail at all, or the trail leads to a river which raises the delicate question: Do we cross it or follow it? Or the water in the river is too high for crossing it at that point... The tour descriptions give you some ideas, but they must remain incomplete by necessity. A valuable help are GPS data which we are giving for a few routes. This requires a GPS receiver (from $200) and knowing how to use it safely.

Chile's central region has one great advantage for finding your way on mountain trails: Between Santiago and San Fernando, vegetation is limited to spindly brush, and even the forests of Nothofagus (a type of beech tree) between San Fernando and Los Angeles do not have dense underbrush – unlike the ones south of there. The terrain provides an excellent view making it easier to bypass obstacles.

GPS-Data

For the recording of GPS data, the modern WGS 84 (World Geodetic System) with its degrees and minutes format for positions was used. The Chilean maps in this book, however, are based on the 1956 Canoa system resulting in major deviations in some cases. Our GPS data should not be transferred directly onto the maps; it is only meant for your orientation during the hike.

Data Collection

For the purpose of improving and expanding this book, we would like to ask other hikers for help. Please write to us with your suggestions, experiences, and GPS data – those following in your tracks will be grateful! E-mail us at turismocaminante@hotmail.com (Franz Schubert) or malte@contactchile.cl (Malte Sieber).

Maps

Unfortunately, maps for hikers are rare in Chile. For a rough overview, the best maps are issued by IGM (Instituto Geográfico Militar, Dieciocho 369, Metro Toesca, Santiago Centro, Tel. 4606963) on a scale of 1:250.000; also try the series "JLM-Mapas" that is available in specialized stores. No. 06 in this series, "Andes Centrales", and No. 09, "Araucanía", even contain some useful detail maps. Those who like more precise maps will have to get the IGM maps on the scale of 1:50.000, but it may take several of these pricey maps for a single tour. Note though that these are not foolproof, either. Not only are they outdated, but they also rarely show mountain trails. Some National Parks have rough overview maps, but they will usually just have run out of them when you get there.

The various maps also give a confusing array of altitudes for the same spots; for some peaks, they differ by several hundred meters because most of these mountains were surveyed decades ago without our modern, satellite-based methods. In this book, you will find either our own GPS-based data, or, if those are not available, data from the IGM maps.

On the Internet

IGM and JLM maps can be ordered ahead of time from: www.omnimap.com/catalog/int/chile.htm

Difficulty

The routes are divided by degree of difficulty (see p. 68). It is important to judge one's abilities correctly. If you are planning a longer tour, start practicing on shorter routes or parts of the longer route so you can gauge your body's and mind's stamina. Even though these tours – with a few exceptions – do not require technical climbing, only very few are appropriate for total novices to hiking in the wilderness.

Mountain Guides and Packhorses

Those who want to make their hiking experience more pleasant should try to hire an arriero, as well as a packhorse or mule. The cost is about $20 per day and horse, and you'll need one for the arriero, too – they never walk! One horse can carry about 4 backpacks. The advantages are obvious: Your backpack won't weigh you down, you can take better food, you can make contact with the locals, and you won't get lost.

Another option is joining a club tour. The German Andean Club Santiago invites non-members (you don't need to know any German) to participate in its program. The only cost will be your share of transportation. Those interested in a weekend tour meet on Thursdays at 8 p.m. For more information, call: Club Alemán Andino, Arrayán 2735, Ph. (2) 232 43 38. For other clubs, see under Addresses.

Hiking Weather

Chile's central region has an extremely stable climate and easily predictable weather. The "climatic border" with the rainier south runs roughly along the 38th parallel, to the south of Los Angeles. North of it summer rains are extremely rare, and short. Bad weather is often triggered by a warm front and can be predicted by watching the cloud formations carefully (see sidebar).

Spring in central Chile starts at the end of August or early September, and it truly makes the Andes sparkle. The lower slopes boast a verdant green, and the snowcover reaches way down the mountains. The ski season runs until mid-October. And yet, in the Pre-Cordillera, you can already go on hikes as early as September. Starting in November, a few of the higher tours will become accessible. The mountain passes are often still covered in snow, which is why you cannot take pack horses, and you should carry light crampons and an iceaxe. The rivers are swollen from the snowmelt. It is essential that you gather detailed information about the conditions beforehand!

The weather can already be very stable in November, with temperatures reaching 25 °C. Occasional bad spells can interrupt the permanent high for a few days. From December on, only the high passes are snowed in. From now until March, sunshine is practically guaranteed in the central region, with temperatures in the lower valleys reaching 35 °C. In the height of summer, afternoon thunderstorms may form more frequently, and at night it cools off pleasantly.

Starting in January, all the passes will be open; there shouldn't be any snow until May. The rising temperatures will make hikers break into a sweat, so you might want to choose the early morning hours and the shaded southern slopes for your ascents.

March with its lower temperatures makes trekking easier. Starting in mid-April, Fall turns the mountains south of San Fernando with their southern beech forests a bright yellow and red – an attractive view for hikes through the end of May. Days will remain mostly sunny, but nights will get quite chilly. Morning fog will shroud the low-lying areas, while the vistas in the mountains will be clear. From mid-May on, the weather turns increasingly cool and rainy. You can go on ski tours from July until the middle of October, with sunny and warm days in the second half of Winter.

Clouds, Wind, and Weather

⚠ With approaching warm fronts, the winds will blow from northerly or westerly directions. The first signals are very high cirrus clouds. If they are moving fast with the barometer falling, you can count on bad weather for the next two days. The sky will then cover itself in a thin, milky blanket of cirrostratus, which will place halos around the Sun or the Moon. It is still safe to continue hiking under those conditions.

Rippling, wavy clouds (cirrocumulus) are a sign for an imminent change in weather. If they are followed by grey, washed-out altostratus that make the sun look like a dim disk, rain won't be far behind. The deep-hanging clouds form a denser layer (nimbostratus) which blocks the sun completely. Below, "raggedy clouds" often race across the sky. It is high time now to find a good campsite; let's hope you brought a good book to read! The end of the bad weather front will be announced by dense, sunny cumulus clouds with cauliflower-like edges, and by a rising barometer.

In the height of Summer, electric storms and rain are frequent in the Andes, with cumulus clouds forming in the morning, and towering clouds mushrooming around noon. Towards the afternoon, anvil-shaped heads will form at their top (cumulonimbus): your thunderstorm has arrived.

The mountain hiker's best friends are dense cumulonimbus clouds with a dark lower rim which dissolve at night. They are formed by cool and dry air masses brought in from the Antarctic by southerly winds.

Hiking days are longest at the height of Summer (December/January) when it is light from about 6 in the morning until 10 at night, while in September or May, hiking hours are shortened from 8 until 6.

Current weather forecasts in the daily papers, and from Dirección Meteorológica de Chile, Ph. (2) 601 90 01.

On the Internet

www.meteochile.cl
Official Chilean meteorological service, not very helpful; in Spanish

www.cnn.com/WEATHER/sa/Chile/SantiagoSCEL.html
Santiago weather from CNN website

Equipment

Given the lack of excitement for hiking among the Chileans, it is hardly surprising that the mountain gear available on location is not much to write home about. The few specialized stores are limited to the Santiago area, articles from Chilean production can be of questionable quality, and imported brand name articles are scarce and grossly overpriced. If at all possible, you should purchase basic equipment before your trip to Chile.

When choosing luggage, weight savings are most important, especially if you have to carry it yourself. Unfortunately, "lighter" almost always means "more expensive", too. As far as food is concerned, all you need to do is choose the right things *(see Provisions)*.

Backpack

Depending on the length of your tour, at least 70 to 100 Liters (4,300 to 6,100 cu.in). Strapping your tent and mat to the outside of the pack will allow choosing a smaller pack, but it will also make it bulkier. If the pack is not coated on the inside or if it's worn, you will need a waterproof cover or a large poncho. Important requirements are an inner frame and a wide, firm, and adjustable hip belt. For carrying equipment on horseback, we recommend a sturdy duffel bag, as well as a smaller hiking pack for the day's needs.

Tent

Given the sunny climate, you won't need a four-season expedition-grade tent. There are good tents available that weigh only 4 to 6 pounds. They save weight by replacing tent fabric with mosquito netting, and fiberglass poles with aluminum ones.

Mat

We recommend a self-inflating, three quarter-length mat. You can make up for the missing part by using your clothes as a pillow or under your feet.

Sleeping Bag

Compared to synthetic fill, down-filled bags are lighter and will work well here because of the dry climate. As for the comfort rating, there is no need to go below 5 °C unless you like to sleep warm.

Hiking Boots

Your most important piece of gear! We recommend taking leather boots with as few seams as possible, and ones that will accept crampons if necessary. We don't recommend Goretex linings because you may get too hot, they might make your feet smell, and sweaty socks are likely to cause blisters. Boots with cordura inserts won't provide enough support.

Rain Jacket

While a Goretex jacket works best, it will only keep you dry a little longer in a real downpour.

Rain Pants

You won't need those often, and if, it will be against the cold. However, don't leave without them, especially for tours at higher altitudes.

Fleece

Cotton T-shirts get soaked with sweat fast in the Summer, and you might catch cold if the wind blows. Synthetic T's, shirts or – best – thin turtle-necks are better. Keep the cold at bay with a fleece jacket.

Sun Protection

Foreigners tend to underestimate the sun in Chile. Even in the central valley, a few minutes of sun exposure will be sufficient to cause sunburn in fair-skinned people (most Europeans and North Americans). The ozone hole over the Antarctic stretches all the way to southern Chile in the Summer, which results in more UV radiation and thus, increased risk of skin cancer. Take long-sleeved shirts, a cap or hat with a broad bill or rim, quality sunglasses (especially for snowfields and glaciers), sun cream (at least SPF 30), as well as lip balm with sun protection.

Protection Against the Cold

For Spring and Fall tours, or for regions above 2,000 m, wool caps and gloves are advisable.

Cooking Gear

You'll need: stove, pots, a water sack (4 liters), a water bottle (at least 2 liters), knife, fork and spoon, a cup and a lighter. We recommend taking a lightweight stove with an extra fuel bottle and adjustable flame control. White gas[oline]

(bencina blanca) can be bought in Chile in pharmacies or (for a little less) in hardware stores. Gasoline has a higher energy value than gas, and a lower volume. A rule of thumb is, one liter of gasoline per person per week.

Flashlight

Because of the longer daylight hours in Summer you will only need a small flashlight with extra batteries. The new flashlights with LED's are ideal.

Laundry and Clothes Bags

We recommend taking two differently-colored bags, one for clean clothes and one for laundry. If you also choose different textures, you will be able to tell your bags apart even in the dark.

Protection for Documents

A waterproof cover for your passports, money and maps.

Trekking Poles

Adjustable aluminum poles are absolutely essential on longer tours. On downhills, they take several pounds worth of weight off your knees, which will add up to several tons over the duration of your trip. Besides, good poles are essential for crossing rivers.

Provisions

Good grub no doubt distinguishes the ho-hum from the great hike. Experience will teach you how much to take. A 150-pound hiker will easily polish off 200 grams of pasta at the end of the day. You can save weight by doing without canned goods and fresh fruit, and by taking dried products. It's a good idea to distribute your food among three bags – here are a few recommendations:

Breakfast

Powdered coffee and milk, tea, sugar/honey, muesli, rolled oats, dried fruit

fortable with camping underneath the stars, and you will find many pleasant and quiet places to pitch your tents. Occasionally, you will also find simple wood cabins owned by *arrieros* or National Park rangers, but be careful – the refugios which have not been aired out or cleaned for weeks may harbor the Hanta virus *(see below)*. When in doubt, choose to sleep in your tent!

The Hanta Virus

This topic pops up regularly in the Chilean media; this dangerous virus has, after all, killed several dozen people over the last few years. Scientists think that the virus is thousands of years old and has always existed. It was not until the 90's that it was identified as a cause of death. The symptoms of the illness were described as early as around 980 A.D. in a Chinese medical handbook, and the virus may have spread from Asia, too.

In Chile there have been about 70 cases so far, with most of them occuring in Regions XI and IX (southern Chile). The Hanta virus is probably passed on by a number of rodents occuring in the wild, and in Chile it has been mostly asscoiated with the longtailed mouse (ratón de cola larga). It's enough to come into contact with the excrement or to breathe the air in which infected mice have been living; the disease can also be transmitted by a mouse bite or by contact with a dead mouse.

An infection leads to death from pulmonary edema in more than 50% of all cases. Since the virus has an incubation period of several days, the first symptoms – headaches, nausea, fever – are rarely diagnosed correctly.

But there is no reason to panic; you can protect yourself effectively with simple means. It is essential to avoid all dark and stuffy rooms that have not been used for a while; in broad daylight, the virus cannot survive outside its host for more than a few minutes, and it can be easily killed with disinfectants. Here are a few safety rules:

While Hiking

Chocolate, cookies, dried fruit, nuts, bread, sausage, cheese, fruit-drink-mix

Dinner

Easiest: Pasta (e.g. spirals) with packaged soups as a sauce. Good: instant mashed potatoes with soy "meat" and tomato sauce (from a bag), pasta with salami cubes and cheese sauce, dried lentils (soak them 2-3 hours before and then cook with packaged soup.)

Overnights

Those who need the comfort of mountain hotels and huts will be disappointed by the Andes. Except for very few places which are listed, there is very little tourism-related infrastructure in the central region of Chile. You will need to be com-

Drinking Water

⚠ Most people will tell you that the water from the clear, cold mountain streams and rivers is very potable – given a proper distance from human settlements. For those who don't trust it, you might want to carry treatment tablets or a water filter. The stronger the current, the better oxygen is at killing bacteria. Suspect water is indicated by light green, filament-shaped algae (Spirogyra). You should always boil or treat water from lakes.

Protection against Hanta

△ Never touch dead rodents

△ Keep food and garbage in closed containers

△ Dig a hole for food that rodents have chewed on and cover with soil, discard leftovers

△ Clean all dishes thoroughly

△ If at all possible, only use cabins that are being used continuously and cared for

△ Before entering cabins and huts, air them out well

△ Never sleep on the floor of a cabin.

Environmental Issues

This should be a moot point for trekkers, but unfortunately, experience has taught us otherwise. In Chile, environmental consciousness is not very highly developed; piles of trash and wads of toilet paper alongside the roads are proof of that just as the annual wildfires caused by humans.

Even trekkers and nature lovers leave traces – whether they are aware of it or not. Especially where areas are virtually untouched we should strive to keep it that way. That means mostly - minimize your impact on nature as much as possible.

And it is so easy: Don't leave anything, not even organic waste. Someone who is strong enough to haul food by the pound into the mountains cannot possibly be too weak to carry out the leftovers or cover his excrement with dirt. Camp-

On the Internet

www.cdc.gov
US-Centers for Disease Control and Prevention, search for: Hanta

www.samexplo.org/hanta.htm
South American Explorers

www.lnt.org
Further principles of outdoor ethics according to the motto "Leave No Trace"

Franz Schubert

Campfires can cause devastating wildfires

fires may be very romantic, but they are also very dangerous – again and again, campfires that were not extinguished carefully have started devastating wildfires. In Natural Parks, campfires are entirely illegal, and in some places you may not be admitted if you don't bring your own stove. So you will need to refrain from playing with fire, and just enjoy the starry sky!

Leave no Traces

△ Collect all garbage in a strong bag and carry it out

△ Dig a hole for organic waste and cover with soil or carry it out, too

△ Don't pour dishwater with food leftovers into streams or lakes; dig a hole for it, too

△ Do not wash cookpots directly in streams or lakes

△ Build campfires only outside of forests, burn dead wood only, keep the fire small, surround it with rocks, and extinguish it with lots of water before you turn in. When leaving your camp, cover the fire pit with sand or soil

△ If possible, avoid using soap, shampoo and detergent

△ Do not destroy plants intentionally; the fragile groundcover in the High Andes is easily destroyed just by stepping on it. Make a habit of stepping around it!

△ Observe wild animals only from a distance; do not try to approach or feed them

Safety

As mentioned before, the tours described here are true wilderness tours. In case of an accident, help will be far; you could be days from the nearest settlement with a phone or transportation! The following rules are important:

● Prepare for each tour thoroughly; don't improvise, but plan your destination and route precisely

● Leave detailed information about the route and your schedule with relatives, acquaintances, or friends

● Sign in and out with National Park rangers or the police; Never go alone! Many people have overestimated their mountain savvy, only to get lost or hurt in the Andes

● Watch the weather report in the media before your tour, or ask for a forecast from: Dirección Meteorológica de Chile, Ph. (2) 601 90 01

Especially for the more demanding tours (Trekking, Alpine, Expedition) you will absolutely need to know how to use all equipment, how to behave during electrical storms, how to cross rivers, and if necessary, how to cross snowfields and glaciers. If you don't want to run any risk, you are better off hiring a knowledgeable guide *(see Addresses)*.

On some tours there will be stretches without water for hours. Especially in the Summer, we need enormous quantities of water; dehydration weakens the body and leads to muscle cramps. So, don't ever walk past a spring without filling your water bottle (at least 2 liters)!

Your First Aid kit should emphasize supplies that are useful in case of blisters, cuts and scrapes: gauze and bandages, a disinfectant, and tape. Do not leave without a strong analgesic.

The only mountain rescue team in Chile in the Santiago area is a volunteer team based in Baños Morales, Ph. (2) 699 47 64, in all other areas you are better off calling the police (133) in case of emergency. Oftentimes, a cell phone has come in handy for calling help. In steep valleys or remote areas you may not be able to get a connection, but sometimes you can succeed from a peak or a pass, esp. in the Santiago area *(Cell phones see Useful Information, p. 214)*.

Emergency Phone Numbers	
△ 133	Police (Carabineros)
△ 138	Airforce Rescue Service (Servicio de Búsqueda y Salvamento, Fuerza Aérea)
△ 6994764	Mountain Rescue Service (Cuerpo de Socorro Andino)
△ 130	Wildfires (Conaf, Forest rangers)

Crossing Rivers

In the Spring and after extended rainfall, rivers and streams often turn into raging waters that can endanger your life. It's easy to underestimate current, depth, and temperature. Ice cold water causes muscles to cramp, which can have unpleasant effects. Crossing is easiest in places where the river branches out. Try to walk at a 45 degree angle against the current. Trekking poles will help you keep your balance. Never cross a river barefoot! Even a small cut can get infected and make the rest of your trip an ordeal. Especially in the Spring, you should carry a thin 20 m rope for river crossings.

Altitude Sickness

Even technically savvy, "experienced" mountain climbers often fail in the Andes because they are not acclimated to the altitude. And contrary to the peoples of the Himalaya region, even the native peoples who have lived on the Altiplano for thousands of years are not entirely adapted to their environment. For many trekkers and climbers it is precisely that altitude that attracts them and gives them the opportunity to test their mettle. However, you will only have a successful tour if you can gauge your abilities realistically.

Acute mountain sickness can be felt – depending on rate of altitude gain - starting at a height of 3,000 m; the problematic zone starts at 3,500 m. This isn't really a disease, rather an accident, which is not without interest from the point of view of your insurance. Compared to diseases, accidents have a great advantage: they are easier to prevent. Some people carry a higher risk: those who suffer from hemorrhoids, chronic sinobronchitis, hidden infection, seizures, cardiopulmonary problems, Raynaud's syndrome, migraine, tooth infection, or circulatory problems of the arteries should discuss their plans with a specialist.

Among the factors that can trigger acute mountain sickness are: gaining altitude too quickly, exhaustion, insufficient breathing, infections of the ear, nose, throat or intestines, sleeping pills, alcohol, dehydration, and the pill. Cigarettes may have a lot of disadvantages, but they do not have an impact on acute mountain sickness. Nor do conditioning or blood pressure. But since your performance decreases by about 10% for every 1,500 meters gained in altitude, a good cardiovascular training background is a great advantage.

As a rule, anyone can feel acute mountain sickness coming. The first symptoms are easy to recognize; they are most pronounced at night. It starts with headaches and loss of appetite, followed by loss of sleep and nausea. A look in the mirror occasionally reveals retinal bleeding and swelling from subcutaneous edemas.

The best measures against initial signs of mountain sickness are:

- Do not continue climbing, rather descend a few hundred meters in altitude

- Observe a day of rest

- Sleep with your upper body propped up

- Lots of fluid

- Avoid alcohol

- Meals must be easy to digest

- If possible, don't take medications.

Pills will only mask the symptoms, the cause remains. They may make ascending easier, but they make the sickness more dangerous because you seem to feel better. Do not use oxygen to support a continued ascent; just as the various diuretics available in pharmacies against the edemas, oxygen should only be used to support the descent of a person with acute mountain sickness.

The body can acclimate best if the ascent is slow. The difference between camps should not be more than 500 meters in altitude. Despite optimal acclimation, the human body has its limits. That's why the altitude of 5,500 m is called the deadly limit. The body cannot take in enough energy at this level.

On the Internet

www.princeton.edu/~oa/safety/altitude.html
Reliable information about altitude sickness; in English

www.multisportsa.com/injuries/altitudesick.htm
Overview of the most important aspects of this topic; in English

Acute Lack of Oxygen

△ It was only at the end of the 19th century that the French physiologist Paul Bert and his Italian colleague Angelo Mosso recognized the correlation between altitude sickness and thin air. Since the brain uses 15-20% of the oxygen intake of the body, it reacts most acutely to thin air. It is assumed that this directs more arterial blood into the brain which leads to the frequently occuring headaches from the resulting pressure on other parts of the brain. Nausea, vomiting and loss of sleep are probably caused by a change in blood supply to the hypothalamus, which regulates these functions.

Another typical phenomenon at high altitude is the Cheyne-Stokes Respiration, a disruption of the normal breathing frequency named after two Dublin doctors, John Cheyne and William Stokes. Breathing changes from deeper to more shallow, and it can even stop for up to 10 seconds. Edemas are formed by complex intracellular processes. If this accumulation of fluids happens to be in someone's lungs, the person may actually die from asphyxiation. A cerebral edema causes insecure gait, loss of fine motor skills, and mental confusion. If pulmonary or cerebral edemas are suspected, the best choice is immediate descent.

Trekking & Mountaineering

2

Hikes & Climbs

On the following pages, you will find 23 hikes and climbs in the Central Andes. In selecting them, we have tried to balance all interests and expectations; however, we cannot possibly cover the entire area. It is just too varied, large and unexplored. Often, we will only describe one of many options for climbing a mountain, and often, a valley or a road will provide more than one tour. Especially in the Cordillera near Santiago, there are numerous valleys, passes, and peaks waiting for the avid hiker. The local Andean clubs will be happy to provide more information *(see Addresses and the websites listed on next page)*.

The tours are listed from north to south; and they carry symbols for difficulty, duration, equipment and attractiveness. For some tours, we have collected GPS data, and for others, they will be included in future updates.

Even though we have collected our information as thoroughly as possible, we cannot give any guarantees as to their accuracy *(see disclaimer on page 2)*.

Photo: At the crater of Descabezado Grande (Tour 14)

Difficulty

 Hiking: Easy terrain without major grades, obvious and easy-to-walk trail, but not a stroll, day tour with small pack, max. length: 6 hours.

 Trekking: Demanding terrain, more grades, trail not always obvious, easy river crossings; longer day tour or multi-day tour with pack.

 Alpine: Difficult terrain, major grades, no obvious trails in places, difficult river crossings, glaciers or snowfields, special equipment and mountaineering experience needed; multi-day tour with pack.

 Expedition: Long climbs on peaks in the High Andes that are not easily accessible, demanding preparation and equipment needs, may require pack animal support, pitching several camps; only for mountaineers with excellent conditioning and sufficient logistical and technical experience.

Equipment	Duration

Overnight camping

Special equipment needed

 Duration in days

🕐 3 Hiking time in hours (estimated)

Our point of view

☺ Worth doing

☺ Great

☺ Don't miss

On the Internet

www.trekkingchile.com
The website related to this book, updated regularly; in English, German & Spanish

www2.ing.puc.cl/~cseebach/mountain/andes.en.html
Detailed information about climbing and mountaineering in Chile, in English & Spanish

http://w3.infotech.cl/andinismo/
Information about ascents and hiking tours, in Spanish only

La Campana National Park
Darwin's Mountain

The very first tour forms an exception: it is the only one located in the Coastal Cordillera. La Campana National Park situated between the 1,880 m peak of the same name and 2,222 m Cerro El Roble protects the last stands of the formerly common Chilean Palm. In addition, in its southern half, there is a vast area of virgin forest with tall Boldo, Peumo, Lingue and Canelo trees, as well as the northernmost Roble stands in the Americas – a botanist's dream. And an animal lover's – hardly a natural park can boast as many bird species, and as for mammals, the cute rodent Degú will vie for visitors' attention with the curious fox zorro culpeo. In 1834, Charles Darwin climbed this mountain, which is noted on a memorial plaque in the upper part. This National Park, which can be accessed from two directions, has several easy, interesting hikes, as well as a special treat: from the top of Mt. La Campana, on a clear day, you can see the Pacific Ocean and the main Cordillera with the impressive peak of Aconcagua.

On the Internet

www.parquelacampana.cl
Excellent description of fauna, flora and hiking trails in the park; in English and Spanish

Photo: View from the summit of Campana towards the Cordillera of the Andes

One of the last preserves for the Chilean palm tree

The threatened Chilean palm

△ There used to be millions of these huge palm trees (jubaea chilensis), which are unique to Chile, between Illapel and Curicó. However, since palm honey and palm wine were popular, the stand is down to a mere 50,000 trees. The trunk, which is reminiscent of an elephant's leg, can reach a diameter of 2 m, and a height of 20 m. At age 60, this palm tree flowers for the first time, and it can become 1,000 years old. The bud explodes with a loud bang, and the walnut-sized fruit are sold in supermarkets.

hour by car inland from Valparaíso/Viña del Mar. There are buses (via Villa Alemana/Limache) to the hamlet of Granizo (6 km east of Olmué), and from there, it's about another 2 km to either of the Park entrances where pretty campsites by bubbling brooks under a dense canopy of trees will be waiting for you, and where you will find people picnicking in the Summer.

Fees

Admission: USD 2.50; Tent camping: USD 10.00 per site (6 people).

View of La Campana from the Portezuelo trail

Point of Departure

Santiago or Valparaíso/Viña del Mar.

Approach by Road

The northern part of the Park (Sector Ocoa) is accessed via the Panamericana Norte (Ruta 5). 94 km north of Santiago a gravel road veers off to the left (to Palmares de Ocoa) and reaches the park entrance after 14 km. Right up to the spot where that road branches off the Panamericana you can take all buses that go to La Ligua from Santiago. From Valparaíso/Viña, public transport will take you within 4 and 2 km respectively of the Park entrance via Quillota – La Calera to Hualcapo or Escuela Las Palmas. Another 1,500 m from the entrance, in the midst of palm trees, is the tent campsite La Buitrera.

The two southern entrances of the Park (Granizo and Cajón Grande) near Olmué are 60 km or an

Through the National Park 4

From the Ocoa park entrance, take the road for about two kilometers to a place named 'Casino' (don't worry, there's no such thing); then take the well sign-posted "Portezuelo" trail (to the right) along Quebrada El Amasijo. There, you will have numerous picturesque views of Cerro La Campana and the palm forests below. The well-marked trail climbs right through the "elephant's legs" to the highest elevation of this tour, Portezuelo Ocoa, at approx. 1,100 m (7 km, 2.5 hrs.). From there, either backtrack or take "Granizo" trail down to the southern Park entrance, passing through dense old growth forest (4.5 km, 1.5 hrs.). The trail merges for a brief while with a road before it leads directly into the valley (Sendero Los Peumos). This day tour has an elevation gain of approx. 700 m.

Alternate Route: A somewhat longer descent follows Cajón Grande valley down to the park entrance of the same name (about 2 hrs.).

Ascent of La Campana, 1,880 m 6

From the southern Park entrance, the ascent to the summit consists of a relatively steep trail signposted as Sendero El Andinista, which runs through dense natural forests with thickets of bamboo (quila), a plant that does not usually grow this far north. It's about three to four hours to the summit, and another two to three hours to get back. Over a distance of 7 km, the altitude gain is approx. 1,400 m.

Darwin on La Campana: "I never enjoyed one day more thoroughly"

▲ Early in the morning of August 16, 1834, Charles Darwin set out on horseback for the summit of Campana. He had been graciously offered the use of horses by the owner of San Isidro Hacienda, which lies to the northwest of this mountain, near Quillota. Darwin gladly left the actual climbing of the muddy trail to these well-rested animals.

Compared to the many other expeditions on this journey during which he studied, among others, Argentina, Chile, and the Galapagos Islands from 1831 until 1836, this two-day tour turned out to be a cinch. Darwin, just 25 years old at the time, was above all interested in the vegetation: While he had found the Quillota Valley a verdant green, full of blooms and plantations, the slopes of La Campana had only brush and hundreds of thousands of Chilean palm trees. "These palms are, for their family, ugly trees", he wrote because of their unusually barrel-shaped trunks. And he described at length how the Chileans made syrup from its sap.

However, the young Darwin was above all a geologist; animals and plants came second. It wasn't until the second day that he saw what he was really excited about. After the ascent to the summit, he wrote into his diary, "I never enjoyed one [day] more thoroughly. Chile, bounded by the Andes and the Pacific, was seen as in a map." He could see all the way to Valparaíso, where even the masts of the schooners in the port were visible as thin black lines. And when he turned his head, the peaks of the Andes glistened like an army of whipped cream-monsters. "Who can avoid wondering at the force which has upheaved these mountains", he wrote breathlessly.

The earthquakes he experienced in Chile, as well as this view utterly convinced the explorer that the world was constantly changing, that it created and buried mountains, and that it had not been unchanged since the days of creation – contrary to the rigidly held views of the captain of his research vessel 'Beagle' and most scientists of his time. Thus, Darwin's journey became the key experience for developing his Theory of Evolution which revolutionized science.

Darwin's arduous northern route to the peak of Campana is hardly used anymore. The Coastal Cordillera und the Andes proper are as impressive as ever. Only the palm trees have become scarcer, and the cloud of smog that hovers over Santiago blocks the view further south. (Marcus Franken)

www.literature.org/authors/darwin-charles/the-voyage-of-the-beagle/
Read the complete version of Darwin's travel log; in English

Yerba Loca Valley
At the Altar of the Andes

  Ascent of Paloma   1-3

Map on page 74

This well-known nature preserve close to Santiago received its name from Yerba Loca (Astragalus Bergii in the same Leguminosae family as peas), literally "crazy herb". In the Summer, there are a lot of day users, families with their picnic baskets who crowd the barbecue pits at the entrance. But a few hundred meters into the park, you will only find other hikers. This Santuario de la Naturaleza (Nature Sanctuary) protects the long valley with its Estero Yerba Loca, a lively stream between steep barren slopes. The trail runs gently uphill along its bank. While the lower part of the tour is characterized by brushy vegetation, the upper areas are filled with vast stony areas and small pastures. At the end of the valley rule glaciated 4,930 m La Paloma and impressive 5,222 m peak El Altar, whose summit is not only reminiscent of an altar, but also of Matterhorn. Experienced mountain climbers wil find an El Dorado of diverse tours, but even if you "only" hike, the easy trail is worth it because of the rugged scenery.

Photo: Hiking between scree slopes in the High Andes valley of Yerba Loca

Point of Departure

Santiago.

Approach by Road

At the end of Av. Las Condes (busses to Lo Barnechea) a narrow blacktop takes off towards the ski region of Farellones. The road switchbacks precipitously. After 25 km (about 40 min. by car), at Curve No. 15, take the turn-off to Yerba Loca / Villa Paulina. Right after that, you have to sign-in at the Conaf post, and then it's 4 more km to Villa Paulina where the dirt road ends. There is no public transport; in Winter, busses run to the ski region. You can hitch-hike from the turn-off to Farellones.

Fees

Admission: USD 2.00, tents free.

Cerro Altar beckons at the end of the valley

Villa Paulina, a former mining camp, which is very popular now as a camping and picnic area, especially on Summer weekends, is at 1,940 m altitude. From here, the easy trail runs entirely on the eastern side of Yerba Loca creek. After roughly 4 hours you will reach a mountain valley at about 3,000 m, with pastures below the rock of Casa de Piedra Carvajal – the best campsite. Before the halfway point, you can fill your water bottle in Agua Larga Creek. This hike to Casa de Piedra and back can easily be done as a day tour (7-8 hours).

From the camp, you can get to the hanging glacier of Cerro Paloma by walking up the valley, in another hour and 500 m in altitude.

Optional tour: Mountain climbers with sufficient experience can climb the peak of Paloma from here in a day. To do so, walk around the rocky hill in front of the mountain to the West following the culoir above the glacier up to the ridge between Paloma (4,930 m) and Altar (5,222 m). From there, it's another 300 m in altitude to the peak via the western side of Paloma.

Day 2 3

Take the same route back to Villa Paulina.

Alternate Tour: Cordón de Yerba Loca

This strenuous day tour takes you from Villa Paulina to the peak of Cerro del Manchón (3,871 m). Right after Villa Paulina, you will cross a bridge, and after a few hundred meters, turn left uphill (no trail here) to Cordón de Yerba Loca. Once at the top, follow the ridge in a northerly direction (parallel to the trail in the valley) all the way to Cerro del Manchón, which provides an impressive view of the glaciers of Plomo (5,424 m), Altar, and Paloma. Take the same route back (approx. 7-8 hours total).

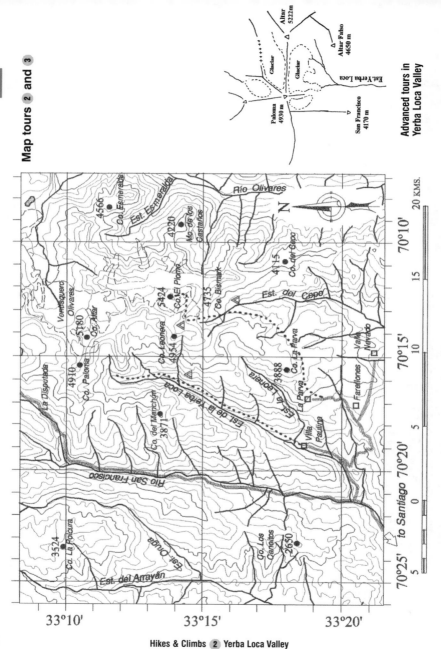

Advanced tours in Yerba Loca Valley

Cerro El Plomo (5,424 m)
Dome Above the City

Map on page 74

Santiago's landmark mountain – unmistakable with its dome-shaped, glaciated back – towers high above the city. It has always lured mountain climbers who want to try an "easy" 5,000 m peak after all those mountains at 3,000 m and 4,000 m to enjoy the panoramic view of the roofs of the Andes. Indeed, technically, the "lead-colored one" is said to be easy to climb. However, do not underestimate the altitude: El Plomo is known for frequent occurrence of acute mountain sickness. There are supposed to have been guys who run up and down this mountain in three days. We recommend, however, that you take your time and climb 4954 m Leonera on day 3 to get acclimated.

The Incas already knew about the fascination of these mountains and considered them the residence of their deities. They used El Plomo as a height sanctuary: In 1954 the well preserved body of a child who had been sacrificed to the gods was found under a stone building in the summit area.

Photo: View of the south-west flank of Plomo with its glaciers

Point of Departure

Santiago.

Approach by Road

You will need a car to get to the trailhead. Where Avenida Las Condes ends, take the turn that leads to Farellones. The road to the skiing region of La Parva winds its way through the mountains for about one and a half hours. When the snow is gone, you can try to take your car up the gravel switchbacks of the skirun, all the way to the upper end of the last lift at an altitude of about 3,400 m.

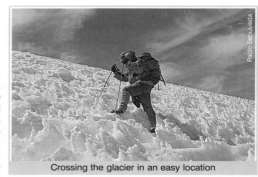
Crossing the glacier in an easy location

Pablo Sepúlveda

Fees

None.

Day 1 ● 3-4

From the end of the skirun, an initially obvious path leads up to Portezuelo Franciscano. Getting there, you will see the lagoon of the same name. From here, the path runs in a north-easterly direction. After several ups and downs totalling about 400 m in altitude, you will reach Piedra Numerada in three to four hours. Here, at an altitude of 3,350 m, you will find excellent camping on the sweeping pasture stretching along Estero Molina, or Cepo.

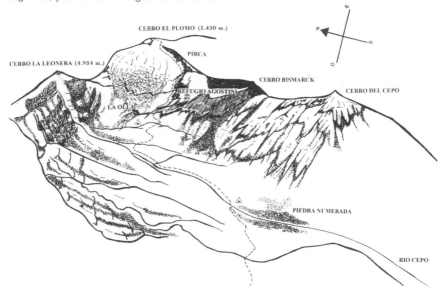

CERRO EL PLOMO (5.430 m.)

CERRO LA LEONERA (4.954 m.)

PIRCA

CERRO BISMARCK

CERRO DEL CEPO

REFUGIO AGOSTINI

LA OLLA

PIEDRA NUMERADA

RIO CEPO

Day 2 4

Today's tour is rather short. The trail becomes quite steep and runs in a northerly direction, to a spot close to Plomo's Iver Glacier at about 4,300 m. *Andinistas* call this camp La Olla (The Pot); it is definitely preferable to the bivouacs Hermandad and Agostini further up. Short excursions to the glacier through the numerous fields of "penitents" or a day tour climbing Leonera will help you get acclimated.

Day 3 5-6

Add a day for acclimating by climbing 4,954 m Leonera, which towers right to the northwest of camp. It's well worth it: After about two or three hours of clambering, you will get to enjoy the phantastic panoramic view of Cerro Plomo with its massive glacier, and you can even spot the next day's route.

Back at La Olla, grab your packs and continue along the Plomo route for roughly another 1.5 hours to an altitude of 4,600 m, where you will find some good spots for pitching your tents near the delapidated Agostini bivouac.

As an alternative, those who are less acclimated could spend another night at La Olla. Another day of getting used to the altitude will do you good, and you will not only be more likely to make the summit, but the ascent will also be more fun!

Day 4 9-11

It is about 850 m in altitude to the summit, and 300 more meters if you start the climb at La Olla. The trail is clearly visible; it runs along the right side of the glacier steeply on talus to an easy spot above where you can cross the glacier using crampons and iceaxes. At an altitude of 5,140 m, you will pass an Inca altar; up further, at about 5,200 m, there is a circular platform where the offering was held. At 5,400 m, the child was found in 1954.

As you get to the last few meters, your legs will turn to lead – is that why this mountain is called El Plomo? However, the ordeal will have been well worth it – from the summit at 5,424 m, there is an unobstructed view of the Andes and their varied peaks and mountain chains reaching all the way to Aconcagua, the highest mountain in the Americas at 6,959 m. Figure on 5 to 7 hours for this climb, and another four hours for the way back.

Day 5 5

Backtrack from La Olla via Piedra Numerada to the upper part of La Parva ski region.

Little Prince in the Frost

△ The Incas, who conquered what is Chile today from the north down to Río Maule in the 15th century, venerated the high peaks of the Andes. Archeological finds have shown that the Incas sacrificed people on the highest peaks in order to communicate with heaven. This was also the fate of the 8 year-old boy who was taken to Cerro El Plomo about 500 years ago. Most likely being of nobility, he was wearing fancy clothes and precious silver jewelry. His face had been painted red and yellow, and his jetblack hair had been fashioned into more than 200 braids festooned with black tassels and condor feathers. On an altar built for this occasion at 5,200 m altitude, he was sacrificed, and then buried at 5,400 m.

In 1954, arrieros unearthed the body that had been freeze-dried naturally in the carefully fashioned tomb built in the permafrost soil, where he was consequently very well preserved. The mummy was on exhibit until 1980 at the Museum of Natural History in Santiago, after which it had to be removed to storage because of conditions not conducive to preservation. The museum has been hoping to be able to afford building a climate-controlled exhibit ever since.

 www.mnhn.cl
Information about mummies found in Chile, on the Museum's website; in Spanish only

Malte Sieber

Cerro Provincia (2,751 m)
Santiago at your feet

4

East of Santiago the Pre-Cordillera chain of Sierra San Ramón abruptly blocks the unbridled growth of the monstrous capital. Especially in the Winter and Spring, when the chain is powdered white, its signature summit line including Cerro Provincia (2,751 m), Cerro San Ramón (3,249 m), and Punta de Damas (3,144 m) sharply contrasts with the concrete jungle of the capital. On a clear day, the mountains seem close enough to touch, beckoning you on a seemingly easy tour. And indeed, ascents of Provincia and San Ramón are relatively easy to organize. At the same time, they are very demanding in terms of conditioning, since none of the access roads brings you closer than an altitude of 1,000 m, which means you will face major altitude gains. And especially in the Summer, the high daytime temperatures make these tours a strenuous undertaking.

We have described the easier ascent of Cerro Provincia (or Providencia), which can be done in a day. Its lower portion is especially gorgeous in Spring, when the slopes are clad in a verdant green and everything seems to be in bloom. The exceptionally well-marked trail climbs to the ridge through a forest of deciduous trees, and from the top, you can either see the city itself, or else its smog cover.

Photo: The Pre-Cordillera chain east of the capital; to the left (not in the photo), Cerro Provincia (2751 m), followed by the long ridge leading up to Cerro San Ramón (3249 m), and on the very right Punta de Damas (3144 m)

Point of Departure

Santiago.

Access by Road

Option 1: After going 5 km on the road to Farellones *(see Yerba Loca Valley, p. 73)*, a gravel road takes off to the right which continues parallel to the main road until you get to an old bridge over the Mapocho river (Puente Ñilhue). Leave the car before the bridge and start your ascent. Several city bus routes (To Lo Barnechea – Plaza San Enrique) run to the end of Av. Las Condes, where the road to Farellones starts. From there, you can either rent a cab or try to hitch-hike.

Option 2: The ascent from San Carlos de Apoquindo is even easier to get to. Bus routes 326 and 327 run all the way to the stadium of the same name that belongs to the Sports club of the Universidad Católica (13,000 block of Av. Las Flores). Get permission at the entrance to the stadium; if you have problems getting in mention the manager's name (Eduardo Barrios.) Continue to the highest point of the road through the club. The well-marked trail starts at a gate behind the equestrian facilities (about 1.5 km).

Fees

None.

Option 1: By the Ñilhue bridge at 970 m a Protege Organization board describes the route which is marked with colored signs. Right at the beginning, you will climb the rocks on the south side of the gorge, with Mapocho creek running way below. The trail first goes up a dry *quebrada* and reaches the first view point after half an hour, with a view of the Mapocho Valley and the peaks beyond. A little while from there, a trail veers off to the left to Vallecito; however, stay on the main trail which follows a ridge and runs next to a concrete irrigation canal briefly – last opportunity for filling your bottles! After a total of two hours of heavy-duty scrambling, you will get to a big saddle at 1,868 m with huge Quillay trees: This place called Alto del Naranjo is the ideal spot for a break; in the Summer, you can find entire groups of scouts camping here.

From Alto del Naranjo, you can already see the summit of Provincia to the south. Right after the restplace our trail is joined by the trail from San Carlos de Apoquindo (Option 2).

Option 2: From San Carlos de Apoquindo stadium (1,010 m) the trail, which is wide initially, is also clearly marked. First it ascends gently until you get to a monolith. This is where the main trail continues to Mirador Las Rocas. Keep to the left, however, on a much steeper trail through dense vegetation. The forest becomes thinner and gives way to enormous cacti. Cross a level area called Cancha de Carrera (racecourse) and clamber up to the ridge right behind Alto del Naranjo where the

Especially in the winter, smog is a problem in Santiago

Alexander Schneider

Unlike others, the Provincia trail is marked

ous in foggy conditions!) – bear right! The trail now becomes steeper again, and before the last major grade, you have to climb through easy rocks. If you think that you made it to the top after 2.5 more hours, you will see that it is another 150 m to the actual summit. But you can do that – now that it's also relatively flat. To the northwest, you can see Santiago suffocating under its smog, to the south, the ridge continues to San Ramón, and to the northeast, Plomo, Pintor, and Colorado are lined up nicely.

The descent is along the same route; about 2.5 to 3 hrs.

trail meets up with Option 1. Altogether, Option 2 is shorter, but steeper (also 2 hrs.) There is no water on the entire trail, even in the spring.

The route continues at first with only minor ups and downs along the ridge, giving you some rest. After about 20-25 minutes you have to cross a fence, after which the trail branches (treacher-

An **optional route** goes from Provincia all the way along the ridge to San Ramón, and west from there along a well visible trail down to Quebrada de Peñalolén and the upper end of Avenida Larraín. If you want to complete this tour in two days, you need to be in great shape and take lots of water.

The "Protege" Project: Dreaming of a Summit Restaurant

△ The gondola of the funicular glides slowly upward escaping the city smog, while in the east, glaciated peaks become visible. Once at the top, people enjoy the panoramic view explained by plaques next to the telescopes. A group of managers in casual dress exit the conference center and amble over to the restaurant … This scene reminiscent of the Austrian Alps is simply utopian for Chile. And yet, the vision is supposed to become reality according to the plans of the Protege ("Protect") project. By the Bicentennial of the Republic of Chile in 2010, Cerro San Ramón is supposed to be turned into a great attraction just outside the capital – with a funicular, view platform, restaurant, and memorial chapel.

So far, Protege has progressed rather modestly, and yet, it has made a difference in the process. In 1993 a group of idealists started convincing the communities of eastern Santiago that there is a tremendous natural potential hidden in "their" Pre-Cordillera that should be developed and protected at the same time. The communal association started marking hiking trails, forming environmental protection programs and developing a sort of "mountain culture" among Santiago's citizens. So far, there are three 'senderos' – the two access trails to Provincia, as well as the first part from Peñalolén to San Ramón. In 2001, a transverse route was started halfway up the slope at Peñalolén, which was declared a part of Sendero de Chile.

Constantly in financial difficulties, Protege has had to shelve numerous projects. The group that started the initiative is now hoping for more impetus from government projects such as Sendero de Chile and the Bicentennial of the Republic.

www.protege.cl
Projects and trails of the Protege organization; in Spanish only

Volcanoes
Tupungato (6,550 m) & Tupungatito (5,640 m)
Like a Himalaya Expedition

(5)

Map on page 86

Even though this area is a lot more attractive as far as scenery than the area around Aconcagua, the volcano Tupungato is not climbed very often. Nestled between Río Aconcagua to the north and Río Maipo to the south, this cone-shaped volcanic giant is only about 70 km from Santiago as the crow flies. However, the area is not easily accessible; the long march to the base camp and the enormous difference in altitude of the last stages give the rather easy climb the characteristics of a tour in the Himalayas. We recommend it (at least any summit attempts) only for experienced mountaineers. Around the base camp, however, trekking types can also have lots of fun.

The regular summit route is over the relatively monotonous north side. We have, however, described the more demanding (since it's glaciated) southwest route over the pass between Tupungato and its little brother, Tupungatito. From the pass, you can do an acclimation tour of much lower Tupungatito, whose 5 km diameter caldera extends its glacier's tongues westward. At its northeastern corner, eight active craters and turquoise lagoons have flocked together like chicks in a nest.

Given the expedition character and the high altitudes, it is hard to give durations of hikes.

Photo: Impressive Tupungato volcano from the south-west, with "penitents" in the foreground

Point of Departure

Santiago.

Organizational Details

For climbing Tupungato you will need permits from the utility company Chilgener S.A., Miraflores 222, Santiago Centro, Ph. (2) 686 84 70, Fax (2) 686 86 68 that runs a hydroelectric powerplant on the lower portion of the Colorado, and from the Chilean border control agency, Dirección Nacional de Fronteras y Límites del Estado, Bandera 52, Santiago Centro, Ph. (2) 671 41 10, Fax (2) 697 19 09. For the long approach to the base camp (with gear and provisions for 10 days) and because of the dangers of crossing Río Azufre (especially in the Spring) it is advisable to rent horses. In mid-Summer, you can always find *arrieros* around Los Maitenes and Alfalfal, but this is best done a few days before the start of your expedition.

Approach by Road

Coming from Santiago take the exit via Avenida La Florida to Las Vizchachas, then follow the road to the Maipo Valley to the bridge across Río Colorado. Immediately after that, a 22 km paved access road turns off towards Los Maitenes/Alfalfal. Get or present the permit for driving through at the Alfalfal power plant; then a good gravel road takes you another 20 km to the starting point at Chacayal at 2,200 m altitude. Plan on 2-3 hours.

Fees

None.

Stage 1: Approach to Base Camp

First hike up the long valley of Río Colorado to its end. The route always stays close to the river and is clearly recognizable as a trail, with few exceptions. You will have to cross several tributaries on this portion of the trail. It is best to divide this approach up over two days. There is a good campsite at the mouth of Río Museo at 2,400 m, which you will reach after approx. three hours. This option allows you to cross Río Azufre the next morning when it will have less water (it

is fed by a glacier). The current will still be very strong, and the water will easily come up to your hips. That's why it's so much more pleasant to be on horseback!

There are several places to choose from for the base camp. We chose a spot on the edge of the marshy pastures on the upper portion of Colorado at about 3,200 m. This area, which is known as Vegas del Flojo, is easy to find because of its verdant vegetation in the midst of this desert of rocks. The water from the watering holes next to the pasture will need to be treated. Without backpacks, it will take about 9-10 hours from Chacayal to here.

From here, you have access to the northern and southwesterly routes, and in addition, you can do nice practice tours. One of those, which is also appropriate for trekkers, goes up the crest to the east of the camp. This small peak reveals a spectacular view of the Tupungato massif.

The northern route follows the trail along Río Colorado further upstream. You can pitch altitude camps at 4,000 m or at Paso Tupungato (4,760 m).

The first obstacle: Río Azufre

Trekking & Mountaineering

2

GPS Waypoints Stage 1

1. Chacayal, al 2,200 m	S 33º 27.107'	W 70º 01.289'
2. Approach base camp	33º 25.347'	W 70º 00.057'
3. Río Museo	S 33º 24.559'	W 69º 58.446'
4. Río Azufre	S 33º 24.068'	W 69º 57.849'
5. Approach base camp	S 33º 22.793'	W 69º 55.293'
6. Creek crossing	S 33º 22.153'	W 69º 54.568'
7. View Tupungatito	S 33º 21.046'	W 69º 53.214'
8. Gorge	S 33º 20.730'	W 69º 52.416'
9. Base camp 3,200 m	S 33º 20.227'	W 69º 51.906'

Stage 2: Approach to Altitude Camp 1

For climbing Tupungato over the southwesterly route, first follow Río Colorado a little way downstream to Quebrada Paso Malo. From the mouth of the creek a trail switchbacks up the western wall of the gorge. You will find one red marker on this trail. After the half-day point, at about 4,300 m, you will find several spots for pitching your tent above a small creek and directly against the side of the vast Tupungatito, with a great view of the surrounding mountains. A short walk will suffice to catch a glimpse of the massive block of Aconcagua.

GPS Waypoints Stage 2

Base Camp	S 33º 20.227'	W 69º 51.906'
10. Paso Malo Gorge	S 33º 20.929'	W 69º 52.700'
11. Ascent C1	S 33º 21.113'	W 69º 51.919'
12. Ascent C1	S 33º 21.402'	W 69º 51.788'
13. Ascent C1	S 33º 21.613'	W 69º 51.564'
14. Ascent C1	S 33º 21.992'	W 69º 51.495'
15. Ascent C1 red	S 33º 21.962'	W 69º 51.082'
16. Altitude Camp 1, 4,300 m	S 33º 22.228'	W 69º 50.198'

Stage 3: Side Trip to Tupungatito

From the first altitude camp let's climb to the crater rim of Tupungatito at 5,300 m – just for practice. The strenuous ascent that leads partly through scree will take three to four hours. It's all the way up the slope that lies to the south of the camp. At the rim of the caldera, you will be shocked to see that you are not at the summit yet, this is not the highest spot. But let's forget about the summit; let's just clamber a bit further to the east so we can see the lime-green crater lake. To the south, you will see the vast glaciers of Piuquenes.

GPS Waypoints Stage 3

Altitude Camp 1, 4,300 m	S 33º 22.228'	W 69º 50.198'
17. Crater, 5,300 m	S 33º 23.029'	W 69º 50.079'
18. Crater rim, Tupungatito, 5,300 m	S 33º 23.201'	W 69º 49.644'

Stage 4: Ascent to Altitude Camp 2

Climb the face ahead of you to the east. Depending on the season, vast fields of "penitents" can make walking very difficult. That might be one of those moments when you ask yourself, "Why am I doing this to myself?" It's hard to squeeze through between the snow and ice towers that are taller than a meter, and when you step on them, they break and fall over. And all this at an altitude of over 5,000 m where every step requires an effort!

Grit your teeth! Follow the logical route along the foot of the vast Tupungatito with a view of majestic Tupungato, staying at the same altitude towards the pass between the two mountains. After the half-day point, at quite a distance from the pass, at 5,300 m you will find several protected spots for camping in the midst of this desert of rock and snow. Level spots are rare on this grade.

GPS Waypoints Stage 4

Altitude Camp 1	S 33º 22.228'	W 69º 50.198'
19. Ascent C2 mountain ridge, bottom	S 33º 22.142'	W 69º 49.637'
20. Ascent C2 mountain ridge, top	S 33º 22.413'	W 69º 49.576'
21. Ascent C2	S 33º 22.767'	W 69º 48.931'
22. Altitude Camp 2, 5,300 m	S 33º 22.908'	W 69º 48.691'

Stage 5: Ascent to the Summit

The climb to the pass will start from the second altitude camp. From the pass, you will have a gorgeous view of the Argentinian side, and you can study the structure of the summit of Tupungato in detail. Further up, you should pitch another altitude camp; there is a good spot at about 6,100 m.

From there, the ascent is the typical volcano climb on glaciated terrain. Even though it is only a few more hundreds of meters to the summit, don't underestimate the time required for reaching it, given the enormous altitude.

From the summit of Central Chile's highest mountain, you will have a cinemascope view of the Andes with their huge glacier tongues streching out towards Argentina. Note: In the Summer, you have to be prepared for electrical storms in the afternoon, or at least for heavy clouds and snowfall.

GPS Waypoints Stage 5

Altitude Camp 2, 5,300 m	S 33º 22.908'	W 69º 48.691'
Paso Tupungato, 5,350 m	S 33º 23.102'	W 69º 47.219'
Ascent summit, 5,360 m	S 33º 22.689'	W 69º 47.018'
Ascent summit, 5,450 m	S 33º 22.407'	W 69º 46.680'
Ascent summit, 5,700 m	S 33º 22.316'	W 69º 46.544'
Ascent summit, 5,850 m	S 33º 22.064'	W 69º 46.372'
Altitude Camp 3, 6,100 m	No Data	
Summit, 6,550 m	No Data	

Stage 6: Descent to Base Camp

Descend the same route you came up.

Optional route: It is theoretically possible to climb over the summit and back down the standard northern route, but it would not only be a mountaineering challenge, but also a logistical one. You would have to carry all your gear ascending the summit! The northern route goes beyond the summit to an altitude camp at 5,500 m that is protected by large boulders, and from there down to Portezuelo Tupungato at 4,800 m. You would reach the base camp of Vegas del Flojo on a well-trodden path.

Stage 7: Return to Chacayal

The return from base camp to the starting point at Chacayal can be done in one long day.

Be prepared for snow even in the summer

Lost in the Andes

△ Tupungato kept its secret for 53 years. In August of 1947, a British passenger plane enroute to Santiago from London via Buenos Aires disappeared in this area during an electrical storm. It was the first regular flight on this route since World War II. Despite a thorough search, the plane – a retrofitted WWII bomber – remained missing in the Andes.

It was not until January of 2000 that Argentinian andinistas found remnants of the Lancaster Stardust and its eleven passengers killed in the accident at an altitude of 5,000 m.

There are many wild speculations about the cause of the crash. The most probable one, however, was that the pilot lost his bearings in heavy turbulences and crashed into the mountain.

 http://europe.cnn.com/2000/WORLD/americas/02/23/argentina.wreckage/ CNN report about the find on Tupungato, with other links

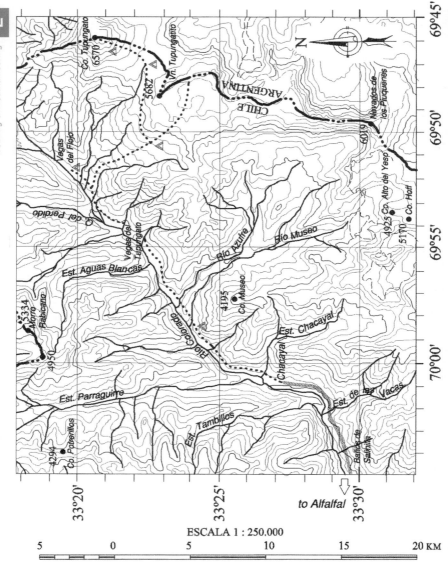

ESCALA 1 : 250.000

5   0   5   10   15   20 KM

Malte Sieber

2

Trekking & Mountaineering

El Morado National Park
Our Cover Star

6

 other tours   1-3 ☺ Map on page 90

This miniature National Park in the upper part of Cajón del Maipo has turned into a popular destination over the last few years. And for a reason, since it can boast easy hikes in a colorful mountain valley fairly easy to reach from Santiago. In addition, the resort of Baños Morales at the Park entrance provides a minimum of tourist attractions with simple accommodations, restaurants, and horse rentals. The hot springs here, however, fail the test miserably – they are barely 20 degrees; those who like it hotter should visit picturesque Baños Colina at the end of the main road (about half an hour by car from Baños Morales).

The park, which was named after the jagged teeth of Cerro Morado (4,490 m) at the valley's end, can be hiked in a day tour or more leisurely in two days. You cannot fail to be impressed by the rock layers on the steep walls that keep changing colors from red to green to ochre. Especially in the Spring, the ground is covered with a multitude of wildflowers – among them orchids, amaryllis, and Inca lilies. This is also where you might be able to observe condors.

The trail leads past green moors and a small lagoon to the glacier tongue of San Francisco, under which a small ice cave will form occasionally that you can walk into. Advanced climbers can participate in a glacier tour to 3,883 m Mirador on an extra day.

Photo: Cerro Morado (4,490 m) resides at the end of this green valley in the High Andes

Point of Departure

Santiago.

Approach by Road

The roughly 70 kilometers from Santiago to Baños Morales will take 2.5 to 3 hours by car. This is due to the amount of traffic on Av. La Florida and the winding road through Cajón del Maipo, whose pavement ends at San Gabriel (ca. 50 km). All the way to San Alfonso, the road is lined with numerous small stores, empanada stalls and homey restaurants. In San Gabriel, the police check personal and car documents.

From Parque O'Higgins there is regular bus service via Av. Matta - Av. Vicuña Mackenna (Metro Bellavista La Florida) - Puente Alto to the main town of the valley, San José de Maipo, and once an hour, it also runs to San Alfonso. From there you can try hitch-hiking. Two companies run vans all the way through Cajon de Maipo to the hot springs of Morales and Colina. They leave at 7:30 a.m. from Plaza Italia in front of Teatro Universidad de Chile. Since they do not operate daily (depending on season), call ahead to check and make reservations at ph. (2) 211 71 65, Turismo Arpue,

In the summer, Baños Colina become busy

or (2) 643 56 51, Manzur Expediciones. Both companies also offer special trips and rates for groups.

Fees

Admission USD 2.00, tent camping: free; closed from May until September.

Day 1/2   5-6

In Baños Morales, a small bridge leads to the Conaf building, where you pay your admission fees, and where you can get current information. From there, an obvious trail runs up the valley along the west side of Estero Morales. After the first steep section, the trail levels out more or less for quite a while. After about an hour, you will see red spots on the green pasture: springs with lots of minerals whose water will leave a prickly taste in your mouth.

It is about 2 to 3 hours to crystal-clear Laguna del Morado, along which you can pitch your tent. From there, you can already see the tongue of the glacier of

This hike is attractive early in the spring, too

4,345 m Cerro San Francisco which you will reach after another half hour. Be careful when entering the ice cave; the ice may not be stable!

Return on the same day or the next day by the same route.

For experienced mountain climbers, the ascent of 3,883 m Cerro Mirador via the glacier is well worth it.

On the Internet

www.gochile.cl/eng/Guide/ChileNationalParks/Chile-National-Parks.asp
Good overview of the Chilean natural parks; in English

www.conaf.cl/html/parques/parques.html
Homepage of the government agency for the national parks; in Spanish only

FUNDACION Claudio Gay

Six wonderful works of the wild flora of Chile

by Adriana Hoffmann

FIND THEM IN THE BEST CHILEAN BOOKSTORES
PHONE 56-2-7514901 · abadilla@mercurio.cl

△ Parque Nacional, Monumento Natural, Reserva Nacional or even Santuario de la Naturaleza (Nature Sanctuary) – the many categories for protected areas in Chile can be confusing for the visitor. And the difference between them is apparently not entirely clear even to the officials in charge. The term Nature Sanctuary does not even exist in official documents, but you will find it on signposts on location. And it also happens that nature preserves are not on the lists of protected places totalling 94 units: 31 National Parks, 48 Nature Reserves, and 15 Natural Monuments with a total area of about 30 million acres – covering almost a fifth of Chile. The Central Region has relatively few of them with only 19, mostly small reserves.

For the visitor, the differences between the categories are quite immaterial. They have to do with the size – a park protects a larger area, a monument a smaller one with specific flora or fauna, or geologically interesting formations. And then, while National Parks place the mostly virgin natural area under a strict ban on any use, the natural resources of reserves can be exploited in a sustainable way.

All state protected areas are administered by the Chilean Forest Service CONAF, even if they do not contain a single tree, such as in the desert north. In many places the limited means are barely enough to pay a few park rangers, but they are not sufficient for proper protection. And this despite the fact that Conaf has raised user fees considerably over the past years. Those monies, however, go into the federal coffers and do not directly benefit the parks.

And there is an additional absurd twist: Conaf is responsible for managing the forests and the entire forestry industry. So they issue permits for logging – even for the natural reserves. Environmental protection advocates are demanding that these functions be separated and an independent National Park administration be instituted.

Trekking & Mountaineering

2

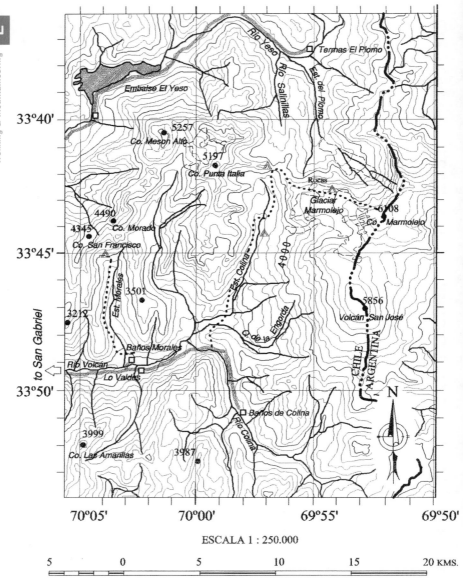

ESCALA 1 : 250.000

5   0   5   10   15   20 KMS.

Cerro Marmolejo (6,109 m) ⑦
The Southernmost 6,000 m Peak

 Summit    Map on page 90

East of El Morado National Park rises Cerro Marmolejo, the southernmost 6,000 m peak in the world. From Maipo Valley the mountain you first see to the south is the volcano San José. Separated only by one pass, Marmolejo and San José form one long mountaneous area. The complex consists of several peaks, out of which only the main peak exceeds 6,000 m. On the west side of the 3 km wide caldera a number of eruption zones document thousands of years of activity of this extinguished volcano. The southern and southeastern sides of the ragged massif are covered by mighty glaciers.

Contrary to Tupungato, this 6,000 m peak is easy to get to and relatively easy to climb. There are four different routes to the summit; we will describe the technically simple one via Estero Marmolejo.

Photo: View of glaciated Marmolejo in the background

Point of Departure

Santiago.

Preparation

The close-by El Morado National Park or Cerro El Plomo, which is also described here, are well suited for acclimation.

Approach by Road

From Santiago take via Av. La Florida to Las Vizcachas, and there turn left up into the Maipo Valley. Register the excursion at the police station in San Gabriel (important: take your personal and car documents!). The gravel road that is passable with regular cars leads past Baños Morales (on the left), and Lo Valdés (on the right, the cabin of the German Andean Club) reaching the bridge across Río Volcán (2,300 m altitude) after 28 km. Immediately behind that, the trail takes off to the left. Up to here, count on about three hours.

Alternate Option: A short distance after San Gabriel, a gravel road turns off to the left into Yeso Valley. Past multi-colored rock formations and the turquoise Yeso reservoir the road leads up to the natural springs of El Plomo at 3,000 m; the last 15 km, however, are extremely bad. From the springs, which are also popular as a point of departure for other tours, a route leads up to Portezuelo Marmolejo *(see Day 2)*.

Fees

None.

Day 1 6-8

The trail leads along the west slope of the volcano San José into the wide Valle de la Engorda (Fattening Valley), where – as the name says – the cows find nourishing pastures. Cross the creek of the same name and then follow the course of Estero Marmolejo in a northerly direction. The trail disappears occasionally and runs first on the westerly, then on the easterly side of the creek. Depending on the season, you may have to cross some tributaries, too. Below a

tongue of the glacier that comes poking down from Marmolejo, you will find good camp spots.

Day 2 5-6

Even though you will be hiking right through the most wonderful mountain area, the approach through the wide valley is quite monotonous. Since you can see most of the trail for most of the time, there are very few surprises as far as change of scenery. The route will take you further in a northerly direction up to Portezuelo Marmolejo (ca. 4,000 m), close to which you can pitch your tent. This is also where the alternate ascent route from Termas El Plomo at the end of Yeso Valley ends.

Day 3 5-6

After a four hour ascent from the pass towards the east you will reach a vast plain which is often covered by fields of "penitents". The best place for the altitude camp is on the opposite side at more than 5,000 m.

Day 4 9-10

From here you can already see the summit which you will reach in about six hours. Even though you do not need technical climbing skills for this ascent, safe handling of crampons and iceaxe, as well as altitude experience are required. The view, especially to the north towards glaciated Nevado de Piuquenes, as well as the mountains of the Morado area will make your heart beat a little faster.

Day 5/6 12-14

Descend by the same route to Colina bridge with one overnight stop.

Maike Sieber

Río Los Cipreses
The Valley of the Parrots

⑧

Map on page 96

In a side valley of the majestic Cachapoal River, Río Los Cipreses has carved its bed into the Andes. River and Nature Preserve owe their name to the dark, slender mountain cypress trees that used to cover the slopes. Today, only a narrow strip of those trees is left. In the lower part of the valley, you will find dense sclerophyll forests and a variety of cactus species. The smell of the sappy plants saturates the air, as do the piercing screeches of Tricahue, the largest of Chile's parrots, nesting in flocks on the steep walls.

The indigenous peoples of this Cordillera who settled here around 6,000 and 3,500 B.C. have left rock drawings in some remote areas. The sides of the valley narrow in some places, in others they allow a view of the mountain chain to the south which leads up to Palomo volcano. The trail wends its way alternately going up- and downhill all along the west side of the river, which provides refreshing coolness on hot Summer days. After the first stage, you will camp in a grove of cypress trees on the river bank, and you can do day tours from here to the surrounding mountains. With some luck, you might even be able to see some of the increasingly rare guanacos in the upper reaches.

Photo: In its lower reaches, the valley is covered in lush vegetation

Point of Departure

Rancagua.

Approach by Road

To get to the mining town of Coya from Rancagua, get on the Carretera Presidente Eduardo Frei Montalva (also called Carretera del Cobre), which was not built and maintained so perfectly for us mortals, but for the El Teniente copper mine further up. Right before the town's edge, the gravel road to the hot springs of Cauquenes turns off to the right. Drive past the fancy facilities (see Day 3) on your left and continue on the gravel road that gets increasingly worse (fourwheel drive or pick-up recommended) crossing the Pre-Cordillera to the entrance of Reserva Nacional Río Los Cipreses (50 km).

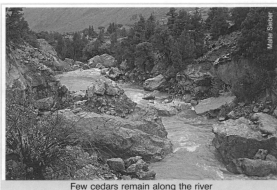
Few cedars remain along the river

Here friendly CONAF staff will give you more detailed information on the route, as well as a somewhat confusing description of how to find the hidden petroglyphs. Six kilometers behind the Conaf building you will find the official Ranchillo campsite. After getting permission from the park rangers, you might be allowed to take the car 6 kilometers further to a spot called Maitenes at an altitude of about 1,200 m. Park your car next to the plantation for indigenous trees and start your tour from there.

From Rancagua to Maitenes it is at least a two hours' drive. Public transport goes only as far as Coya. From there, it is 21 km to the park entrance - most of it uphill - and another 12 km to Maitenes. So you might be better off waiting for a ride!

Fees

Admission: USD 3.00, Camping: USD 7.50 per tent and night

Day 1 6

To the right of the tree plantation, an initially wide trail heads south into the valley of Río Los Cipreses. Early on, there are a few pretty views of the confluence of Los Cipreses and Cachapoal with a backdrop of steeply rising ragged 3,000 m peaks. The trail remains clearly visible throughout, running along the right side of the river. Especially in the lower part with its denser vegetation, it is of interest to the botanically inclined. While the ups and downs of the trail provide some diversion, you will be passing a number of nice campsites, and you will have to cross half a dozen creeks.

After about six hours of hiking, you will reach Camp Urriola at 1,500 m – easy to tell from a distance by its dark green stand of cypress trees. While the park rangers' hut on the other side may look inviting, you would have to cross the river with its strong currents, and it might also be better to try and avoid the potential Hanta virus risk. *(see p. 62-63).*

Day 2 6

You will follow the main trail upstream to Baúl creek, the closest wider valley of a tributary to the west. There, a trail leads up to the bluish mountain lake Piuquenes at about 2,500 m (4 hours). Return by the same route.

Another day tour goes further up Cipreses valley, past the Agua de la Vida / Agua de la Muerte springs, to the glaciated Quebrada Medina.

Return to Maitenes on the same route you ascended.

On the way back, it is worth taking a side trip to Termas de Cauquenes, one of the oldest and fanciest of Chile's spa hotels. Even as a day user, you can relax fabulously in a tub or jacuzzi in this facility that is almost 200 years old. If you want to stay overnight, you will have to make reservations and account for the steep prices. In return, René Acklin, the Swiss owner and his daughter Sabine, who are both world class chefs, will spoil you with exquisite dishes.

Enjoying a rainy day in Cypress valley

GPS Waypoints Río Los Cipreses

1. Starting point Maitenes	S 34° 20.097'	W 070° 24.896'
2. Camp Urriola	S 34° 27.459'	W 070° 25.163'

El Teniente: The Hollow Mountain

▲ Not far from Río Los Cipreses, the Andes harbor an attraction of a different kind: El Teniente, the world¹s largest underground copper mine. Cerro Negro, which has been systematically hollowed out for almost 100 years now, is criss-crossed by 2,200 km of galleries. The mountain is mined from the bottom to the top by means of the block-caving method which blasts the copper ore from the mountain by entire caves, then sends the ore to the crushers and takes it from below to the smelter by train. This impressive and unique sight - all other copper mines in Chile employ strip mining - can be toured. Unfortunately, the day-long tour (approx. USD 30.00) does not show the actual production process, but it does go to the former mining camp of Sewell, now a historic monument. Reservations through Turismo Sewell, ph. Stgo. 698 2270.

🡒 www.codelco.com/ingles/corporacion/f-divisiones.html
Chile's state-owned copper corporation; click on 'El Teniente'; in English

www.sewellturismo.cl
The somewhat clumsy site of the El Teniente tourist agency; the English version doesn't work

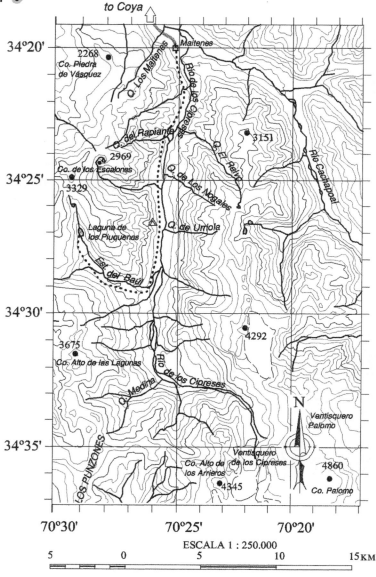

Franz Schubert

Volcán Tinguiririca (4,280 m)
The Tongue Twister

Map on page 100

The further south you get, the lower the Andes. One of the last efforts at a 4,000 m peak is Tinguiririca, a tongue twister of a name which signifies 'brightly shining quartz' or 'emaciated, freezing fox' in the Mapuche language. From the point of view of geology, this mountain is a rarity: The cone of Tinguiririca forms part of a 20 km volcanic fissure, and its crater is only one of at least ten "hot spots" along this line. While the last eruption dates back more than 80 years, the fumaroles inside the crater and to its northwest have kept steaming merrily.

But this volcano's fame is not based on its pyrotechnical skills but on something altogether different. In 1972, a passenger plane crashed on Tinguiririca. The dramatic tale of the survivors who endured 70 days in the glaciated mountains and even resorted to eating their dead was made into a gripping Hollywood thriller titled "Alive!".

It is easy to imagine the drama unfolding in the wild scenery around the peak. The splendid panoramic view that expects you at the summit is a just reward for what is a fairly boring and strenuous ascent.

Photo: The Tinguiririca massif represents a geological rarity

Point of Departure

San Fernando.

Approach by Road

The road that goes from San Fernando up the valley towards Termas del Flaco is an adventure unto itself. In the mornings, you can drive only uphill, and in the afternoons, only downhill – but on Sundays, it's the reverse. Only the first 17 km are paved. A rickety bus runs from San Fernando in the afternoon. Info can be obtained from Buses Yolita, ph. (74) 714 009; Buses Tur Coster, ph. (74) 712 473, and Buses Cordillera, ph. (74) 711 932. If you take the Sunday morning bus, you can go hiking in the afternoon.

Ask the driver to drop you off at the bridge on Fundo Maitenes. Since the first part of the trail is on private land, you will need to get permission from the owners first. Eugenio and Roberto Frank don't mind as long as you ask first and don't leave any trash.

Fees

None.

Day 1 8

A gravel road that starts at the bridge takes you along Río Azufre to the beautifully situated houses of the land owners.That will take a little over an hour on foot. This is where you need to ask for permission. If you have an allwheel drive, you can continue past this point up to where the last cabins are; on foot, that's another two hours. By the way, those are the cabins that two of the survivors of the plane crash were finally able to reach.

Cross the stream and fill your bottles; there will be no more water for a few hours. The most difficult part of the trip is right at the beginning: After you cross the stream, the trail disappears. Follow the trail that's faintly visible, cross a horse paddock, and struggle through the brush above the stream. Stay above a steep drop-off at the stream's bank. After following the edge of the drop-off

for a little while, you will reach a slope. Here the valley narrows to a gorge, and where the stream exits the narrows, you will see the trail again.

Quite obvious now, the trail turns away from the stream and goes uphill to the saddle between "our" stream and Río Azufre. After two hours of a rather steep ascent it will take you another two hours to get to a nice camp site next to the arrieros' camp.

Day 2 10

In the upper part of Río Azufre, three valleys meet. The southernmost one goes down to Termas del Flaco. Starting directly at the arrieros' camp, a trail runs to the right of the stream up the northernmost valley towards the volcano. You won't be able to see the mountain proper from here yet. So, just head towards the lowest point where you can walk on either side of the stream. It will take about 4 hours to get to the pass.

On the other side of the pass, you will be descending a few hundred meters to the next stream where a few old boards are all that's left of a sulphur mine. There are a few level spots for camping here. The great disadvantage: the strong hydrogen sulphide smell. The water is not potable, either! Just melt some snow instead. According to the *arrieros*, there are supposed to be three hot springs a bit further down the stream, which could be easily identified by the vegetation they feed there. Later we regretted not having followed their suggestion, despite the loss in altitude. The night we spent by the smelly sulphur

This is how the physical and mental strain will be rewarded

mine was not a whole lot of fun! But that same day, we made the summit.

There are two mountains ahead, but on this tour, you will head for the one further to the north, Tinguiririca. To get there, head towards the pass between the two mountains and follow the ridge to the crater. While the grade seems mild, and the ascent takes only three hours, it is sheer torture. You will spend the entire time making two steps forward and sliding one step back on the volcanic scree. It's a trial for muscles and nerves, but finally, you are rewarded with a phantastic view from the summit. Towards the north, the glaciated area around Cerro Palomo stretch forever, and to the south, the volcanic complex Peteroa-Azufre can be seen steaming.

It takes us only an hour and a half to get back to our sulphur camp.

Alternate Option: On the first day, only go as far as the sulphur mine, and maybe down to the hot springs, and climb the summit the next day, and return to the arrieros' camp. That way, you will avoid the smells and shorten hiking time.

Day 3 🕐 9

It's another long haul from the campsite at the sulphur mine to the starting point. On weekdays, the bus from San Fernando to Termas de Flaco passes by the bridge around 5 p.m. You can rest your weary bones at the hot springs contained in concrete basins of varying temperatures. There is a number of small places to stay overnight at, and simple restaurants offer decent meals. A two-hour hike will take you to see fossilized dinosaur tracks (Iguanodontes and Camptosaurus).

¡Viven! Alive!

EL MERCURIO
SI QUEDO EL AVION
SE JUEGAN LA VIDA EN EL RESCATE

△ On October 13, 1972 a charter plane from Uruguay's airforce is on its way from Montevideo to Santiago, after a stop in Mendoza, Argentina. On board: an entire high school rugby team with many of their friends and family – all in all, 40 passengers and a crew of five. The plane, a Fairchild FH-227D, has a maximum flying altitude of 6,800 m and so, to cross the Andes, the pilot is headed for Planchón Pass near Curicó. Because of the dense cloud cover, he misses the break and hits the glaciated side of Tinguiririca volcano. 18 of those on board die from the impact or shortly thereafter, the others find themselves – without bearings and with some of them seriously injured – in a hostile high mountain environment. The body of the plane with its tail broken off provides insufficient protection from the icy temperatures at night. More difficult yet, there is not much to eat. When the last chocolate bars are gone, they start eating their dead companions...

Their hopes of being rescued give way to desperation when they hear on the radio that the search for them has been suspended. More people die from their injuries, the cold and exhaustion. Two avalanches hit and almost bury the wrecked plane and kill 8 more passengers. After weeks of a nerve-wrecking wait, two of the rugby players finally risk a desperate excursion: With a homemade sleeping bag they head west. And indeed, they manage to cross the Andes and descend into Chile. After ten days, they meet an *arriero* in a valley. On the following two days, December 22 und 23, 1972, after spending 72 days in the Cordillera, the remaining 14 survivors are flown out on Chilean airforce helicopters.

This story was made into two movies, one in Mexico, and the Hollywood production "Alive!" (1993).

 http://members.aol.com/PorkinsR6/alive.html
An individual's website about the Andean drama; in English

Trekking & Mountaineering

2

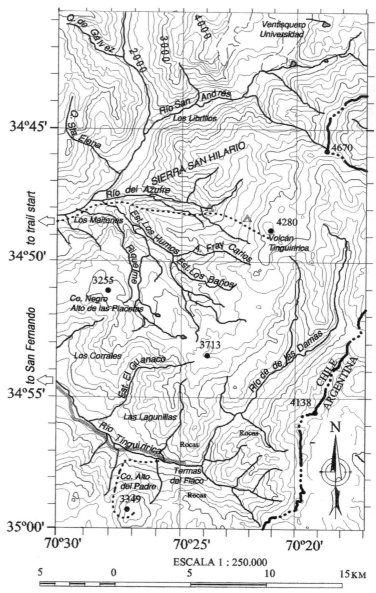

Franz Schubert

Cerro Alto del Padre (3,349 m)
A Summit with a View

⑩

Map on page 100

3,349 m Alto del Padre is one of the easiest peaks in the area of Tinguiririca volcano. This long day tour is rewarded with an impressive view: to the south, the 4,000 m peak Peteroa with Descabezado Grande behind it, and to the north, the Cordillera del Palomo, Chile's second largest glacier area after the Patagonian Icefield. A plus of this little developed region: The starting point of this hike, Termas del Flaco, is easy to reach by public transport.

Photo: View from the summit of Alto del Padre towards Tinguiririca Valley

Point of Departure

San Fernando.

Approach by Road

The approach by road to Termas del Flaco is described under "Volcán Tinguiririca" *(see p. 97)*. In addition to the hot springs with a temperature of up to 96 °C, this miniature resort at 1,720 m altitude has a number of stores and cheap accommodations. A worthwhile excursion of about two hours goes to fossilized dinosaur footprints.

Fees

None.

Day 1 🕐 10

Due to the length of this tour, we suggest starting out early. The trip's only difficulty will have to be faced right at the start while still in town: Not far from the campsite, you will have to cross Río Tinguiririca – not much fun given its temperature barely above freezing and the fact that it takes several minutes. A solution to this problem is hiring local *arrieros* to take you across on horseback.

Once on the other side, follow a road downhill along the river until you get to the next tributary's valley. Take the trail that branches off there and then switchbacks through a grassy area towards a pass. There are several springs where you can fill your bottles. Just before you get to the pass, leave the trail and start walking east uphill. In the upper reaches, the sparse vegetation yields to rock.

Don't forget to fill your bottles!

After about six hours, you will reach the 3,349 m summit. For a good view of Tinguiririca valley, climb down a bit towards the north where you can enjoy a view of the valley stretching all the way to the Argentinian border as well as Peteroa, an active volcano.

Return by the same route.

GPS Waypoints Alto del Padre		
Pass	S 34° 59.289'	W 070° 28.374'
Summit	S 34° 59.426'	W 070º 27.461'

© Franz Schubert

Volcanoes
Planchón - Peteroa - Azufre (4,100 m) ⑪
The Sulphur Monsters

 V. Peteroa V. Azufre

Map on page 106

As for rugged beauty, no other mountains in this area can match this group of volcanoes. The massif unfolds along the border east of Curicó over an area of 130 square kilometers. Its highest point is the stratovolcano Azufre at 4,100 m, which is easily identified from as far away as the Panamericana, given its longish shape and, above all, its icefields – about 60 percent of the volcano is covered by glaciers. Crampons, an iceaxe, and – depending on the route – a rope are essential.

From the Argentinian side, Azufre peak can be climbed in an easy, if slightly boring, long day's tour. The Chilean route, however, will spoil you with views of the glacier area around Cerro Palomo. It goes past picturesque Laguna Teno; first, up to the impressive craters of 3,603 m volcano Peteroa. This monster has erupted as recently as 1991, and its acid sulphur dioxide and sulphur hydroxide fumes will not let you forget that fact. In one of the craters, you can see caustic sulphuric acid boiling next to the edge of the glacier – a dip is not advisable.

4,090 m volcano Planchón rules the northern edge of this massif. Climbing is made difficult on its upper reaches by extremely porous andesite and basalt rock.

Photo: Boiling sulphuric acid in the crater of Peteroa

Point of Departure

Curicó.

Approach by Road

It is a 100 km trip from Curicó on the international road to Vergara Pass at approx. 2,500 m. Public transport only goes as far as Los Queñes resort (km 46), where you will also find the police station. If you want to climb the mountain from the Argentinian side, a Salvoconducto is required, which you will have to get in advance from the Policía de Investigaciones in Curicó since the border patrol office is not connected to the central computer. If your car documents are not in your name, you will need to bring a notarized letter from the owner giving you permission to take the car across the border. The hot springs of Azufre would be a good starting point for the Argentinian route.

Those who choose the Chilean route will only need the usual papers such as passport and car documents. The hot springs of San Pedro, located on verdant green pastures framed by the sides of the Teno valley, are only a few kilometers from the border, and there is camping. For the route described here you can leave your car right by the border marker to start your tour.

Fees

None.

The trail runs above the shimmering blue Laguna Teno

Day 1 5-6

First of all, while crossing a boggy pasture, you will need to focus on the northernmost point of the volcano Planchón ahead. West of that, you will reach a path that leads directly to the saddle above Laguna Teno; by then, you will have climbed for about an hour and a half. The backdrop behind the glistening blue lake is formed by the large glacier zone around Cerro Palomo. The slopes stay covered in snow all the way down to the lake until late in the Summer. Some of the snowpack, which can be several meters strong, has broken off and floats as 'iceberg' in the lake.

The path, which is clearly visible at first, starts snaking south towards the peak of Planchón; then, far above the lake, it turns in a westerly direction. Progress is made difficult by steep gorges *(quebradas)*, and it's easy to lose the path on the pasture far below the mountain side. Whatever you do, don't descend into the valley of Río Claro! There are flat places for pitching a tent all along the *quebradas*. To make it that far, count on another four hours of hiking.

Day 2 4-6

All the ridges between the *quebradas* lead uphill towards the summit of Peteroa. Right from the outset, you will be able to spot four characteristic peaks. Choose the ridge leading to the center, and after less than four hours of tough climbing you will reach the craters of Peteroa. The first one butts right up to the glacier, with sulphuric acid simmering... Don't get too close, the edge is very crumbly! In good weather, southerly and westerly winds will help scatter the toxic fumes of the crater in the background towards the east so that you can approach the edge all the way from the other side.

Walk around the mouth of the volcano to its south, and descend east of the ridge for a few hundred meters in altitude. This is where you can find a makeshift place below the snowline for pitching your tent.

Alternate Option: Climb the highest point of the caldera of Peteroa to the south, round the crumbly summit on ice somewhat below, and continue south down to the saddle between Peteroa and Azufre. From there, Azufre can be climbed on the following day. However, that means spending a night on the glacier, or else a megatour with the ascent and descent on the same day. We suggest you descend immediately if the weather turns bad. Under those conditions, the northerly winds will blow the sulphuric fumes from the crater directly towards you.

Day 3 (ascent of Azufre) 7

Following the trail from the camp below Peteroa to Azufre you will first get to its glacier. Right beside, a bit further to the left, small waterfalls tumble towards the valley. The entrance to the lower part of the glacier is steep with a 50 degree incline, but that's only for a short stretch. Right above this steep drop-off you will reach an area with huge crevasses. Round the lower part of a rock of several hundred meters' height separating you from the summit to its south. (If you try to circumvent it to the north you will hit an impassable crevasse.) Behind this rock, continue uphill.

The continuation of the route is now easy to see. It will lead over a steep side up to the shallow ridge, and on it, up to the summit proper (4,100 m). Depending on the season, you will find high towers of "penitents" which make the passage arduous. Under normal conditions, this ascent will take about four hours.

The descent to today's starting point will take two to three hours. If you want you can descend to the first camp the same day (another 3-4 hours) and after sleeping there that night, backtrack to the starting point the next day (4-5 hours.)

Alternate Route: From the second camp, head north to the east of the volcano complex while staying at the same altitude, cross several *quebradas*, and after as little as two or three hours, you will spot Laguna Teno. Descending while walking towards it will take you to the trail you know from ascending (about 1 hr.)

For those who want to descend all the way to Argentina and the Termas de Azufre: You will definitely need the Salvoconducto described above, as well as the exit stamp from the Los Queñes police. You will already be partly passing over Argentinian soil while rounding the mountain on the tour described.

Penitentes: The Jagged Penitents

△ On an Andean crossing from Santiago to Mendoza, Charles Darwin first described these snow formations known as penitents (Spanish: 'penitentes') in 1835. The name was derived from the white habits worn in Spanish Easter processions. The jagged forms are found primarily at altitudes above 4,000 m. They will also make climbers "repent" since they can make walking very difficult. The formations can range from few inches to 30 meters in height – the latter were observed on Mt. Everest's Khumbu glacier.

It is not quite clear how the penitents form. Possibly, this phenomenon that occurs mainly in tropical and subtropical areas, has something to do with vertical exposure to the sun; the penitents found in Chile all lean a little towards the north. In addition to altitude and latitude, there may be other factors such as the relief of the terrain, meteorological radiation, a dewpoint below zero degrees Celsius or dry air. Snow will clump together during short rises in temperature into particles of 3 to 6 mm in diameter. The resulting slight unevenness is enough to cause different sublimation rates (direct change from the solid to the gaseous stage). The snow won't melt, it evaporates instead – but to a varying degree, because of the unevenness. This causes the formation of micro-penitents which then keep growing through increased sublimation in the small hollows. The closer to vertical the sunlight hits them, the greater the sublimation. This causes jagged shapes with minimum surface exposure to the radiation.

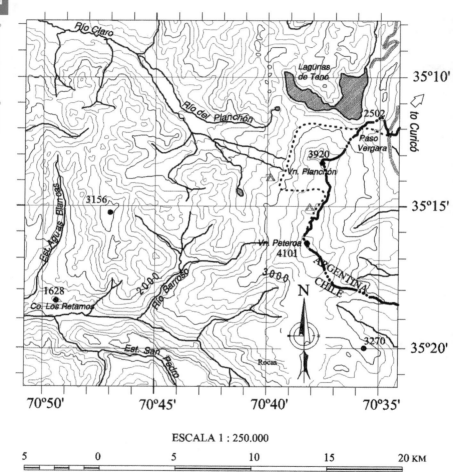

ESCALA 1 : 250.000

Please note: This map does not show Azufre volcano since on officially sanctioned Chilean maps, it is considered part of Peteroa volcano.

Mondaca Trail
Mountain Lakes and Hot Springs

12

Map on page 114

This is one of those rare cases in which getting there on the trail is as worthwhile as your actual destination. Mondaca Trail could have been named in many different ways since this lagoon is not the only one along the trail, and since the trail also leads to hot springs, through vast roble forests and way beyond the treeline. 'Condor trail' would have been a good name, too, since Chile's state bird is frequently spotted in the pass area between the Claro and Lontué valleys. On this easily organized hike you will be constantly rewarded with views of the mountains, especially of the glaciated giant Azufre to the north. At the same time, you will get a good impression of the various zones of vegetation in Chile. From the hot springs on the banks of Estero Volcán there is also an optional day tour to charming Laguna Mondaca, the source of Río Lontué.

Photo: Past Laguna Las Animas to Sulphur valley

Point of Departure

Curicó.

Approach by Road

A gravel road that is passable by regular cars in the Summer runs from Curicó via Molina to the Nature Preserve of Siete Tazas 65 km away. About 10 km from the park entrance at Parque Inglés you can stop the car and scramble down to the spectacular cascading falls of Siete Tazas *(see sidebar on p. 110)*. However, if you came by bus, it won't wait for you.

From Curicó to Molina, you can take the frequent minibus service. During high season (January/February) there is one bus daily that leaves at 5 p.m. from Molina and returns the following morning, leaving at 8 a.m. from Parque Inglés. During the rest of the year, the bus only goes as far as Radal near Siete Tazas. For more detailed information, call Buses Hernández, Ph. (75) 491 179.

Fees

Admission: USD 1.60, tent camping: USD 13.00 per tent (campsite at Parque Inglés)

Day 1 5

Starting at the Information Center of the Nature Preserve, a sign-posted trail leads to Valle del Indio. After about one and a half to two hours, you will reach a sandy spot with a distinct tree with several trunks. From here, you can take a worth-while short sidetrip to the narrow gorge of Río Claro. At that tree, simply turn to the right and start walking through the brush following the sound of the river. In a few minutes you will be at the top edge of the gorge. Keep looking for a place to make a quick descent. Once at the bottom, you can cool off and take a welcome break.

Back on the main trail, after about another two hours, you will pass by the spot where the Vilches hike descends from the pass to Río Radal *(see Tour 13, p. 112)*.

After another 30 minutes on the same trail you can already pick out Valle de Indio located to the north. However, keep following Río Claro, past the remnants of a stone hut, and a small waterfall. After about half an hour, a verdant green valley with Ñirre brush beckons you to camp at 1,800 m.

If you still have something left (especially, air) you can add another two hours' walk to a pretty camp-site by Laguna Las Animas at 2,300 m.

Río Claro gorge near Parque Inglés

From the camp in the valley, the trail runs up the valley along its left side. After about 40 minutes it starts switchbacking uphill, and it will take about an hour to the first pass at 2,300 m. From here, it's only 15 more minutes to Laguna Las Animas, which is far above the treeline. Then there is another hour and a half of strenuous scrambling over pumice rock to the second pass (2,500 m). From there, you will have a dynamite view of the glaciers on Peteroa, Laguna Mondaca, and the waterfalls of Estero San José.

Then it's basically downhill to the northeast on the sandy slope, with just a few short uphills interspersed. In the midst of this environment hostile to all vegetation, you will find colorful flowers along the banks of the clear streams. After about three hours, you will arrive at the hot springs in the sulphur valley at about 1,900 m. Solfataras shoot up from the ground and four natural basins with 40° Celsius water beckon you to take a relaxing bath. By these springs, the young *arriero* Cristián can be found living until mid-March.

Alternate Options: If you have only three days, leave your tent at Ñirre valley and take a day trip to the lagoon and back. If you have four days, you can stay overnight in sulphur valley and backtrack the next day.

Off you go, without your packs, from the sulphur camp to Laguna Mondaca. Follow the southern bank of Río Azufre with the trail leading away from the hot springs. After about an hour's worth of downhill hiking, you will have to cross the river. On the other side, the trail disappears in the river gravel. After half an hour, the trail becomes easier to see, but now it's on the other side of the river; so you will have to cross again. Keep to the edge of Azufre gorge which is about 100 m deep here, and after a little over an hour, start descending to Laguna Mondaca at 1,550 m.

A dream of a mountain lake! Intensely turquoise water before a wildly scenic backdrop with countless small waterfalls in the green San Pedro valley, and tall basalt columns that Río Lontue has carved its bed through.

Return to the sulphur camp the way you came.

Alternate Option: According to the *arrieros*, you can follow Río Lontué from Laguna Mondaca, where you will reach Radal and the road to Molina in two days making this a roundtrip option.

Day 4/5

Return via the same route as Day 1/2.

GPS Waypoints Mondaca Trail

Roughly same altitude as descent from Vilches, see p. 112	S 35º 30.125'	W 070º 54.816'
Stone hut	S 35º 29.862'	W 070º 54.283'
Plain with Ñirre brush, Camping	S 35º 29.867'	W 070º 53.460'
Switchbacks start	S 35º 29.524'	W 070º 52.110'
First pass at approx. 2,300 m	S 35º 29.066'	W 070º 51.673'
Laguna Las Animas	S 35º 29.077'	W 070º 50.937'
Second pass at approx. 2,500 m	S 35º 28.805'	W 070º 49.434'
Valle Azufre, Camp	S 35º 29.752'	W 070º 45.847'
Crossing Azufre river	S 35º 28.885'	W 070º 46.265'
Laguna Mondaca	S 35º 27.704'	W 070º 45.527'

Siete Tazas Daytrip: Seven or Seventy Cups

△ There are really only six and a half "cups" or – if you count along a longer stretch – maybe several dozen round basins Río Claro has carved into the black basalt rock of the Pre-Cordillera. However many there may be, this narrow gorge in the midst of green virgin forest is an impressive sight to behold. Since this nature preserve is easily reached from Curicó, it is a good place for a nice daytrip. Above and below Siete Tazas there are several pretty places for taking a dip in this clear, green-shimmering river. If you come outside high season, you will have picturesque places such as Velo de la Novia (Bridal Veil) waterfalls all to yourself. In January/February, the area around Parque Inglés (Conaf Center, Restaurant[1], Hostería[1]) sees an increase in Summer visitors; during that time, the campsites overflow with trash. You can also book trips on horseback from here.

From the Conaf building, a trail leads to Valle del Indio following the Claro gorge all the way. Even a short hike through the awe-inspiring Southern Beech forest is well worth it; especially starting from mid-April, when the leaves start turning, and in early Spring, because of the snowy mountain panorama.

1 Burnt down in winter 2001

Sketch tour 12

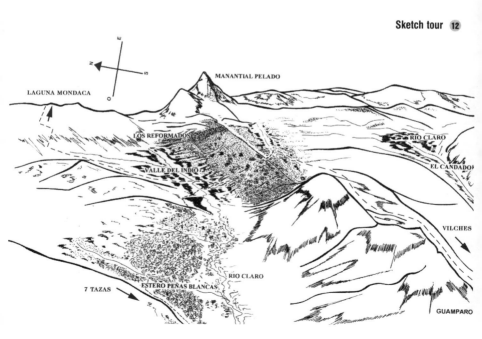

Vilches - Siete Tazas
From Park to Park

(13)

Sketch on page 110, map on page 114

This very special trek from one Nature Preserve to another will take you from the lush Nothofagus forests of the Vilches reserve (also called Altos del Lircay) to a 2,000 mountain ridge to the upper section of Río Claro and the famous Siete Tazas waterfalls. Starting point and end point are relatively easily accessible, and the scenery offers a change of vegetation zones and great views. Almost every time we were there, we saw condors. Even though both parks get heavy visitor traffic in Summer, on this tour that is not known to many you will hardly meet a soul. Among its highlights is the narrow gorge of Río Claro that is only a short sidetrip away towards the end of this tour. Strong trekkers can do this tour in two days, but why would anyone want to? Give yourself at least three days.

From Siete Tazas, the entry point for the trail is relatively hard to find, which is why you should start from Vilches.

Photo: This hike does not reach much more than 2,000 m, but offers great views of peaks like Descabezado Grande (to the right)

Point of Departure

Talca.

Approach by Road

The paved international highway to Argentina goes through the quiet little town of San Clemente. This is where you can load up on food for this tour. At the 40 km marker, a well-kept gravel road starts to Vilches. After another 26 km and a total of about an hour, you will get to Vilches resort with its Conaf Information Center at an altitude of over 1,000 m.

From Talca bus station, there are several buses daily in both directions; riding time: 2.5 hours approx. For information, call Buses Vilches, ph. (71) 235 327.

Fees

Admission: USD 1.60, tent camping: USD 13 per site (official campsite) or USD 1.60/day and person in certain places inside the reserve.

Day 1 6

At the entrance to Vilches you will find current information at the Conaf post. The trail leading east is clearly sign-posted "Mirador" and "Valle Venado". After about 4.5 hours of strenuous uphill hiking through the rare forest type of Maulino, you will reach the Refugio, or what little is left of it. There is drinking water and campsites close by; a few spots are right by the water a few hundred me-ters before you get to the Refugio. In late Summer, however, the stream often runs dry.

It is definitely worth taking a sidetrip to the spectacular view point of Claro Canyon. Without packs, it is about an hour to Mirador (see p. 116).

Day 2 7

From the campsite on the stream a trail leads uphill that runs to the left of the densely over-grown hill called El Fraile with the typical shape of a volcano. Along the side of the mountain, the trail disappears at times. Just stay at the same altitude and look for tracks. On the opposite side, you will already be able to see the ascent route for the drawn-out ridge north of us. There are two options for doing this: either up the switchbacks from here, or following the valley in a westerly direction. It's definitely nicer in the valley. Both routes lead to the long, flat ridge Guamparo which has great views in store for you.

The next section is the most beautiful one of this tour. Stay on the ridge as long as you can and keep going east; the trail will keep disappearing. Right before the descent, you have to cross onto the steep northern slope of Radal Valley. It looks more difficult than it actually is; there is an easy trail up to the last pass at 2,200 m.

From the pass, the trail switchbacks down through a grove of trees visible from afar. Lower down, keep to the right of the stream and simply make your way through the brush down to Río Radal at 1,650 m, where you will be treated to great camping spots in the shady forest and a refreshing bath in the crystal-clear stream.

Again and again, splendid views such as this will open up

Day 3 4

Can't find a trail, but somehow you've got to get to the opposite side of the valley! Let's use the distinct shape of Cerro Bolsón to the north for orientation. That's where Río Claro runs, which is merged by Río Radal further downstream. Before you get to Río Claro, you will find the trail again leading down to Radal/Siete Tazas. You'll have to cross the river here, which can be a wet and chilly affair depending on the time of year. Make sure you cross where the trail does; lower down the river becomes very deep in places.

After only four hours you will reach the resort of Parque Inglés at 1,050 m. There is a tree-shaded campsite that can be busy in January and February, a restaurant, a simple hotel (burnt down in winter 2001), and nice swimming holes in Río Claro. Following the road about an hour on foot from here, you will get to the photogenic cascading falls of the "Seven Cups" *(see p. 110)*.

In the Summer, there is a daily bus from Parque Inglés to Molina near Curicó *(see p. 108)*. Off season, you will have to hike another 10 km to Radal, which has daily bus service, or try hitch-hiking.

GPS Waypoints Vilches – Siete Tazas

Vilches, Starting point	S 35º 36.285'	W 071º 04.335'
Stream crossing	S 35º 35.719'	W 071º 02.186'
Volcano, turn to pass	S 35º 35.089'	W 070º 59.883'
Pass	S 35º 32.128'	W 070º 59.002'
View of the end of Radal Valley	S 35º 31.460'	W 070º 56.150'
Turn-off Siete Tazas	S 35º 31.314'	W 070º 55.401'
Second camp on Radal River	S 35º 30.822'	W 070º 54.754'
Restaurant	S 35º 28.582'	W 070º 59.658'

Vilches Day Tour: Something for Everyone

△ This charming nature reserve in the midst of a Southern Beech forest, Vilches/Altos del Lircay, offers several easy hiking trails for nature lovers. It's so pretty, you won't even mind an occasional shower in the Fall, when the leaves turn yellow and red, or in the Spring, when the peaks glisten white.

Only a few steps behind the Conaf building, you will find a remarkable witness of pre-hispanic times. A number of granite rocks called Piedras Tacitas have shallow man-made indentations the aboriginal population probably used as mortars for grinding grain and pigments. You can continue through a majestic Coihue forest to the rock named Piedra de Aguila towering over a deep gorge (40 min approx.), or to moor Majadilla on a mountain ridge with a nice view (2 hrs.). For mountain lovers, a side trip to the outlook Peine (2,448 m, 6-7 hrs.) is a treat.

At the Park entrance and a few kilometers before you get to the park, there are campsites along the road, and small kiosks sell basic stuff. The Conaf officials can give you information, as will Don Tito, who sells refreshments and sandwiches from a small stall before you get to the park. Several *arrieros* offer tours on horseback for half or whole days.

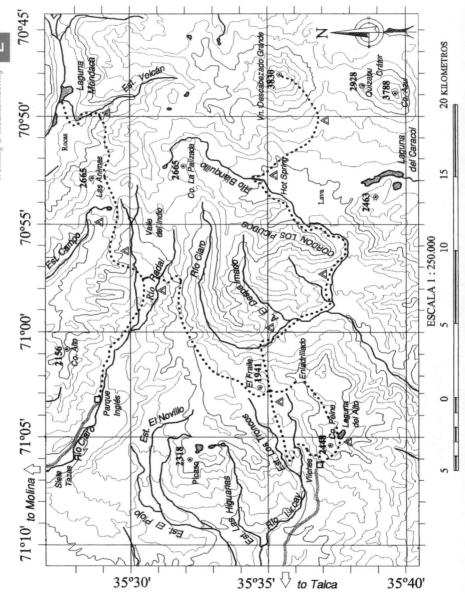

Descabezado Grande (3,830 m) (14)
The Decapitated Volcano

 with snow cover   5

Map on page 114, sketches on p. 118-119

"The Great Decapitated One", which is visible from afar as a literally "decapitated" volcano, is a truly impressive specimen of its kind with a base 10 to 12 kilometers long and a crater measuring 1.5 km across. On April 10, 1932, in one powerful eruption, its side crater Quizapu spread 25 cubic kilometers of volcanic matter all over creation: The ashes even fell on South Africa. Legend has it that the name of the 700 m wide crater comes from the colloquial expression "Quién sabe, pu!" (Who knows!), supposedly the answer to the question for the name of the crater on its south side.

This technically easy climb is not only worth doing for volcanologists. The extremely variable scenery makes this a Dorado popular with hikers and climbers alike. Descabezado rules with its ice-filled main crater over clear streams, waterfalls and hot springs, jungles with flocks of parrots, and a white ash desert. You need to be prepared for fields of hard snow until well into early Summer, so take crampons and iceaxe.

Photo: Camp in the ash desert at Descabezado

Point of Departure

Talca.

Approach by Road

Same as Vilches – Siete Tazas, *see p. 112.*

Same as Vilches – Siete Tazas, *see p. 112.*

Fees

Same as Vilches – Siete Tazas, *see p. 112.*

Same as Vilches – Siete Tazas, *see p. 112.*

Day 1 8

The first part corresponds to the Vilches – Siete Tazas hike. From the Park entrance a trail leading east is clearly sign-posted "Mirador" and "Valle Venado". After about 4.5 hours of strenuous uphill hiking you will reach the Refugio, or what little is left of it. There is drinking water and campsites close by; a few spots are right by the water a few hundred meters before you get to the Refugio.

Then you will have to pay extra attention on the stony stretch that follows; the path branches off several times. Keep to the right throughout, towards where the downhill to the north becomes flatter. After about an hour you will get to a Mirador with a gorgeous view of Río Claro valley. There, the clearly visible and sign-posted path zig-zags down to the Claro gorge. Follow the river downstream in order to climb up the next valley, Río Blanquillo, in an easterly direction. The turn-off is sign-posted and you will recognize it from afar by the lavafield. Occasionally, the path disappears; but finally you will reach a hut next to which you can camp.

Day 2   8-9

From here, the path leads steeply uphill, always staying to the north of the hardened lavaflows in Blanquillo Valley. The first great view of Descabezado can be had from Laguna Blanquillo which will also refresh you with a cool dip. After another short climb, and after crossing the river three times, you will have a view over a wide pasture at the foot of the mountain. Then follow the little stream to the little stone house of the *arriero*, who can also give you current information about the

ascent. He lives right next to the hot springs that invite you for a nice break after a 6 to 7 hour hike.

But don't give in to the urge yet; better hike another two hours so that you can camp as close as possible to the mountain. The trail is obvious and visible to the most part. Except in the Spring, you cannot count on finding drinking water once you have passed the hot springs, take at least five liters per person from here! (The white spots on the slopes are not snow, but pumice rock.)

Day 3 7

Leaving your packs behind, first climb up the slope of the volcano towards the saddle between Cerro Azul and Descabezado; then climb your destination from its southern side. The rocky part of the ascent snaking upward like a band in the porous volcanic rock looks quite difficult from afar. However, it is actually easy to tackle; you will hardly need to use your hands. Once again, you will be climbing through pumice rock, up to

Looks like snow, but it's pumice rock

a spot with a view of the giant crater of Quizapu between Cerro Azul and Descabezado.

On the last stretch, choose the rocky part since the loose pumice rock is tiring. When you finally have arrived at the crater's edge at 3,815 m, you will see that all the toiling was worth it! From here, you have an excellent view across the Central Andes towards the north, far into Argentina, of glaciated mountain peaks, and of the huge crater of Descabezado.

Return the same day to the cozy campsite by the hot springs.

Day 4 3-4

Descend to Río Claro the same way you ascended via the valley of Río Blanquillo. Walk upstream along Río Claro, and after about an hour, turn into the second valley to the east for a few hundred meters, where Despalmado waterfalls have formed a pretty lagoon. A great place for a swim and for pitching your tent – the most beautiful campsite on the whole tour!

Day 5 8

On the last day, climb back up to Mirador (1,800 m) and backtrack to Vilches, where you will arrive after a long day's hiking.

A dip in the hot springs

GPS Waypoints Descabezado Grande

Vilches, Starting point	S 35º 36.285'	W 071º 04.335'
Stream	S 35º 35.719'	W 071º 02.186'
Volcano-s haped hill on left, right before Refugio	S 35º 35.089'	W 070º 59.883'
Water	S 35º 34.780'	W 070º 58.731'
View point Mirador, 1,800 m	S 35º 34.652'	W 070º 58.002'
Camp 4 at the waterfall	S 35º 35.174'	W 070º 55.932'
Turn-off at lavafield Río Blanquillo	S 35º 36.866'	W 070º 55.443'
Small lake	S 35º 36.229'	W 070º 51.835'
Hot springs	S 35º 35.688'	W 070º 49.570'
Camp 2, 2,300 m	S 35º 36.060'	W 070º 48.028'
Ascent 1	S 35º 36.055'	W 070º 46.896'
Ascent 2	S 35º 35.865'	W 070º 46.168'
South slope	S 35º 35.709'	W 070º 45.425'
Crater rim, 3,815 m	S 35º 35.537'	W 070º 45.265'

Trekking & Mountaineering

2

CERRO AZUL

QUIZAPÚ

DESCABEZADO GRANDE (3.830 m.)

MANANTIAL PELADO

RÍO BLANQUILLO

EL LLANO

ESCORIALES

LAS JUNTAS

LA PLAYA

ENLADRILLADO

EL SALTO

QUEBRADA LAS BANDURRIAS

RÍO CLARO

MIRADOR

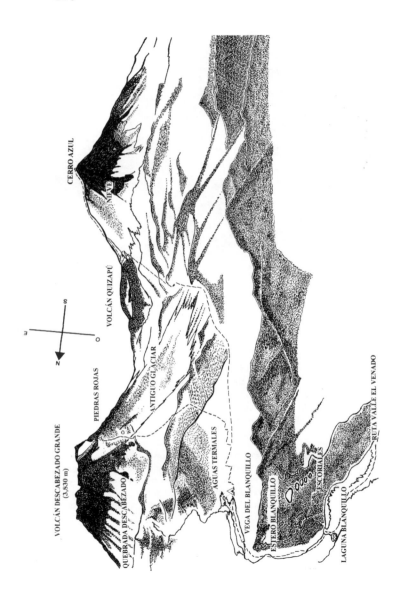

CERRO AZUL

NIEVE

VOLCÁN QUIZAPÚ

PIEDRAS ROJAS

ANTIGUO GLACIAR

VOLCÁN DESCABEZADO GRANDE
(3.830 m)

QUEBRADA DESCABEZADO

AGUAS TERMALES

VEGA DEL BLANQUILLO

ESTERO BLANQUILLO

ESCORIALES

LAGUNA BLANQUILLO

RUTA VALLE EL VENADO

S

E

O

N

Enladrillado Trek
Remember E.T.?

15

Map on page 114, sketch on page 123

We've probably all wished we could see extraterrestrials in action! The Enladrillado Trek, no doubt one of the most beautiful tours between Santiago and Temuco, makes anyone smile who is interested in UFO's. Most locals have absolutely no doubt that the high plain, which looks as if it had been tiled by 'someone', is being used as a landing strip by extraterrestrials, and just about every *arriero* has had some supernatural experience involving strange lights and unusual flying machines.

It really doesn't take a belief in galactic beings for a person to become enthralled with the natural beauty of the Andes on this tour. It leads to the spectacular drop-off of Claro gorge 1,000 m down below, and again and again, it offers great views of the mountains. In the woods at the lower altitudes, flocks of parrots will accompany hikers, and Laguna del Alto, a small mountain lake, invites you for a dip. With all that magical beauty around, it's no wonder that you might see an OVNI (*objeto volante no identificado*, UFO)!

Photo: At the Enladrillado "UFO pad" above the Claro gorge

Point of Departure

Talca.

Approach by Road

See Vilches – Siete Tazas, *see p. 112.*

Day 1 4-6

From the information center of the nature pre-serve, a sign-posted trail leads past white rocks (Piedras Blancas), up to Laguna del Alto, through dense Southern Beech woods with huge Coihue trees. On the way, you can enjoy a beautiful view of the Pre-Cordillera and the Central Valley. Then the trail switchbacks upwards over the grassy slope, and sometimes it's hard to see. After some strenuous scrambling over about 1,100 m of al-titude gain and three to four hours, you will get to a narrow pass behind which you can see La-guna del Alto. (In the Summer you might want to do this tough ascent early in the day to escape the heat.) From the pass, there is a phantastic sidetrip of 1.5 hours to the summit of 2,448 m Cerro El Peine with a panoramic view of moun-tain peaks.

Another 300 m down in altitude on a switchback and scree for about an hour, and you will find several tent sites around this lake that lies sur-rounded by mountains as in a bowl.

Alternate Option: If you don't want to end the day's stage here, you can climb Enladrillado and

Breakfast near Enladrillado

descend back down into the valley – all on the same day. Make sure you take enough water! The only water is from snow along the trail – if there is any.

Day 2 5-6

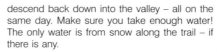

A narrow trail runs up the steep slope on the northern side of the lake. You will reach a broad ridge with a view of Lircay Valley and then follow the course of a small stream. Cross it before it tumbles down the north side of the ridge, and keep walking along the highest line of the ridge. The ridge will end abruptly at the edge of the gorge of Río Claro with its 1,000 m drop-off. There is a small plain that looks as if it had been tiled by human hands, partially with hexagonal tiles – the famous Enladrillado. Even strong UFO skep-tics such as we cannot help experiencing a strange feeling in our gut …

A little ways before you get there, a rock named Piedra La Coneja juts up like a finger into the sky (the sign-post for the UFO's, of course!). Only a few meters further to the west, a trail descends to Lircay Valley. Lower down, this trail will cross a small stream, where you might pitch your tent that night. This day's stage gains 560 m in alti-tude, and you lose 870 m.

Alternate Option: Those in a hurry can still make it back on the same day to the entrance of the nature reserve.

Day 3 4

From your camp follow the trail a little bit further to the north. There you will come across a trail leading to Mirador as described in the Descabezado Tour (Day 1, *see p. 116*), right before the rem-nants of the delapidated Refugio. To get back to Vilches, turn left here and stay on the wide trail. Be careful! In one place, there is a confusing turn-off: All of a sudden, the trail turns down to-wards the river, and ends there. A few meters behind the turn-off the trail con-tinues more clearly visible. After a total of about four hours, you will reach the park entrance.

UFO's over Chile

△ It happened on September 21, 1999: Three extraterrestrial spaceships were approaching Cajón de Maipo south of Santiago and began strange maneuvers in the sky. A reporter from a radio station reported live on location ("They are changing! They are changing their shape! What does that mean?"), he interviewed 'eye witnesses', and back at the studio, 'experts' explained the phenomenon. Within a short period of time, the phones at the radio station were ringing off the hook, and the only road leading to Maipo Valley was jammed almost immediately. Hundreds of rubbernecks wanted to witness the spectacle with their own eyes. And faith makes believers: Some people swore later they had indeed seen something. But everything had only been a show: Because of the tremendous impact, the station hastened to tell the audience the truth: they had only been joking – they had put on a radio play.

This episode is symptomatic for the widespread belief in extraterrestrial phenomena among Chileans. Again and again, even the serious media will report on un-identified flying objects (UFO's) or even about abductions of humans into space. The national TV networks evening news regularly show images of inexplicable light effects in the Cordillera, and the moderator always keeps a straight face. The ratings are assured. Even the airforce has its own department for the investigation of mysterious apparitions in the sky.

Why are Chileans of all people so ready to believe in extraterrestrials? The overwhelming night skies are probably just as much a part of the answer as the futuristic observatories in northern Chile and the generally widespread 'heathen' beliefs in miracles and the devil. Whatever the reason, If you see a UFO on an Andean trip, don't be scared – point your camera at it and sell the pictures to the TV station!

 www.ovni.cl
The latest "news" on Ufo's in Chile, in Spanish only

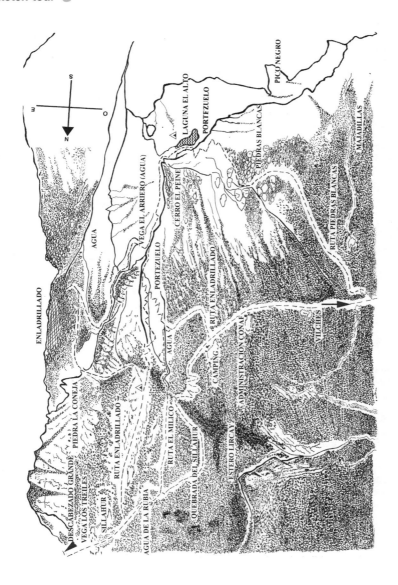

Pellado Trek

16

Three Cute 3,000 m Peaks

 Descent Río de la Plata   4-5   Map on page 127

After the tours at comparatively low altitude around Vilches and Siete Tazas it's back to the rugged world of the High Andes now. The Pellado trek above the tree line is chock-full of lava flows, glaciers, volcanoes, mountain lagoons and what is maybe Chile's most beautiful waterfall. From a small lagoon that is usually iced up, you can climb three big 3,000 m peaks - San Pedro (3,621 m), Pellado (3,121 m), and San Pablo (3,325 m) – crampons and iceaxes are a must! Pellado is the easiest to climb, and from its summit, you will have a panoramic dream view of the entire area.

Apart from running into some *arrieros* occasionally, you can bank on being far from the crowds on this little-known hiking tour. If you backtrack the same way, the tour can be made easier; if you do a round trip via Río de la Plata Valley, it will be more demanding.

Photo: A challenge for andinistas - San Pedro, Pellado, and San Pablo

Point of Departure

Talca.

Approach by Road

Take the international highway to Argentina from Talca. Last opportunity for shopping in San Clemente (km 20). The pavement ends after you have passed Colbún reservoir; continue on a gravel road along Río Maule. After a total of about 100 km, precisely on the other side of the bridge across Río Maule, a road turns off to the right. It takes you across Río Colorado up a pass and down into Río Melado Valley. Once at Melado, the road gets quite a bit worse, and the last part can only be negotiated by allwheel-drive vehicles. During the 35 km from the bridge to La Huerta you will gain about 500 meters in altitude. After La Huerta (about four hours total for the approach by road) you can only continue on foot.

The ascent to Pellado is relatively simple

Buses run only rarely from Talca to the bridge over Río Maule mentioned above. The road to La Huerta, a gravel road, is very pretty in scenery, but it would take one and a half days on foot. A long boulevard lined with poplar trees distinguishes the hamlet of La Huerta; you will find plenty of good camping all along the way.

Fees

None.

Day 1 5

In La Huerta, stick to the continuation of the road, and you will get to the bridge across Río de la Puente after about three hours. The bridge is already above the treeline making for an excellent view of the long valley and the surrounding mountains. Behind the bridge, the trail goes uphill for another half an hour to – of all things, in this wilderness – a police station where you should sign in.

And on you go, always slightly uphill, until you find yourselves at what may well be Chile's most beautiful waterfall. (Of course, it is not signposted, so you'll never know its name.) The water from the snowmelt drops down in two cascades and on into the gorge over steep basalt columns, framed by cypress trees. To make it picture perfect, the appropriate backdrop is provided by the snowy slopes of San Pedro volcano. Right after the waterfalls, to the left of the trail, there are some fenced pastures with a few houses. The owner will gladly give you permission to camp there, but of course you should still ask before.

Day 2 8

The trail is still hard to miss; and after two hours, you will get to Río Yegua: brace yourself and wade through the icy cold water! Your calves will just barely have warmed up again when you will have to take off your shoes again after about half an hour. This "bath" is called Río Botacura. After you've crossed it, the trail is harder to find but this shouldn't bother you: Just walk up Valle Chico staying on the right side of Río San Pedro, always due north. After about 30 minutes, the trail goes up a grassy ridge; when you are on top, you will see that this is an old lavaflow from Pellado volcano.

After another half hour you will get to a small lagoon. The local arriero who lives there in a cabin will be happy to give you directions. Then it's another hour and a half of climbing along the ridge until you get to a piece of rangeland on the upper San Pedro. Cross the river here and simply walk uphill (without a trail) for about three hours, always heading towards Cerro Pellado. There will be several potential camping spots, mostly along small lagoons.

Alternate Option: To get to the pass, simply hike up the valley from the pasture without crossing the river. In the upper section of the stream, you will find a pretty lake, great for camping. For those who get tired earlier, there is camping at the lower lagoon or at the pasture.

Day 3 3

You can use the day for exploring the area without your pack. There are three peaks to choose from: The furthest east is San Pablo (3,325 m); there is a demanding tour (for experienced mountain climbers only!) via the southeastern side – crampons, rope and iceaxe are mandatory – to the summit.

The ascent of neighboring Pellado (3,121 m) proves to be a lot easier. The route is obvious, and you will be able to enjoy the view from the top after only a two hour hike. And yet, for the snowy side, you will need crampons here, too.

The much harder ascent of San Pedro (3,621 m) will take two days from here.

Day 4 (-5)   6-7

For the return, an easier but longer option is backtracking to La Huerta, which will take two days. If there is no car waiting for you there, plan on another day for getting down to the road to Talca.

Only experienced hikers should take the plunge for the shorter, but more complicated round trip. If you come from the camp at the foot of Cerro Pellado, start following the highest of the ridges running down from the peak to get to the west-

A little too cold for a dip

Franz Schubert

ern part of the Plata valley. If you have camped at the lagoon on the upper section of Río San Pedro, just cross the relatively flat pass to the north, to get to the wide basin of Río del la Plata where the descent starts.

The most difficult – alpine - section is encountered right at the beginning. There is no trail to be seen anywhere; you will have to follow your intuition while watching your step constantly. Once you see the Plata valley, it becomes easier. According to an arriero's information, you can descend on either side of the stream. Choosing the left or western side will get you to the valley floor in about two hours. On the last section, there is a defined trail that crosses the stream where it exits a narrow gorge.

After another two hours, you will get to the valley of Río Bahamondes, which runs in an easterly direction. Just before you get there, you will have to cross Río de la Plata again to get to the left side (as seen downstream). From the Bahamondes valley it is only another hour and a half to the international highway, and you can hitchhike back to Talca.

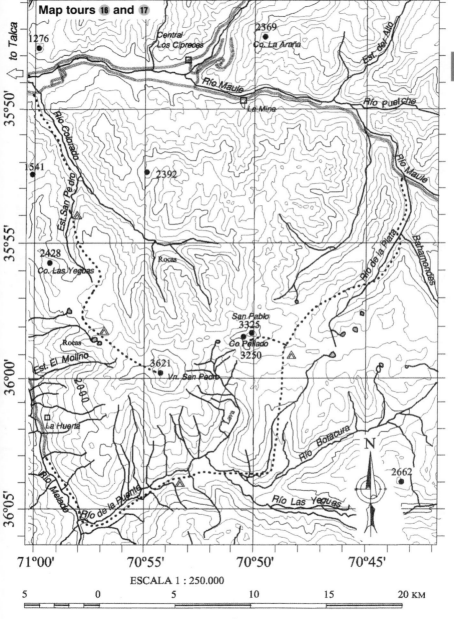

to Talca

1276

Central
Los Cipreses

2369
Co. La Araña

Est. del Alto

Río Maule

La Mina

Río Puelche

Río Maule

35°50'

Río Colorada

1541

2392

Est. San Pedro

Río de la Plata

Bahamondes

35°55'

2428
Co. Las Yeguas

Rocas

San Pablo
3325

Est. El Molino

Rocas

3621

Co Pellado
3250

36°00'

Vn. San Pedro

2.000

Lava

La Huerta

Río Botacura

N

2662

Río Meldo

Río de la Puente

Río Las Yeguas

36°05'

71°00'   70°55'   70°50'   70°45'

ESCALA 1 : 250.000

5   0   5   10   15   20 KM

Volcán San Pedro (3,621 m)
No Pain, no Gain

 summit   4-5 Map on page 127

Throughout its history, San Pedro's cone has been more popular with volcanologists than with mountain climbers, which is unfortunate since the mountain offers great variety in scenery. However, it is still more of a paradise for scientists, since the innards of the mountain are revealed by canyons that have been carved deep into this stratovolcano – like cutting through a torte. The lavaflows full of andesite and basalt from this now extinct volcano did not only create the mountain proper, but also an area of about 200 square kilometers.

There are several routes to choose from for the ascent. The one described here is only recommended when there is enough snow to cover the steep scree slopes in the upper section that make the climb tiring and dangerous because of the inherent danger of rockfall.

Photo: It helps if there is sufficient snow when climbing over volcanic scree

Point of Departure

Talca.

Approach by Road

From Talca, take the international highway towards Pehuenche Pass/Argentina. After about 100 km there is a bridge across Río Maule; turn right immediately behind the bridge. After a few kilometers and a total of two hours of driving, you will get to the bridge over Río Colorado, the starting point of our tour at an altitude of about 750 m. For public transport options, *see Pellado Trek p. 125.*

Fees

None.

Day 1

After crossing the bridge, follow the road upriver on the right hand side. About 2.5 hours of wading through an area of mostly brush vegetation will get you to the confluence of Río San Pedro and Río Colorado at 1,040 m. About 100 m before the bridge, an obvious trail starts to your right and switchbacks up to a cypress grove where you need to turn left, walk over a saddle and downhill a bit to Río San Pedro at 1,430 m.

Time for a break now since you will have been climbing from the confluence for an hour and a half, and there is no water the entire time.

From here on, the trail becomes invisible at times, but only for short stretches. Follow the stream and start switchbacking uphill after about 20 minutes. Try to stay on the trail because the

slope is too steep to go straight up. Soon you will reach a forest with a nice campsite by a stream at 1,740 m.

Day 2

You only need to cross Río San Pedro once throughout the entire ascent, but this can be very difficult depending on the season – but didn't you come here for an adventure? The spot is easy to recognize, and the trail leads right up to it. Continue on the other (left) side of the stream through a forest of Southern beech. Above the treeline, there is a marshy area in which it's hard not to lose sight of the trail. Just stay close to the stream!

You can already see the tall waterfall from quite a distance as it heads towards the valley over basalt columns. To its left, a trail leads over a small ridge to the falls at 1,930 m. Head for the saddle opposite and cross some marshy rangeland. At the deepest point of the saddle you will find the trail again. Continue on past a pretty lake down into a green valley where the trail finally ends.

After crossing the marshy valley, climb up the slope on the other side. At the top, there is a mountain lake at 2,500 m, at whose opposite bank you can pitch your tent. Follow the ridge

A look back – but not in anger

GPS Waypoints San Pedro Volcano		
Starting point Río Colorado	S 35° 48.708'	W 070° 56.311'
Confluence with Río San Pedro	S 35° 52.297'	W 070° 54.930'
Acces to water	S 35° 53.438'	W 070° 55.237'
Switchback uphill on Río San Pedro	S 35° 53.891'	W 070° 55.324'
Camp site in the grove	S 35° 54.615'	W 070° 55.555'
Descent into valley	S 35° 57.510'	W 070° 54.852'
Lake at 2,500 m	S 35° 58.265'	W 070° 54.247'
Camp above lake at 2,600 m	S 35° 58.427'	W 070° 53.716'
Ridge at 2,970 m	S 35° 59.002'	W 070° 52.558'
Top of steep side, 3,150 m, at foot of volcano	S 35° 59.444'	W 070° 51.928'
Summit	S 35° 59.578'	W 070° 51.106'
Camp site at top of waterfalls	S 35° 55.663'	W 070° 55.146'

for an altitude gain of about 100 m to two smaller lagoons that also offer good camping.

Day 3 6

Summit day! Head straight for your goal whose upper portion is already visible, and you will get to a small ridge after about an hour (at 2,970 m). Stay at that altitude until you get to the side leading to the main ridge of San Pedro. Without snow, the further ascent is an ordeal across a steep scree slope leading to the foot of the volcano's cone at 3,150 m – Caution: high danger of rockfall!

It's easy to see the route for your further ascent. A hump-shaped crater towers over the summit area; you will have climbed it after a total of 4 hours. All your efforts will be rewarded by a stunning view of the Andes from this 3,621 m volcano. Towards the east, a desert-like area stretches all the way to Argentina, to the north Cerro Azul appears in front of Descabezado, to the west you'll recognize the hanging glaciers of Cerro Toro, and to the south resides Longaví.

It takes only two hours to get back to the camp at the lagoon. If your legs are still strong enough, you can continue on to the waterfall the same day so that you can get all the way back in two days.

Day 4/5 8-10

Backtrack to the starting point on Río Colorado. The distance from the waterfall can easily be done in one day.

△ When the Incas pushed south from Cuzco, only decades before the Spanish, they met with little resistance in sparsely populated Central Chile. South of there, the Mapuche gave them more trouble, and so their conquest was stopped at the water-rich Río Maule, which thus became the natural southern border of their empire. Legend has it that this was due to the charm of the women from the Maule area: "The strangers, tired and thirsty from all the fighting and marching, threw themselves down at the river and drank until their thirst was sated. One after another, they fell asleep, hexed as it were by the effects of the murmuring river. The next morning, as the sun rose in the east, they were awakened by the sound of beautiful songs and dances with exotic rhythm. What they saw made them ecstatic – women dancing bathed in the morning sun with waistlong, silky hair, ruby-colored eyes and strong lips, as purple as the Copihue flower. And that's why these courageous men who had conquered the north and the center of the country succumbed to the lure of the Maule women (....) and forgot the Konquista."[1]

500 years later, the sirens of the Maule river have not lost their magic. Many a gringo who came to conquer the mountains of this region fell in love and stayed here forever...

[1] quoted from: Oreste Plath

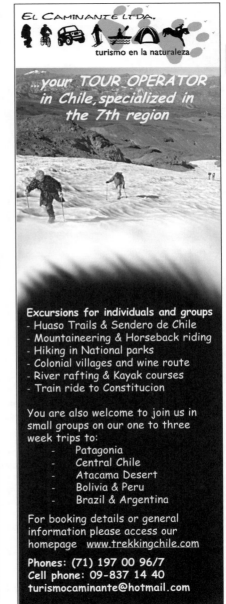
Trekking & Mountaineering

2

Franz Schubert

Belloto Trail
Through an Enchanted Forest

18

Those who hike through the quiet old Southern Beech forests of the Bellotos El Melado Nature Preserve might both wonder about and rejoice in the fact that hardly anyone else seems to have discovered the unsullied beauty of this valley and its natural features. The 417 hectare preserve, donated to the state by an individual, is home to the last stands of the highly threatened Belloto *(see p. 25/27)*.

An easy trekking route accompanies Río Ancoa, which rages in some places, and just placidly flows dark green in others. At its source, it cascades down the northern slope of the snow moun-tain El Toro, and then disappears underground from the surface under its stony, dry bed only to reappear another kilometer downstream. Several small lagoons by the cascading falls make perfect swimming holes, and there is great camping in a small wooded area.

The only obstacle on the way there is, you have to cross the river four times one way. But that's a small price to pay if you want to just hike without scrambling over rocks, and if you like the varied fauna. And in the Fall, when the leaves turn, their reddish cast truly turns this into an Enchanted Forest!

Photo: This light-green lake at the source of Río Ancoa beckons for a swim

Point of Departure

Linares.

Approach by Road

A well-maintained gravel road sign-posted as "El Peñasco" runs along Río Ancoa to the nature preserve of Bellotos El Melado. On the last six kilometers, the road clings to the steep slope of picturesque Ancoa gorge right below the rocky tooth of Peñasco; from here, you will need a pick-up to continue. Figure on two hours from Linares. Buses only run to Ancoa bridge about 10 kilometers before you get to the nature preserve.

One km before you get to the park entrance, there is a hotel (Hotel Melado at about 800 m); in the park, there is plenty of camping.

Fees

None.

The dark green Ancoa rushs through the forest

At the entrance to the reserve you will see the park ranger's house; it might be a good idea to sign in even though there is no admission fee. Then follow the road, which will end at Río Ancoa after about 20 minutes. It's really a bit early and too cold for a bath, but you don't really have a choice: you need to get to the other side! The trail continues but alas! After only a few minutes it runs down to the river again and demands that you take off your shoes again. A few meters above, right by the trail, you can find a few cacti of the genus "curvispina", one of only five cactus species of the region *(see p. 27)*.

As was to be expected, after only 20 minutes you will get to prove your fording skills again. Back on the right side of the river, you will soon reach a small lagoon in a shady Arrayán forest; this tree in the Myrtaceae family is easily recognized by its cinnamon-colored bark. Then hike uphill for about 20 minutes and back down to the river where - as you probably know by now – you will do another one of those river crossings, the fourth and last one of the day. The trail then runs mostly through sparse forest and will remain on the left side of the river.

Then a big boulder right by the trail hints that it will get difficult now. The grade that follows will make you break into a sweat for the first time that day! Please note: There will be a trail that turns off to the left and uphill on the way; don't take it but stay above the river! Your trail will descend to Río Ancoa eventually. Up to here, it's been about 1.5 hours from the last river crossing. Another 20 minutes later, you will pass a small cave; you might want to check whether the troll is in! After another hour's hike through the woods, you will get to a nice campsite, where anglers can test their luck anywhere along the river.

Take a well-deserved break, then leave your packs here and walk up the stony river bed. Only a few hundred meters further, you will find the place where the river emerges from its underground bed (at least, that's what we found in March of 2001). You can see it cascading from afar, it's another half hour's walk to what is an idyllic sight: the waterfalls splash into a green lagoon. Don't let this opportunity for a dip pass!

It is also worth climbing up a little where the waterfall cascades down. Right by the lagoon, there are several good campsites in the forest.

Day 2 🕐 4

Backtrack the same way.

Optional Day

Another day tour goes from Melado Hotel to a rocky vantage point at 1,800 m with a view of the turquoise colored Melado reservoir, Descabezado to the north, and San Pedro volcano to the east. The unmarked trail is hard to find; a local guide is recommended (ask at the hotel).

Andean Legends: Of Nightbirds, Monsters and Devils

△ When hiking in the Enchanted Forest, you'd better know the local witches, dragons, and ghosts. The Chilean Andes are full of magic birds, monsters, and devils in all kinds of shapes. Beware of **Cuca Negra**, a black nightbird that bleats like a donkey. If you are as much as grazed by its shadow on a full moon, you will die before the year is over. That's nothing compared to **Chonchón**, a flying head with ears for wings that announces a person's death with blood-curdling cries of 'tué tué'. The white bird **Cuca Blanca**, however, is a good one: it shows hikers who got lost the way at night crying, 'Cuca! Cuca!' Hollow trees are the home of the terrifying **Pihuchén**, a greenish snake that sucks the blood from humans and animals - from a distance, no less! Trekkers especially should beware of **Lola**. This woman shrouded in white lures hikers into gorges and cliffs in blizzards. But lucky are those who discover **Ciudad de los Césares**, the Emperors' City, which is supposed to be glittering with splendor and wealth somewhere in the Andes – but it has not revealed itself to anyone yet.

None of these legends, however, is as alive among country folks as is the belief in **devils**. Witness to that are not only numerous place names containing the word *diablo*, but also the lengthy stories any *arriero* will tell around the campfire.

Franz Schubert

Longaví Trek
River Crossing Championship

19

 Climbing Longaví    6 Map on page 138, sketch on p. 139

This mountain trek provides a lot of variety, and it is one of the most demanding ones described in this book. In addition, this circumnavigation and ascent of 3,240 m Nevado de Longaví (Nevado = snow mountain, Longaví = snake's head) no doubt deserves its place among the ten most beautiful tours in Chile. Virgin forests and glaciers, a quiet camp on the bank of Laguna Achibueno and stands of rare cypress trees south of the snowy Toro Massif more than compensate for the exertion. And if you are someone who likes to practice crossing rivers, this is the tour for you! Only for experienced mountain trekkers or with a guide.

Photo: On the snow fields on the eastern slope of Longaví

Point of Departure

Parral.

Approach by Road

Without your own transportation, even the first stage will be difficult. There is a bus once a day from Parral to the Malcho bridge over Río Longaví. From here, it is 8 km to the entrance of Fundo Castillo, where you have to get permission to enter the private grounds. There are two different gravel roads that take you another 5 km down to Río Blanco. Better take the one to the north, the manager can give precise directions. This will be the actual starting point at an altitude of about 750 m.

Fees

None.

Day 1 3

First follow the road, which will end after about 30 minutes. It continues on the other side of Río Blanco, which carries a lot of water, especially in the Spring. You should have solid experience with river crossings, or you might get into serious trouble! Once on the other (eastern) side of the river, walk uphill for about half an hour and then another 1.5 hours on relatively level ground back down to the river, which you will have to cross here again. There is also a nice spot for camping here. Since this stretch is densely forested, you can catch only occasional glimpses of snow-covered Toro.

Day 2 5

You should be able to hit the trail well-rested, and soon you will arrive at Río Martín. After crossing it, continue to follow Río Blanco upstream. It's important to stay close to the escarpment until you are back on the trail. Then it's uphill steeply to the summer pastures which the locals call *potrero*; you will pass a wooden cabin. Stay on the left edge of the pasture and climb a cattle fence to get back on the trail. After about another hour, and two more stream crossings, you will find a good campsite in a forest near a stream.

By now, you've been hiking 5 hours total.

Those who feel like a bath can hike to La Turbia without their packs. A few minutes after you have crossed the second stream, a trail starts switchbacking uphill following the stream at some distance. On a small level plain colored sediments right next to the stream will signal the small warm springs.

Day 3 6

A few hundred meters behind the camp you will pass "Crying Rock" where water emerges from the volcanic rock. The trail leads back to Río Blanco, and you'll have to cross it again. A little ways up, the same thing all over, and then it's further up the valley without a trail, over big river rocks.

Loma de arena (Sand Hill) can be seen from quite a distance ahead. The ascent is a little tiring because of the shifting sand. Once at the top, you

Don't know how to do this yet? You'll learn it!

will find a trail on relatively level ground. After crossing a tributary, you will get to a nice campsite next to a huge rock that you simply can't miss. Since you will have been above the treeline starting at Loma de arena, you will have an unobstructed view of Longaví.

Day 4   6-7

It's mountain climbing today; a day tour to 3,240 m Nevado de Longaví, no less. On the eastern slope, snowfields descend until well into the Summer, so you might need crampons and iceaxe. If there is no snow, the ascent will be all the more difficult because of the scree on the steep slopes. From the camp, follow the stream towards the mountain hiking through an impressive gorge. In its lower portion, it consists of silt, and further uphill, head for the hilly part that is about 100 meters below the actual summit. Beware of rockfall! Pick your route carefully.

The upper part of the summit is for experienced mountaineers only; it is climbed from the north. But even from the spot where you are now, you can already see for about 300 kilometers on clear days, over numerous snowy peaks close by and all the way into Argentina. The altitude gain between camp and summit is about 800 m.

Return by the same route.

Day 5 6

You can already see the trail on the other side of Río Blanco leading to the 2,000 m pass. Once on the pass, hike for about an hour to get to Laguna Achibueno nestled among the dwarf pine that feeds the river of the same name. There is nothing like a mountain lake for cooling off in the heat of the Summer!

The trail follows Río Achibueno down into the valley. At the mouth of Río Nacimiento you will find a good campsite at 1,200 m.

GPS Waypoints Longaví Trek		
Fundo Castillo, Starting point on Río blanco	S 36º 15.171	W 071º 17.182
After first river crossing, before as cending main trail	S 36º 14.816	W 071º 15.799
Second river crossing, east again	S 36º 14.297	W 071º 14.376
First camp	S 36º 14.663	W 071º 10.357
Hot springs "La Turbia"	S 36º 13.966	W 071º 10.141
Trail ends, crossing Río Blanco	S 36º 14.717	W 071º 09.064
Trail to camp on upper part of sand hill	S 36º 13.037	W 071º 07.553
Ascent Longaví 1	S 36º 12.729	W 071º 07.576
Ascent Longaví 2	S 36º 12.356	W 071º 08.282
Ascent Longaví 3	S 36º 12.280	W 071º 08.988
Ascent Longaví 4	S 36º 12.246	W 071º 09.408
Ascent Longaví 5	S 36º 12.283	W 071º 09.567
Hilly part of peak	S 36º 12.118	W 071º 09.755
Pass between Laguna Achibueno and Río Blanco Valley	S 36º 12.958'	W 071º 06.764'
Laguna Achibueno	S 36º 12.996'	W 071º 04.647'
Pass to upper section of Río Achibueno, close to lake	S 36º 12.391'	W 071º 03.837'
Río Nacimiento, camp	S 36º 09.747'	W 071º 05.787'
Río Pato	S 36º 08.165'	W 071º 06.948'
Río Potrero	S 36º 07.203'	W 071º 07.472'

Day 6 6

Following what has by now turned into a well-trodden path that meanders along Río Achi-bueno, you will get to a hotel that is located in beautiful natural surroundings. This is an ideal place for relaxing a bit before you head back for civilization.

The gravel road to Linares is awful. There is no public transport; you'll have to hitch-hike or find transport from the hotel.

Map tour 19

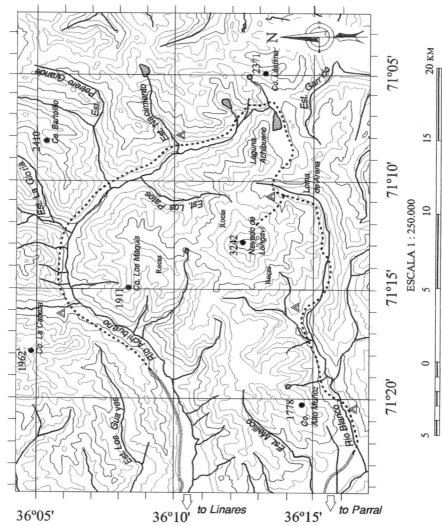

36°05'   36°10' to Linares   36°15' to Parral

NEVADO LONGAVÍ (3,240 m)

LAGUNAS DEL ACHIBUENO

RÍO ACHIBUENO

CAJÓN DE LOS PERROS

RÍO ACHIBUENO

CAJÓN DE LAS ÁNIMAS

MONTE OSCURO

Trekking & Mountaineering

2

Franz-Schubert

Laguna Trucha
Hermit Lake

20

Map on page 142

Would you like to be far from any sign of civilization, all by yourself in rugged nature? With nothing but the whispering of the leaves, the singing of the birds, the murmuring of the brook? If so, you will find the two-day ascent to the isolated Laguna Trucha well worth the effort, especially since in the Fall, you will be hiking through splendidly colored forests. It would be easy to spend a few days here.

Photo: Solitude is guaranteed at this picturesque mountain lake

Point of Departure

San Carlos.

Approach by Road

A road whose pavement soon ends runs from San Carlos to a small settlement on Río Los Sauces via San Fabián de Alico (police station). A daily bus from San Carlos also makes it that far; the stop is right by the spot where the water level is measured. In El Sauce, horses and guides can be hired. It's about 2 to 3 hours from San Carlos.

Fees

None.

Day 1 8

At the water measuring station close to where Río Los Sauces flows into Río Ñuble, you can either ford the former or take the cable car if the water is too high. On the other side is the home of Alfredo Sandoval, the official "water level measuring man"; he also organizes tours into the surrounding areas.

Follow Río Ñuble past lots of nice swimming holes, and you will get to the hamlet of Los Robles after about 4 hours of easy hiking on level ground. At the other end of Los Robles, slip through a wooden gate and head up a rough gravel path leading steeply up the side of the mountain. Then a good trail will take you slightly downhill through beautiful forested areas. After about 4 hours of hiking, you will find a camp spot by the second stream that needs to be crossed, right by Río de las Truchas.

Day 2 4

You will spend today following the "trout river" through pretty forests with views of the north side of Chillán volcano. After four hours, you will reach Laguna Trucha located in a "bowl" of steeply rising mountain walls. You shouldn't need much convincing for a refreshing bath!

Time just flies at this mountain lake in the midst of gorgeous Southern Beech forests. There is great camping at the bank, and if you are tired of resting, you can go on a variety of tours from here.

Day 3-4 10

Backtrack the same way. The adventuresome or those with a guide can test their mettle with a crossing of the pass to Río de la Tragedia and a return via Río González.

An easy hike through the forest

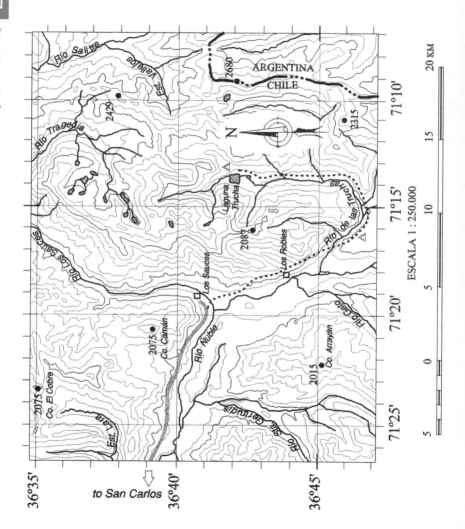

Valle Aguas Calientes
Hot Springs under Starry Skies

21

Map on page 148

Close to the famous, but very touristy thermal spa of Chillán, there is a valley that steals its thunder. The hot springs in Valle de Aguas Calientes use the same underground furnace of Chillán volcano just like their "rich" neighbors. Among the prettiest natural hot springs in Chile, Aguas Calientes are only an easy day tour over a 2,000 m pass away. This is an ideal practice tour for other treks! Amateur photographers will love the phantastic views of the glaciated Sierra Velluda to the south, and the snowy chain of Chillán to the north. And for romantic sorts: How about a night by the hot springs by candlelight under the stars with your significant other?

Photo: The hot springs are a short ways up from here; in the background, Antuco volcano (on the left) and Sierra Velluda

Point of Departure

Chillán.

Approach by Road

The small resort of Las Trancas is easily reached from Chillán by public transport (73 km). You will find campsites, accommodations of several categories, bicycle and horse rentals and a small grocery store. There is lots of traffic on the last 9 km to Termas de Chillán, and so hitch-hiking is easy. Once or twice in the morning, there is a bus from Chillán to the hot springs. The road passes fancy hotels (a ski center in the Winter) on its way to the public hot springs, from whose parking lot this tour starts.

Fees

None.

Day 1 ⏱ 4–5

Above the swimming pools, a wide path runs along the left bank of a stream. Turn right after a few hundred meters, cross the stream, and start your ascent on a trail that switchbacks up the grassy slope. There are several confusing branches, but after about 45 minutes, they eventually all reach the sulfur springs called "Pozones" (basins) where you can enjoy the questionable pleasure of rolling around in warm volcanic mud with total strangers, but who knows, you might feel healthier afterwards.

A hiker's life...

Not for everyone: a mud bath half way

Behind those mud holes that are very busy in the Summer, the trail continues in three different directions. Follow the most-used trail up the valley. After two to three hours and an altitude gain of about 600 meters, you will reach the pass at 2,400 m, where you will be rewarded with a splendid view: The mountains to the south are Sierra Velluda, and the volcano Antuco with its trademark conical shape.

Then descend into Valle de Aguas Calientes. After a few hundred meters – here's a hint for a climbing tour – there's a barely visible trail that would take you to the summit of the volcano Chillán. This time, however, follow the main trail, which takes you to the hot springs in about an hour. Several rivers originate in the volcano at a temperature of about 70 °C and flow downhill into the valley. For a stretch of several hundred meters, they beckon for a soothing bath.

If you like, you can start heading back the same day. However, you can find great spots for camping that invite you to bide your time. It can be busy here during the high season, and you might want to look for a quieter spot. If you follow the trail up the valley, you will get to its end after about an hour, where the greenery stops abruptly. This is where the last of the hot streams starts – not quite as spectacular, but definitely quieter.

Day 2 3-4

Return the same way.

How the Hot Springs were discovered

△ Who discovered the Hot Springs at Chillán? There are several myths connected to this event; one of which tells of the infamous gang of the Pincheira brothers that actually did exist. They roamed the mountains near Chillán from 1817 until 1832, stealing cattle on both sides of the Cordillera, plundering, marauding and abducting women. Legend also has it that the Pincheiras were once returning from a pillage from Argentina with a gravely injured man. Since they were not able to take him any further, they left him with some food in a spot called Pirigallo and continued without him. The man laid down expecting certain death, when he felt some warm water on his back. He washed his wounds, drank from it, and lo and behold – he got better every day! When his companions returned, they were surprised to find him alive and well. That's how the Pincheiras discovered the hot springs of Chillán, where now one of the hotels is called 'Pirigallo'.

For those who like it hot: The thermal spa at the Pirigallo Hotel

Franz Schubert

Nevado de Chillán (3,212 m) 22
In the Realm of Lava

 in the
glacier area

Map on page 148

Do not miss this tour if you are into wildly cracked lava landscapes with glaciers, craters, and parasite cones of geological interest. This is actually an entire group of active volcanoes with a number of calderas and lava flows. And over all this towers the partially glaciated 3,212 m Nevado de Chillán. A ski region with expensive hot springs spa hotels has sprung up on its wooded flanks using the hot springs that freely pour forth from the mountain. Chillán's last eruption started in 1973 and lasted, with one interruption, until 1987.

The icing on the cake is the ascent via the glacier, which provides an ideal practice terrain for iceclimbing novices.

Photo: View south from the summit; to the left, Chillán volcano; in the background, Antuco and Sierra Velluda

Point of Departure

Chillán.

Approach by Road

From Chillán, there are several buses a day to the small resort of Las Trancas, nine kilometers below Termas de Chillán. Las Trancas has a youth hostel with campsites, a number of cabañas, hotels, and a small store for basic food items.

Day 1 5

From the campsite at 1,300 m, go back on the blacktop for a few hundred meters, turn right at the next intersection, and follow the gravel road to Shangri La. After about an hour's walk through pretty Southern Beech (Lenga) forests, the road crosses a lava flow. Right after that, leave the road and follow the edge of the lava flow uphill. The trail runs between the lava flow and the lenga bushes, disappearing a few times, which turns the ascent into a constant search. After about four hours, you will reach a dilapidated cabin where you can pitch your tent in a few very nice spots right by a waterfall, with a view of the volcano and the Central Valley.

Day 2 8

Leave your tent up and follow the creek uphill over the volcanic rock. After a few hundred meters, there will be a sandy depression with some vegetation to your left. This is where you will come upon a trail marked with a cairn. And right behind it, there is a morain, which you will follow to the glacier. So far, it has been about an hour.

This is followed by a 4 hour (approx.) ascent over the glacier with crampons and iceaxe all the way to the summit at 3,212 m. Keep climbing towards the pass between Nevado and its neighbor peak to the west, cross below the pass and climb your target from the west. The route is relatively easy to see, but you have to know how to use your crampons and iceaxe.

At the top, there is not only a specially designed summit cross to greet you, but there is also a summit log, which is unusual for the Chilean Andes. The view of the vast glacier, the towering ice masses and the forested green valleys are definitely worth the climb.

Descend by the same route; about three hours back to the camp.

Day 3 4

Return to Las Trancas the same way.

Ideal for beginners: The ascent over the glacier

Trekking & Mountaineering

2

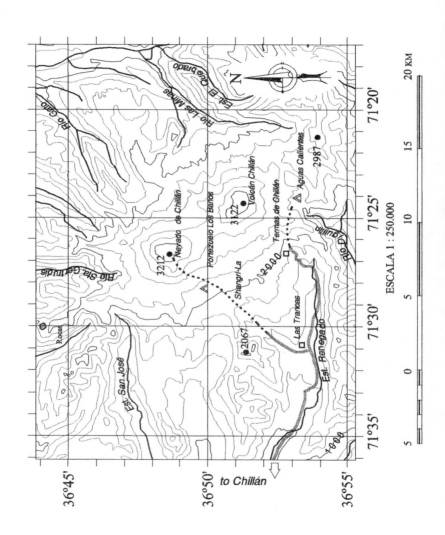

Franz Schubert

Volcán Antuco (2,985 m)
Sugar Cone in a Moonscape

23

Between dark blue Laguna del Laja and glaciated Sierra Velluda, the perfectly shaped sugarcone of the volcano Antuco juts up, falling only a few meters short of the 3,000 m mark. At its 1752 eruption, a lavaflow cut off the entire valley damming the huge lake – one of the largest drinking water reservoirs of the Central Region. The water has found its way out of this porous barrier underground and shoots down several hundred meters from a vertical rockface – thus forming the picturesque source of Río Laja.

Theoretically, this volcano can be climbed from all sides. The southern route is the most interesting one since it runs on a small glacier, and not just on boring lava sand. From the top, you will have an interesting view of the moonscape created by volcanic action. The quiet of Antuco is deceiving: Even if the most recent activity was recorded 70 years ago, the volcano is not extinct. Experts expect new eruptions of lava every 100 to 150 years.

There are several multi-day tours that can be done in Laguna del Laja National Park, a place not to be missed on any tour of Chile. Among those are a hike to the foot of Sierra Velluda, on which you will cross the lava flows from the last major eruption in 1853, or a tour around the entire volcano.

Photo: The quiet may be deceiving - Antuco is among the most active volcanoes of Chile

Point of Departure

Los Angeles.

Approach by Road

From Los Angeles there is a good road leading via Antuco (66 km) to the National Park at the foot of the volcano. Right after Antuco, the road surface turns to gravel which can, however, be negotiated by regular cars. The ERS bus company, ph. (43) 322 356, makes several runs daily from Los Angeles to the hydropower plant of Abanico, 11 km from the park entrance (about 2 hrs.); from there, you can try hitchhiking. Right before you get to the park, there is a narrow trail that takes off to the left and gets you within minutes to the impressive waterfalls of Ojos del Laja, the underground drain of the lagoon.

At the Park entrance, after a 91 km drive, you should sign in at Conaf. There is a small cafetería and a simple hostel. A gravel road that gets worse and worse leads around the volcano, past good camp sites at the sandy edge of Laguna del Laja. Before the road leads south from the volcano and crosses Aguada (also: El Volcán) creek, the trail uphill starts. From Los Angeles to this point, figure at least three hours by car.

Fees

Admission: USD 1.25/day, incl. tent camping

Day 1 5-6

Alternate Options: The ascent via the northern flank is much more easily accessible. It starts right before the lagoon at the tiny ski area (1 lift). The manager of the Hostería offers his services as a guide. Scrambling up 30 to 40 degree slopes of loose lava rocks is arduous; in the Spring, snowfields make it easier. Plan on three to four hours to the summit. You can connect both routes by having someone drop you off at the foot of

The source of Río Laja in a lava flow

The ascent does not require much of a description since the route is easy to see. You should take crampons, but you won't need a rope or iceaxe. We only came across one crevasse, and that was easy to spot. From the starting point at 1,500 m to the summit it takes about three hours, and count on about 2.5 hours for the descent.

the southern slope and pick you up on the northern side.

Another option is the climb from the saddle between Sierra Velluda and Antuco on a multi-day tour.

△ Self-confidence was one of the things German explorer Eduard Friedrich Poeppig (1798-1868) did not exactly lack. So when he climbed Antuco on February 19, 1829, he did not only think that he was the first person to do so, but he actually thought he was the first person ever on any Chilean volcano. Together with two *arrieros* – one turned back on the way - he had dragged himself to the summit that had erupted again only the year before. Apart from his delusions of grandeur – the Incas knew the Andean peaks very well – Poeppig's report makes for interesting reading:

"The closer we got to the crater, the more terrifying the strong trembling of the ground became, and finally, thick clouds of sand fell dangerously hot down upon us as an accidental change in the direction of the wind blew the crater's smoke column our way. The steepness of the terrain and our weakness led to falls, and our hands were bleeding when we reached the summit. It was steeper than we had been able to see before we actually arrived there, and it announced its presence sufficiently by the thin columns of smoke that emerged everywhere from out of the sand, and by the heat of the treacherous ground, which, however, after hours of walking over snow and ice appeared pleasant to us. After three hours of uninterrupted and continued effort the high goal was finally reached; we were standing only a few steps from the crater, the first humans ever to scale a volcano in Chile. However, our triumph was only of brief duration, for soon we found the ground too hot, and the thick clouds of steam were blown towards us by the wind in such quantities as to make us seek salvation from asphyxiation by swiftly throwing ourselves down on the ground. We walked a few more steps, but we were soon forced to throw ourselves down again. However, we finally succeeded after all in reaching the northern edge, where the wind protected us from the smoke that was hurled from the abyss, and the rocks that were intermittently expelled along with it with great force."

After studying medicine and natural sciences at the University of Leipzig, Poeppig had left for a multi-year reseach journey to Chile and Peru. He returned with numerous botanical and zoological finds to Leipzig, where he founded the university's Natural History collection. Despite his groundbreaking work – he discovered and categorized numerous South American plant and animal species - Poeppig always stood in the shadow of his great colleague, Alexander von Humboldt.

Alfredo Escobar

Rock Climbing
Tackling Steep Walls

3

The Andes -
A Climbers' Dorado

What is climbing? Different people will define this term in different ways. Mountaineers will be thinking of tackling steep peaks or difficult walls, sometimes including multi-day "assaults" with elaborate logistics and technical detail. Chilean andinistas have only just discovered the lure of conquering hard-to-access climbs in the as yet unexplored Cordillera, and lots of tough routes have not been completed yet at all.

It was not until the 90's that sport climbing became popular in Chile. Its fans enjoy the athletic challenge and the kick they get from climbing shorter routes equipped with a number of diverse anchors. In Santiago, a crowd of enthusiasts got into climbing indoor walls (escalada deportiva), and the best of them now participate successfully in international competitions. In this chapter, we will distinguish between the following types of climbing:

Sport Climbing: Shorter, prepared routes on rock with fixed anchors

Traditional Rock Climbing: Longer routes on rock without existing anchors

Alpine Climbing: Climbing peaks involving considerable efforts in logistics and time, rocks and glaciers.

Access

In Greater Santiago, there are about 100 to 120 climbing routes with varying degrees of difficulty and equipped with reliable bolts and anchors. Traditional climbers will find about half a dozen walls that have been done before. Beyond that, there is no limit to your imagination when looking for new routes. One of the greatest obstacles is presented by the challenges to accessing potential climbing areas. In some cases, an all-terrain vehicle is indispensable, and usually you will face a long approach on foot. In addition, you will often have to negotiate permission for access with the landowner (see Access to Hiking Routes, p. 56). And if you plan to climb in border areas, get permission beforehand at Dirección de Fronteras y Límites, Bandera 52, Santiago Centro , ph. (2) 671 41 10, fax (2) 697 19 09, and remember to sign in at the border police.

Difficulty

Chilean climbers use primarily the Yosemite Decimal Scale (YDS).

Conditions

The Andes are a comparatively old, very eroded chain of mountains with poor rock quality. The predominant rock is heavily eroded, crumbly andesite. In some areas, you will also

Five Golden Rules for Climbing

△ Never go on a climbing tour by yourself.

△ If at all possible, find a knowledgeable local guide.

△ Plan longer tours thoroughly, get information ahead of time, and take sufficient provisions and gear.

△ Wear a helmet!

△ For emergencies, take a cell phone or a two-way radio.

find a conglomerate rock with lots of holes and holds. The rare granite rocks, such as in Yerba Loca Valley, at Cerro San Gabriel in Cajón del Maipo, and at Cordón Granito in the Cordillera near Rancagua, provide good surfaces. The best rock for climbing, consisting of tuff like famous Smith Rock in Oregon, can be found at the rocks of El Manzano.

The region provides an excellent climate for climbing comparable to that of California *(see Hiking Weather, p. 58-59)*. Consistently hot and sunny summers make a shirt and shorts sufficient gear, and depending on the wall's orientation, you may be able to climb in the shade.

An infrastructure of hostels, stores for supplies, as well as emergency services are largely non-existent. So, it's important to bring along sufficient provisions, water, and possibly a tent and sleeping bag!

Safety

In addition to all the usual safety measures for this risky sport, two considerations are important to keep in mind for Central Chile: Because of the frequent rock fall, wearing a helmet is essential, and prior arrangements should be made to account for the fact that no swift rescue services are available. It is important to have a vehicle at your disposal for getting help or transporting an injured person. While cell

phones will not work everywhere, they can be helpful in some areas. Leave word with an Andean Club before you go on long tours. The emergency number to call is 133 (police) or the air rescue service (SAR) at 138.

Equipment

Besides climbing shoes, ropes and quickdraws, a helmet is part of the basic equipment for climbing in Central Chile (except for El Manzano). Depending on your climbing route, you should always take a set of anchors and rappelling slings, and possibly nails and bolts. Before installing new bolts on established walls, ask about the local procedure! A number of stores in Santiago offer climbing gear, but the selection is limited. In the capital, you can rent equipment at Climbing Planet (also an indoor climbing wall, *see Addresses*).

Indoor Climbing Walls

Indoor climbing facilities are the best places for finding other enthusiasts, as well as knowledgeable guides for climbing in the Andes. *See Addresses p. 227.*

On the Internet

www.escalando.cl
Lots of and good info from experts, not very functional, but in English

http://www2.ing.puc.cl/~cseebach/mountain/andes.en.html
Homepage of a Chilean climber and mountaineer, some drawings of climbing walls; in English and Spanish

www.tricuspide.cl
Lots of current info and discussions about climbing and mountaineering in Chile; in Spanish only

Climbs in Central Chile

Sport Climbing

Established rock routes with fixed anchors can be found at:

Las Chilcas

Popular rock area 75 km north of Santiago, on the left side of the Panamericana before you get to Llaillay. Crumbly conglomerate, 90 solid routes of up to three pitches, 5.5 to 5.14. A 50-60 m-rope and a dozen quickdraws are sufficient to have some fun here! Very hot in the Summer, no water. You can camp here. Beware of the vinchuca bug that is found here *(see p. 49)*!

Los Dominicos (Piedra Rajada)

A boulder for a Sunday morning on the eastern edge of Santiago, at the end of Camino Otoñal in Los Dominicos (Las Condes district), behind a school, 15 min. walk. Eight short routes on very crumbly andesite, hardly to be recommended. 5.8 to 5.11.

Las Palestras del Manzano

A real climbing paradise with many varied options for all tastes, as well as some of the most difficult routes in Central Chile. Easy to get to via the road to Cajón de Maipo, about 25 km from Santiago. Access 800 m past El Manzano bridge (a sign says, "Bienvenidos jóvenes pente-costales"), through a gate (Admission: USD 0.40), then proceed uphill to a powerline; follow it east for about 300 m until you reach a trail leading up to the foot of the walls. About 40 routes of up to 30 m, 5.3 to 5.13 (many 5.9 and 5.10), tuff with lots of finger pockets. Lots of wind, room for two tents, more at Torrecillas.

Piedra Rommel

Five minutes by car / 20 on foot from the road, up the valley, at the foot of the Torrecillas, there

Hot and dry: Climbing on the rocks at Las Chilcas

are two big boulders right on Río Manzano. Accessed from about 500 m past the bridge over the Manzano. The land owner charges USD 3.00 admission. About 20 short routes from 5.7 to 5.12d.

Torrecillas del Manzano

The two high rock walls in Manzano Valley are another paradise for sport and traditional rock climbing, and they also provide very beautiful scenery. They are well worth the hike from the road (about an hour) or from Piedra Rommel through the sclerophyll forest. Access is also possible via a gravel road by car (approach same as for Piedra Rommel, Admission: USD 3.00).

About 30 sport routes of up to 8 pitches in hard tuff with lots of small holes and holds, with bolts everywhere, 5.8 to 5.12. Bring two ropes for rappelling and plenty of quickdraws. Some routes lead all the way to a ridge from which you can descend via the opposite side. Good tent camping, no water in summer.

Coast

Outside Santiago, sport climbing is a neglected sport. There is a single rock for climbing with rusty anchors at **Punta de Tralca** on the coast south of Algarrobo; beware of high waves! The seaside resort of **Reñaca** also has its rock, Piedra Oceánica. At **Constitución**, you will find some boulders with routes of 10 to 18 m close to the harbor, and more routes on Elephant Rock south of the beach walk. Bring enough slings and cams; nice cracks.

Traditional Rock Climbing

For this sport, you will need a lot more knowledge about the locations, as well as more gear. Your best bet for finding information and experienced climbing partners are the Andean Clubs, *Addresses see p. 224*. We have only listed a selection of well-known routes, most of which have no fixed anchors.

Yerba Loca

Little-climbed granite wall in Yerba Loca Valley east of Santiago, about one and a half hours past Villa Paulina on the left side of the river. Approach by road *see trekking tour 2, p. 73*. A variety of face and crack routes, 5.7 to 5.10, up to ten pitches. In Winter, good ice falls will form here.

Cerro San Gabriel

One of the few granite walls in Central Chile, approach by road through Cajón de Maipo as far as San Gabriel (about 50 km from Santiago). From the police station, it's about an hour on foot to the 400 m high wall. It is full of cracks, and it has about six routes, the most popular one of

which is called 'Ruta de los colombianos' (5.9) with 10 pitches; others go up to 5.11 in difficulty. There are more 3-pitch routes in the craggy Quebrada Los Espolones, which starts by the police station (about 30 minutes on foot).

Las Melosas

Several granite walls on upper Río Maipo, about 8 km above San Gabriel (turn right off the main road a few kilometers beyond the police station, and go past Los Queltehues hydropower station). Roughly 20 routes on eroded granite, max. 70 m, 5.8 to 5.12. Natural protection necessary almost everywhere, long runouts and some breath-taking passages; only for experienced rock climbers. Take enough cams and stoppers, as well as two ropes for rappelling down.

This popular route on the Torrecillas is called 'Microclima'

Placa Roja / Placa Gris

Basic rock climbing on vertical plates. Two kilometers behind the hut of the German Andean Club (Refugio Alemán) at Lo Valdés (25 km above San Gabriel). 15 min walk to Placa Roja, one hour to Placa Gris. Several routes along the edges of the plates with fixed rappels, up to eight pitches, standard equipment. North face of Placa Gris 5.8 has beautiful view, south face is very eroded, not recommended. The homey Refugio Alemán is the only "real" hut in all of Central Chile.

Punta Zanzi

Hard to access, very demanding walls above Lo Valdés. Starting three kilometers past Refugio Alemán, a two-hour steep switchback climb will get you to the starting point. Several long routes of up to 10 pitches, vertically layered basalt rock, loose in places, lots of cracks and chimneys. Recommended routes: 'Concierto para Bongs', 'Diedro', 'Directísima', and 'Ira de Thor', 5.9 to 5.11.

Alpine Climbing

Only a handful of climbers is into this sport in Chile. Again, your best bet for finding experts to prepare expeditions with are the Andean Clubs. Among the classic routes is Cerro Arenas above Baños Morales. Only few have attempted scaling the steep peak of Cerro Morado *(title page photo, trekking tour 6)*. Equally demanding are Cerro Altar and Cerro Paloma at the end of Yerba Loca Valley *(trekking tour 2)*, as well as the crags of Cajón de la Casa Piedra northwest of El Yeso dam. The legendary walls of Cordón Granito near Rancagua are hard to get to. The granite area of Cordillera Lástima near Linares remains yet to be explored.

Ice Climbing

Especially in Winter, fanciers of ice climbing will find options galore, the best at Yerba Loca Valley (see above), but also at Cerro Plomo glacier, and in Cajón del Morado. Giant blue ice walls cover a side of Cerro Negro in Río Blanco Valley above Los Andes all year round. Unfortunately, you will have to "fight" for admission at Codelco, Division Andina, who mine copper there. More easily accessed are the ice formations at San José volcano above Refugio Plantat (approach about 6 hrs.)

See also chapter 2, routes 2 (Yerba Loca), 5 (Tupungato), 6 (El Morado), 7 (Marmolejo), 11 (Azufre), 16 (San Pablo - Pellado - San Pedro), 19 (Longaví), and 22 (Nevado de Chillán).

Claudio Seebach

Punta Zanzi, one of the most difficult rocks in Central Chile

Riding Tours
High on a Horse

4

If you want to give your legs a break, you can also do many of the tours described in Chapter 2 on horseback, and you can feel like a real *huaso (see p. 14)* doing so. The easier routes can also be done by beginners. However, a multi-day riding tour in the Andes can be every bit as exhausting as a trekking tour – especially for your behind. The occasional horseperson will also be challenged quite a bit by river crossings, steep slopes, and scree.

The horse continues to be an important means of transportation in rural areas of the Central Region. Many people own horses and are often willing to rent them out for a small fee, such as the *arrieros*, who always travel on horseback in the mountains. If you like things catered, you can turn to one of the horse ranches providing guided rides with accommodations and food.

Photo: Absolute top - crossing the Andes in the tracks of the conquistadores

Travelling like the Huasos

Conditions

The rural population's horses are usually the small, sturdy and easy to handle kind who are used to daily work, and as such, they are well suited to beginners – provided those have received the requisite instructions. But in the Andes, even experienced horseback riders should not tour without a knowledgeable guide. As far as preparations and safety are concerned, the same holds true as for trekking tours.

Equipment

Saddle and reins after the Chilean fashion (leather), as well as bags are provided by the tour organizers and those renting horses. In addition to the equipment *(see p. 60)* needed for tours in the mountains, you will need a sturdy pair of long pants and sturdy shoes.

Typical Chilean saddle

(see p. 60)

Package Tours

Several professional providers offer horseback tours in the Pre-Cordillera as well as in the High Andes, some of them with pass crossings into Argentina *(see Addresses)*. A day tour is USD 35 to 50, and on longer tours with gear and food the daily cost can go up to USD 200, depending on service provided and number of participants.

You can often see signs advertising *'Se arriendan caballos'* (horses for rent) on lots and houses in the country, or on simple cabins. Horses are also actively marketed in National Parks and tourist centers. The prices here are around USD 20 per horse and day, without accommodation and food. For longer tours, you also have to figure on the additional cost for the horse and provisions for your guide.

On the Internet

www.gochile.cl/Activ/cabalgata.asp
General information on horseback riding in Chile; in English and Spanish

www.cascadadelasanimas.cl/horserides.htm
Detailed tour descriptions from a tour operator in the central region; in English and Spanish

Riding Tours

4

Cascada Expediciones

Tours on Horseback in Central Chile

As already mentioned, you can find a mount almost anywhere in Central Chile. Below are a few places that are especially well suited as starting points for taking horseback tours from.

Contact information under Addresses, p. 228

Around Santiago

Therese Matthews from the US organizes tours into the Pre-Cordillera from her horse ranch La Ermita located on the road to Farellones (km 11) that range from one hour up to four days, and from simple rides to demanding expeditions.

The Astorga family has explored numerous routes in the Andes around Cajón del Maipo. From their ecologically- and esoteric-minded ranch of 'Cascada de las Animas' in San Alfonso, as well as through the travel provider Cascada Expediciones, they offer one- to multi-day tours. Absolute top: a 12-day crossing of the Andes following the tracks of the conquistadores.

El Morado National Park *(see trekking tour 6, p. 87)* can also be explored from the saddle. Close to the park entrance in Baños Morales, you will find guides and horses waiting for riding enthusiasts on the weekends.

Coast

In most coastal resort towns, you can rent horses from locals waiting patiently for horse-crazy tourists. And the miles of sandy beaches are ideal for practicing your galloping skills!

Riding Tours 4

160   **Tours on Horseback in Central Chile**

Termas de Flaco

From the natural hot springs in the Cordillera near San Fernando *(see trekking tours 9 and 10)*, it is easy to go on horseback tours to the petrified dinosaur tracks and into the immediate surroundings. During the day, the access road to the town is usually lined with people who rent horses.

Siete Tazas Nature Preserve

A provider for riding tours from Santiago offers tours around the famous Siete Tazas area only during the vacation period (January/February) and on off-season weekends *(see p. 110)*.

Vilches Nature Preserve

In the forests of the Vilches Nature Preserve in the mountains near Talca, one- and multi-day rides are easy to arrange and cheap. *Suggestions for tours on p. 113.*

Los Bellotos Nature Preserve

Hotel Melado, a fancy resort in the Cordillera near Linares, offers beautiful rides at reasonable prices; among others, to the cascading falls at the source of Río Ancoa *(see p. 132-134)*.

Río Achibueno

At the confluence of Estero Animas and Río Achibueno a horse ranch is being built in a very pretty area. It is scheduled to open in 2002.

Río Ñuble

From the confluence of Río Los Sauces and Río Ñuble, you can conveniently start multi-day tours on horseback. Destinations well worth heading for are Laguna Trucha or Lago Dial *(see p .141)*.

Termas de Chillán

Las Trancas resort located nine kilometers before you get to Termas de Chillán is a good starting point for a variety of riding excursions, such as a multi-day ride to Laguna El Lobo in Diguillín Valley. The spa hotels themselves rent horses by the hour for excursions into the forested surroundings *(see p. 143-146)*.

A real horseback riding trip is not complete without a singing huaso

Pablo Sepulveda

Mountain Biking
Around the Andes on Two Wheels

5

Over the past few years, bicycling has become increasingly popular in Chile. Whether it's on the outskirts of Santiago, in national parks, or in roadless valleys of the Cordillera – you will meet more and more touring mountain bikers. Those who like this mode of transport will find exciting trails through beautiful natural surroundings, uncrowded trails far from civilization, and a reliable, sunny climate for a large part of the year. Day tours are possible almost anywhere, and there are no limits to longer tours, maybe with the exception of logistical problems.

Photo: The Pre-Cordillera offers a bounty of mountain biking options for all levels

Adventure in the Saddle

Best Season

Mountainbike touring is possible almost year-round. Best times on the Coast and in the Central Valley are the end of Winter and Spring (August to November), when everything is lush and green; and in the mountains, from mid-December (after the snowmelt) into May.

Access

Many easy tours are easily accessible from Santiago; some of them by bus. For more distant locations, your own means of transportation is indispensable, as well as a sag vehicle for longer tours.

Conditions

Touring on busy roads should be avoided; Chilean drivers are not very considerate when it comes to bicyclists. However, there is a vast network of little-traveled gravel and dirt roads waiting for mountain bikers. Just do not expect a well-established infrastructure – there are no sign-posted bike paths, nor a network of cheap accommodations, or support services. Many of the tours described here will take you into remote areas. This makes thorough preparation, taking adequate gear and getting useful information all the more important. It's a good idea to find a knowledgeable guide for this sport, too.

Safety

Besides an obvious awareness of the basic rules for bicycle touring, wilderness touring in unknown territory requires sound judgment when it comes to taking risks. You will need a good deal of experience to tackle critical situations, such as mechanical problems or difficult terrain. Bicycles will need to be watched or locked when camping in crowded areas, especially at beaches. Basically, however, Chile is thought of as a very safe country.

Equipment

If you are planning longer tours, you should bring your own bike. For day tours, you can try and rent a bike, but rental places are few and far in between. Never leave on a tour without the following: Helmet, gloves, tools, replacement inner tube, patch kit, pump, First Aid kit, sufficient water and provisions.

On the Internet

www.gochile.cl/Activ/mountainbike.asp
General information about mountain biking in Chile; in English and Spanish

www.paredsur.cl
A tour operator's tours throughout Chile; in English

Package Tours

A number of agencies offer package tours for mountain bikers, ranging from day tours to multi-day expeditions, with bikes, gear, provisions, accommodations and sag vehicle included.

See Addresses on p. 228.

Five Golden Rules for Mountain Biking

△ Do not overestimate your abilities.

△ Never ride alone.

△ Find a knowledgeable local guide, and get necessary information ahead of time.

△ Match equipment and gear to the route.

△ Carry a cell phone for emergencies.

Mountain Bike Trails
in Central Chile

If you are resourceful, skilled and have the endurance, you can mount your steed just about anywhere. The following routes are some of the best known tours for mountainbike enthusiasts.

Around Santiago

This megalopolis may have its ugly sides – but its surroundings are definitely pretty. Only a few miles from the city, mountain bikers will find the greatest trails and challenges.

Parque Metropolitano

This city park on Cerro San Cristóbal is a popular meeting point for cyclists who don't have much time. You will find tricked-out, partially signposted trails on blacktop and dirt, and even demanding competition-level trails. Access via both parking entrances (Bellavista and Pedro de Valdivia Norte). Beginners and Advanced.

Santuario de la Naturaleza El Arrayán

This Nature Preserve on the northeastern edge of Santiago offers a vast network of diverse trails through its green sclerophyll vegetation along small streams. Ambitious riders can make their way up the valley for 40 to 50 kilometers, with several portages. Access via Av. Las Condes to Plaza San Enrique, where you turn right onto

Photo: "On the road" at Río de los Cipreses

Pastor Fernández, then turn left about 500 m past the bridge (sign-posted), and keep going on Camino El Cajón until it ends. Admission: USD 3.00. Beginners and Advanced.

San Carlos de Apoquindo

A 7 km trail through sclerophyll forests where the climb to Cerro Provincia starts *(see p. 79)*. Access via the stadium of Universidad Católica at the end of Avenida Las Flores in Las Condes, Map posted on-site. Beginners and Advanced.

Camino a Farellones

On weekends, this curvy asphalt road leading to the ski areas east of Santiago is full of cyclists working up a sweat. If you are in good shape, you can do the 40 km and 2,000 m in altitude gain to Farellones (or further). Beware: during the ski season, this road is busy and dangerous! At curve No. 15 (km 25), a gravel road to **Yerba Loca** Nature Preserve starts on the left *(see trekking tour 2, p. 73)*, which is also a worthwhile trip for cyclists (Admission: USD 2.00). Beginners and Advanced.

Piedra Numerada

Because of its altitude of over 3,000 m, this tour to Piedra Numerada Camp, the first camp for climbs of Cerro Plomo *(see trekking tour 3, p. 76)* is only for those in good shape. For this multiday mountain tour, Laguna Franciscano would make a good camp. Access by road via La Parva ski area and then up the switchbacks to the mountainside station of the last lift. Expert.

Cajón del Maipo

The Pre-Cordillera valley of Río Maipo offers a bounty of mountain biking options for all levels. The route between **Maitenes** and **Alfalfal** (take the road out, and the dirt trail on the other side of the river back, all in all 23 km) in the tributary valley of Río Colorado can be done as an easy half-day trip. Beyond San José de Maipo, on the left, a 17 km dirt road switchbacks up to the **Lagunillas** ski area. A demanding day tour leads from San Gabriel through the craggy valley of **Río Yeso** to the lake of the same name (Embalse El Yeso) located in gorgeous surroundings at 3,000 m (22 km). If you want

to proceed all the way to **Baños del Plomo** (another 13 km), you will have to plan on an extra day. A shorter, but no less impressive tour (12 km) goes from Baños Morales to **Baños Colina**, which is located in the midst of a beautiful mountain panorama. Another mountainbike tour exploring the narrow upper end of **Río Maipo** starts 5 km beyond San Gabriel at Queltehues hydropower station (28 km out and back). Advanced.

Fjording a river in Yeso valley

Central Coast

Quebrada El Tigre

From the beach towns of Zapallar and Cachagua you can use your bike to explore the green jungle of the Quebrada El Tigre, a valley in the Coastal Cordillera with dense vegetation. Access is over private land (get permission); the tour requires good technical skills and endurance. Advanced.

La Campana National Park

From the southern entrance to the park at Granizo *(see trekking tour 1, p. 70)* a demanding fourwheel-drive road switchbacks up all the way to an old mine, from where you can continue on foot to the summit. An easier route leads from the northern entrance (Ocoa) through palm tree woods to beautiful waterfalls (Cascada), out and back 12 km. Advanced.

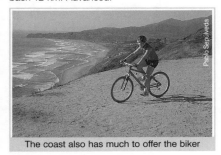

The coast also has much to offer the biker

North of Santiago

Portillo Pass Road

The winding road from Los Andes (820 m) to Portillo ski area at 2880 m (61 km) is only for hardcore riders, who will be rewarded with stunning views of the rugged High Andes. Stay out of the way of the heavy trucks! Expert.

Santiago to Los Angeles

Río Los Cipreses Nature Preserve

This mountain biking tour to Río Los Cipreses Nature Preserve can be linked with a visit of the fancy thermal spa of Cauquenes *(see trekking tour 8, p. 94)*. It is 15 km from the spa to the park entrance, and then another 12 km to Maitenes through pretty sclerophyll forests with a view of Cachapoal Valley. Beginners to Advanced.

Lago Vichuquén

On this mellow tour, you can experience this lake nestled in the Coastal Cordillera. A more demanding option uses the old Camino Real to climb the ridge for a view of both the lake and the ocean. Overnight accommodations in Vichuquén, Llico or a campsite on the lake. Access by road is from Curicó via Hualañe. Beginners to Advanced.

Siete Tazas Nature Reserve

Especially when Fall colors are blazing, this preserve east of Curicó is a paradise for cyclists. Bikes can be rented from the only Hostería in Parque Inglés, above Siete Tazas, and you can also get information there *(see p. 110)*. Advanced.

Termas de Chillán

There are a number of trails around this spa in the Southern Beech forests at Chillán volcano for those who love mountain biking. You can rent bikes and get information at the hotels. Beginners to Advanced.

Laguna La Laja National Park

You can feel as if you are biking on the Moon when riding through the volcanic ashes at Antuco volcano *(see trekking tour 23, p. 150)*. There is a nice trail around the volcano leading along the dark blue lagoon, which offers good camping. Beginners to Advanced.

Horst Simon

Watersports
Catching a Wave

6

What is true for the mountains can also be said to some extent for rivers, lakes, and beaches. Central Chile provides wilderness waters that have hardly been explored, with lots of sunshine, athletic challenges of all kinds, and varied landscapes. Whether you are into rafting or kayaking, surfing or diving – the country has something to offer for every watersport enthusiast.

However, you better not base your expectations on experiences made in Europe or North America; Chilean waters are a totally different matter. This is especially true for kayaking; while every turn, every eddy are documented extensively in Europe, you will find only very sketchy descriptions of Chilean bodies of water. In exchange for that, you will be travelling on some of the most beautiful, unaltered, unpolluted, and uncrowded rivers. Considerable and constant changes in water levels make sure that an old saying holds true: You never get on the same river twice.

The lakes of the Central Region are mostly reservoirs, and they usually store water for drinking, irrigation, or power generating purposes. To the extent that they are accessible they can also be enjoyed by surfing enthusiasts, most of whom, however, congregate on the roughly two dozen beaches of the Central Coast offering tube waves of up to 6 m.

This area also attracts divers who are not deterred by the low temperatures of the Pacific.

Photo: Only for daredevils - "kayaking" the cascades of Siete Tazas

Rafting, Kayaking & Canoeing
Never on the Same River

Every 30 to 40 kilometers, a major whitewater river makes its way from the Andes to the Pacific, altogether about two dozen between Los Andes and Los Angeles, not counting the many small tributaries. Only two of them are run regularly – Río Maipo near Santiago and Río Bío Bío, which forms the southern border of the Central Region and will not be described here. Between these two, numerous rivers are waiting to be explored by adventuresome kayakers and canoeists.

Whitewater only exists east of the Panamericana; the higher up in the mountains, the wilder and more rugged. By the time you get to 'Ruta 5', the rivers are not only very tame, but they also carry with them the effluent from the big cities.

Another rule of thumb: The further south you go, the cleaner the river and the greener the environment. While the rivers in the Santiago area run through a region of fairly sparse vegetation and are strongly colored by greyish-brown sediment, by the time you get to Río Tinguiririca, you will find more and more old growth forests along the banks of the rivers, and the water color will vary between the prettiest shades of green and blue.

While rafting may occasionally look like a really adventurous pursuit, it is not only for skilled white-water athletes. In the Central Region, several outfitters offer rafting trips for ordinary tourists ranging from half-day tours on the relatively mellow Río Maipo (up to Class III of VI) to trips on Teno, Lontué, Maule, and Achibueno rivers (Class III to IV) to multi-day tours on Bío Bío river (up to Class V).

Prices will vary according to distance, level of service and safety precautions *(see Addresses)*.

If you are preparing your own river trip, the same safety rules apply that were listed in Ch. 2 *(see p. 64)*. Since rafting tours can only be done with a registered provider, this chapter will concentrate on kayak and canoe trips.

Best Season

November to April, depending on water level. Generally, kayak tours are also possible in winter; in the spring, they tend to be more difficult because of all the runoff.

Access

You can hear the river rushing down below, but how do you get there? Good places for putting in and taking out are the essence of any kayaking tour, and you should ask about them ahead of time, if possible. In the as yet undeveloped foothills of the Andes, you will find few roads and trails. While those that do exist tend to run through river valleys, they hardly ever come close to the banks. Obvious spots for putting in are at the

Horst Simon

Do you know any other tricks?

morning to evening, from one day to the next, from month to month, and from year to year.

A good rain is enough to turn a harmless trickle into a raging creek. When the sun shines, the heat of the day will let the rivers swell from additional runoff, and so they rise in the afternoons. In general, runoff will make the rivers and streams swell in the Spring making many of them impassable until well into November. How strong the effect of this phenomenon will be depends on how much snow has fallen during the Winter. The amount of precipitation, however, varies considerably from year to year. Consequently in dry years, some rivers may run low as early as in January.

But it is not only the water level that changes; even the course of the river itself will change, too. Gravel will shift, new obstacles will be added, trees will fall into the river... Consequently, describing a section of a river exactly is virtually impossible.

Equipment

Under normal conditions, most whitewater rivers of the Central Region will have a larger volume of water than their smaller, rockier "brothers" in Europe. This means that tours in Chile necessitate the longer boats with their more rugged construction: The heavily rockered and round bottom hulls make them emerge faster from eddies and rolls. Given the low water temperatures, a wetsuit (5-7 mm of neoprene) or a drysuit is mandatory.

If you prefer to travel with your own gear, you better bring everything and the kitchen sink. It is

bridges, while almost everywhere else, direct access will be blocked by fences. Occasionally, gravel roads will also be blocked by gates. Whenever feasible, try to find the owner/manager to get permission to cross their land. If your request is turned down by a guard whose supervisor is far away in Santiago, you will just have to find a different place.

Difficulty

In our descriptions, we are using the US scale from I (easy) to VI (extreme) that is also common in Chile.

Water Level

Contrary to the situation in much of Western Europe and North America, where all or many rivers have been made navigable and can be regulated with a host of locks and dams, the water levels in the natural rivers of Central Chile tend to vary enormously. This presents a major challenge for kayakers since conditions change from

Five Golden Rules for Kayaking

△ Never go alone

△ Get local expert kayakers' information ahead of time

△ Do not rely on just any locals' information

△ Do not trespass on private property

△ Always explore the more difficult stretches of rivers from the bank first.

difficult, expensive, and sometimes plain impossible to find specific parts. Only (very few) athletic stores in Santiago (which does not even have a store specializing in kayaking) carry related gear. Most airlines nowadays will transport boats and paddles without any problems.

Occasional kayakers can rent the necessary equipment; providers can be found in Santiago and Talca *(see Addresses)*. They are also your best source for practical hints, classes, and tours.

Doubling Up in an Open Canoe

If you are looking for a less exciting way of travelling, you can explore quieter sections of rivers or lakes in a double canoe, which may well be one of the most beautiful modes of transport in nature. Inflatable boats of sufficient structural integrity are best suited for this purpose because they are easier to transport. For canoes, Class III rapids are considered the upper safe limit.

If you are willing to portage the boat around the more difficult spots, you can do more difficult sections even as a beginner. When doing so, follow Golden Rule #5, stop at the least indication of danger, get out and explore the stretch ahead from the bank. Make sure you don't ever turn the boat perpendicular to the current; it's really easy to tip the boat over that way, even without help from any obstacles. Make changes in direction by diverting from the direction of the current with the smallest possible angle (<45°), and try to anticipate obstacles.

On the Internet

www.kayaking.cl
Homepage of a kayaking instructor about whitewater in Chile, tours; in English and Spanish

http://www.awa.org/awa/river_project/Chile/
Excerpts from reports by Lars Holbek on the American Whitewater Association site; in English

Whitewater Rivers

The following descriptions are intended to help you choose and plan trips, but they definitely cannot replace knowledge of local conditions and a thorough prior exploration of the river's run. More detailed information is best obtained from Chilean kayaking experts *(see Addresses)*. Places are listed from north to south.

Mapocho

Who would have thought that people would want to practice watersports on what runs through Santiago like a dirty and smelly cesspool! Above the capital, however, Mapocho's waters are still clean, and they form a few interesting eddies. However, unless you have the lofty goal of "doing" all Chilean rivers, this is one you can skip. While its upper reaches are very rocky, lower down it has been altered hopelessly, and it is lined by fierce dogs.

Access is via the road to Farellones. From its confluence with Río San Francisco, the Mapocho drops over 5 km at a rate of about 28 m/km and with Class IV-V rapids all the way to the bridge for the road. Below, there's another 5 km of Class IV until you get to El Arrayán bridge.

Maipo

The best-known river for rafting and kayaking in the Central Region owes its popularity to its proximity

Hang in there!

Getting their adrenaline going

into the upper Maipo valley. This river is hard to get to; it runs for about 4 km at Class V and drops 25 m/km to the bridge. Only for hardcore extreme types.

Colorado

Upper Colorado, also a Maipo tributary, can only be used with permission from the Military. From the checkpoint on the road to Maitenes, this river races at Class IV and with a gradient of more than 20 m/km back towards the main road through the Maipo valley. Its steep gorge makes it practically impossible to get out anywhere on the way. According to some reports, some sections cannot be run anymore; make sure to check it out thoroughly before you go!

Cachapoal

This river is accessed from Rancagua via Coya. The approx. 12 km section between the dam and Coya has Class IV to V rapids and a 12 m/km gradient, however, it often does not have enough water (when it is pumped to the El Teniente copper mine, which then returns it full of chemicals lower down.) Below Termas de Cauquenes the Cachapoal is suitable for beginners' classes.

Tinguiririca

While this river is not recommended for rafting, it offers kayak enthusiasts some technical challenges. To get there, follow the bumpy gravel road from San Fernando to Termas del Flaco (80 km) which is one-way only, depending on the time of day (see p. 98). About 12 km before you get to the hot springs, the road crosses the river; at this bridge is a good put-in.

Starting here, a deep gorge offers 40 km of whitewater distinguished by the fact that it gets harder rather than easier, and that you cannot get out on some sections. The river is rated Class III to IV, and there are several portages. The gradient on the first 20 kilometers, which are entirely above the treeline, is about 24 m/km. The river is guarded by high mountains on either side. It doesn't take much luck to spot condors here.

to Santiago rather than any special attractiveness. The upper Maipo valley has long been densely settled, and there are more and more fences making access to the banks difficult, and the brownish-grey glacier water does not look especially attractive, either.

Access via San José de Maipo further up the valley (see p. 88). The uppermost sections of the river are only for daring experts: Below El Manzanito hydropower station, there is an 8 km Class V section which is easy to scout out from the road. Do not overlook the Class VI spot in the "death gorge"!

The most popular put-in is at the confluence with Río Yeso, which is crossed by a bridge a little ways beyond the police station. This bridge is where a 35 km Class III to V with a gradient of 14 m/km starts. Beware: At the railroad tunnel, there is a difficult Class V+ spot, and soon after, another one. Take out at San José at the latest.

Volcán

This Maipo tributary offers little water, lots of rocks, and Class V+ rapids between Baños Morales and the town of El Volcán. Further below, it runs for about 4 km at Class IV and a gradient of 20-25 m/km.

Yeso

This Maipo tributary is more like a "wet gravel pit". The road to Yeso lake starts at the road

Watersports 6

Following this section, there is another 22 kilometers at 13 m/km to the Negro bridge. The last section down to the Panamericana consists of about 15 km of easy paddling between Class II and III while still offering very scenic views.

Teno

East of Curicó, a good gravel road leads to the resort of Los Queñes. About 17 km upriver, Río Teno squeezes through an enormous gorge. Below these cascades is a good place to put in to do a few kilometers of Class III to V rapids and a few portages. After that, the river runs at Class III to IV to the bridge located about 4 km beyond Los Queñes. The gradient should be around 15 m/km.

In its upper reaches, Río Teno is forced through a narrow valley in between rugged mountains, its lower reaches are partially lined by trees. Its clear tributary Río Claro, that joins in Los Queñes, is also worth checking out for whitewater enthusiasts.

Mataquito

West of the Panamericana the Teno flows into the Lontué and continues as Río Mataquito to the Pacific. Because of its slow current, it can easily be navigated with a canoe. This scenic section that is easily accessed at several bridges is well suited for one- or multi-day tours of the river. Its wide valley can be very windy. Beware at its mouth on the Pacific: High waves and a strong current can easily create dangerous situations.

Lontué

This river is hard to get to, but it's worth a nice kayak tour. There is a road that runs from Curicó southeast towards Upeo; before it turns north, stay on the river and try to put in from one of the properties across from Culenar.

17-20 kilometers of Class III-IV in clear water, through vast fields.

Claro

This Río Claro (one of many with the same name) is known for the famous cascades of Siete Tazas and the Nature Preserve of the same name. There is a good gravel road from Curicó via Molina. These cascades are navigable – but only for professionals. The objective is not so much running the river as plunging down the waterfalls without breaking one's neck. Put-in is either directly above the highest waterfall (at 8 m) or 500 m above that. A sign-posted trail goes from the road to the best take-out by the lowest "Taza".

A visit to the adjacent Nature Preserve is an absolute must. Southern Beech forests with pictureque gorges provide opportunities for several days of hiking (see p. 110).

Maule

From Talca, the international pass road keeps following Río Maule to Argentina. Beyond the La Mina police station lies a resort complex by some hot springs, as well as a bridge which is suitable for put-in. Before you leave, take a look around Laguna del Maule located further up.

From the put-in, Río Maule takes off at Class V+

The upper part of Río Ancoa has demanding Class IV and V rapids

The famous cascades at Siete Tazas

Ancoa. Starting here, the river is Class IV and V, and there are two portages. The gradient on this section is about 19 m/km. For take-out, use the dam or the bridge after it.

If you follow the road up the valley all the way to its end, you will get to Refugio Melado. From here, you can do fascinating tours into the surrounding area, e.g., in Los Bellotos National Preserve: Waterfalls, lakes, horseback riding and rafting in the midst of practically virgin jungle. (see trekking tour 18, p. 132).

down towards La Mina. The next section to where the river joins the reservoir is Class III to IV, and very scenic. Beware: the river has been turned into a canal in order to pump water in two places. Before you get to the Colbún lake, you will pass spectacular falls dropping 80 m over basalt rocks into a lagoon.

The lower portion of Río Maule, which winds its way slowly through the plain between two mountain ranges west of the Panamericana, is well suited for canoes. This is where the Chilean canoe championships are held every year. Put-in is at Talca into Río Claro coming from the north and flowing into Maule further to the southwest. It is followed by a railroad line all the way to the coast, but there is no road. Theoretically you could stop anywhere, flag down the train, and ride it back to Talca.

The last section before you get to Constitución does not have much of a current anymore. Plan on two days for the entire length.

Ancoa

Río Ancoa receives its water through a tunnel from Río Melado. From Linares, take the road to El Peñasco. A logical input is where the water from the Melado surges from the tunnel into

Achibueno

This river that wends its way through one of the wildest sceneries in Central Chile like a turquoise snake, can also be accessed from Linares. The bluish-green lagoons, the cypress forests and granite walls are a little reminiscent of Yosemite National Park in the US, just not as well-known. A poor road follows the river and ends at a horse ranch under construction. From this road, the various sections down to the confluence with Ancoa can be explored easily; Class III to IV – a kayaker's dream!

Ñuble

For purists, the real kayaker's paradise starts with this high water volume, bluish-green river northeast of Chillán. There is a good road from San Carlos to El Sauce via San Fabián de Alico, with good spots for camping along the river. This section is Class III with two passages of Class IV and interesting bends; the gradient is mild at 8 m/km. Starting with Nahueltoro bridge it gets easier, and the valley becomes wider. If you want to, you can rent mules at El Sauce for having your boats carried further upriver to explore the upper reaches.

A gorgeous three to four day trekking tour leads to Laguna Trucha mountain lake – a real insider tip (see trekking tour 20, p. 140).

Surfing & Windsurfing
All A-board!

Just like the mountains and rivers of the Central Region, the lakes and beaches are also part of a hardly developed outdoor paradise. While the few beaches around Viña del Mar, Algarrobo and Cartagena are packed with Chilean and Argentinian vacationers in the summer, windsurfers and surfers will find numerous uncrowded spots along this long and varied coast, with wind and waves suited to any taste. Outside the high season, they even have the sandy beaches all to themselves – apart from some curious dolphins and grumpy sea lions. Windsurfers can also practice their skills on turquoise lakes and lagoons.

Access

Access to ocean beaches and lakes is guaranteed to all citizens. In actual fact, however, this regulation is mostly ignored, and so it can often be hard, especially at inland lakes, to find access to the beach or lakeside between fenced-in lots. At the ocean, access is usually easier. However, not all sections of the coast can be reached by road, and sometimes the existing access routes are gravel roads that are marked poorly or not at all.

Conditions

In general, surfers can practice their sport year-round in Central Chile. Only in the winter months from June through August low pressure and storm systems will frequently spoil your fun, but there will also be the occasional mild day. From November to April, sunny weather is guaranteed; there are almost always good waves (average 2 m).

The Antarctic Humboldt current makes sure that the water temperatures only reach an average of 13 to 15 °C on the Central Coast. A sufficiently thick thermoskin wetsuit (4/3, better yet, 5/3 mm) is recommended for year-round use; in winter, add a hood, too.

The ocean knows no dangerous animals here, and outside the harbor areas, the Pacific is very clean. The strong sun requires a sunscreen with high protection factor.

On some of the beaches popular for surfing, competition for "the ideal wave" can be fierce. We suggest you respect the local surfers and avoid busy beaches such as Reñaca, Puertecillo or Pichilemu on the weekends.

Surfing

The best surf forms in winter right after a storm system has moved through. Due to the sandy underground, place and shape of the waves change constantly. Because of the prevailing lefts Chile is called "Goofy Land". The extreme length of the waves forces surfers to decide whether they want to swim back several hundred meters or walk back on the beach.

Windsurfing

In the Central Region, good winds blow from September to May, mostly from southwesterly directions and side-off. The experts among windsurfers follow the center of the windy high pressure area over the Chilean coast. From October to December it lies directly off the Central Coast, in January it moves south towards Concepción, only to return to Valparaíso in March and finally drift off to the north (Iquique) in May.

Windsurfers can usually find enough wind on the coast from 11 a.m. until 7 p.m. The waves follow each other at fairly large distance, but with a force that can easily break your board and mast if you make a wrong move.

Safety

There is nothing "pacifist" about the Pacific Ocean – it has many surprises up its sleeve, and it can be anything but peaceful. Even on

This takes some skill!

days with little wind, strong surf can form. And especially dangerous are the huge waves that can appear out of the blue to crash on rocks and beaches washing everything in their way out to sea.

If you are out and about in Chile for the first time, look for beaches with other surfers who can teach you about local conditions, or allow you to accompany them. Unknown coasts can harbor many invisible dangers, e.g., underwater reefs and cliffs, strong currents, sea urchins and sharp rocks on the beach, etc. In emergencies, call the Navy rescue service (ph. 137), or ask fishermen for help.

When you are camping on the beach, always keep an eye on your gear to avoid being ripped off by casual thieves.

Equipment

If your airline's regulations allow it, do bring your complete gear. If you want to save money on the way back, you can try and sell your equipment before you leave. While surf gear is more plentiful in the stores compared to kayaking or trekking equipment, the choices are quite limited, and they are only available in few specialty stores in Santiago *(see Addresses)*. Some prices for new equipment are quite a bit cheaper than in North America or Europe, and in addition, here you can find what will be next season's merchandise on the northern hemisphere six months earlier than there. Stores such as Windsurfing Chile in Santiago offer a service through which they will ship parts to the coast by bus against payment by bank draft.

Rental equipment is only available for (board) surfers in a few places (among others, at Cachagua, Maitencillo, Viña del Mar, and Pichilemu), for windsurfers that is next to impossible. In the surfing stores, you can also get information on classes, guides, and package tours.

Regarding wetsuits, see "Conditions". Indispensable for (board) surfers - less so for windsurfers - are rubber boots to protect your feet from sharp rocks or mussels.

Since many places are without the requisite basic infrastructure, always take enough drinking water, food, a First-Aid kit, and, if necessary, a tent and sleeping bag when you go surfing at a remote beach.

Windsurfing: For Course and Racing, large sails (> 9 sq.m.) are recommended, for Wave, sails of 4.5 or 5 sq.m. and a 70-80-liter board.

Surfing: For low waves a 6 ft. board is sufficient, for strong surf, the experts get out boards starting at 6.8 ft.

On the Internet

www.surfchile.cl
Magazine for surfers. Current reports, news, contacts; in Spanish only

www.surfnet.cl
Surfsite with fancy design but not much functionality; lots of advertising; in Spanish only

www.windsurf.cl
Chilean windsurfing site with lots of information and contacts; in Spanish only

Beaches for Surfing

The following list can only name some of the most popular surfing beaches among the many on the Central Coast. Listed from north to south.

Los Molles

This small fishermen's village located on a land spit close to the Panamericana (approx. 190 km northwest of Santiago) offers nice surf. Beginners should head to the mellow point-breaks at Salinas de Pullalli beach, about 15 km further south. In Winter, however, the surf can be strong here.

Maitencillo

Long sandy beach with straight, short lefts and rights (beachbreak), up to 1.5 m ideal for beginners, without major currents. Though quite busy in the summer, the resort of Maitencillo has been able to preserve its original charm. Located about 160 km northwest of Santiago, easy to get to on paved roads; good tourism infrastructure. Cachagua, which is located further north, also has good beachbreaks.

Ritoque

Long sandy beach with some rocks, short, high rights, pointbreak, strong currents, not suitable for beginners. The sleepy resort of Ritoque is separated from the industrial facilities at Concón and the noisy beach resort of Viña del Mar by a 13 km beach dune. Accommodations and provisions in neighboring Quinteros.

Reñaca

This sandy beach near Viña del Mar against the backdrop of highrise hotel and apartment buildings has a beachbreak, and it is packed with a trendy crowd in the summer. While this place is a dream for Baywatch types, anyone into nature will hate it. Short, choppy lefts and rights with tubes forming, dangerous when over 2 m high.

Algarrobo

Very crowded in January/February, the beach at Algarrobo resort, 115 km west of Santiago, is accessed via Ruta 68. Various sections with short lefts and rights, some of which break on rocks. Especially demanding: the reefbreak at El Mejoral.

El Tabo

Quiet vacation resort about 15 km south of Algarrobo; on your way, you will pass Pablo Neruda's famous beach house at Isla Negra. An easy section with perfect lefts and rights (beachbreak) at a sandbank. La Castilla beach, with strong lefts breaking on cliffs, is more suitable for the advanced surfer.

Performing for the masses at Reñaca

Matanzas

Let's move on from the crowded beaches of Region V to these less populous areas. About 160 km southwest of Santiago (take Ruta 78 "Autopista del Sol" to Melipilla, then head southwest on a winding blacktop road via Rapel and Navidad, the final 4 km on gravel) you will find the fishing village of Matanzas. The strong, fast tube waves here (pointbreak) are among the longest in all of Chile.

Puertecillo

Mention of this name makes the eyes of aficionados shine. The perfect tube waves here (pointbreak) that are up to 300 m long are truly world class. Every bit as worthwhile is Topocalma beach 10 kilometers to the south with two great pointbreaks.

However, getting to this isolated part of the coast is quite a challenge. This entire section belongs to the privately owned Hacienda Topocalma, for access to which you will have to get permission ahead of time in Santiago at: Inmobiliaria General S.A., Teatinos 280 p. 15, ph. (2) 695 00 63. Take Autopista del Sol to Melipilla (km 67), then the road to Hacienda Topocalma (km 170) via Central Rapel (this is where the gravel starts) and Litueche. Beware, a good rain will turn these roads into mudpits that are impassable even for jeeps!

Pichilemu

The lively resort of Pichilemu 126 km west of San Fernando is the undisputed surfing capital of Chile. This is where the national championships are held every year, and there are lots of accommodations, campsites and outfitters for surfing enthusiasts.

The places for surfing are "arranged" in order of difficulty. Closest to town lies the vast and extremely flat beginners' beach of La Puntilla whose fast lefts run for up to a kilometer! 500 m further south awaits the rocky beach of El Infiernillo ("little hell") with much stronger lefts that have to be surfed starting above 2 meters' height because otherwise, they break too close to the rocks.

A 6 km gravel road will take you to the landspit of Punta de Lobos. This is only for experts: you have

The surfing paradise of Pichilemu

to climb over rocks, swim through a whitewater canal, climb some more cliffs and then throw yourself off these into the next long left (which can get up to 6 m high) at exactly the right moment.

Constitución

This port located about 110 kilometers west of Talca has two nice pointbreaks right by the beach promenade; they become interesting starting at a height of 2 m. The rocky exit can be a problem, though. If you don't like the polluted waters here, you can go 5 km south to the vicinity of the port where strong and long lefts break on a rocky point and sometimes form tubes.

Punta Pellines

About an hour by car on the coastal road south of Constitución is Punta Pellines. Strong waves (pointbreak), ideal at 1.5 to 2 m high. Difficult exit by the rocks.

Curanipe

150 km southwest of Talca, the picturesque resort of Curanipe rules over a virtually endless strip

of coast occasionally punctuated by rock formations. The beach with its black sand offers long tubes such as at Punta La Sirena. Along the coastal road to the south there is a string of more bays and challenges.

Cobquecura

To get to the quiet fishing village of Cobquecura, either take the unpaved coastal road from Curanipe, or else the 100 km blacktop from Chillán. North of town, within 25 km you will find some of Chile's most attractive surfing beaches with waves up to 6 m high.

The parade starts with the quiet rocky bay of **La Rinconada** (km 6), followed by a sandy beach at **Buchupureo** (km 13), also known as "Chi Land" among insiders (a take-off on the world famous beach of G-Land in Indonesia) that offers formidable walls. At **Pullay** (km 20) a frontal left tube, approx. 60 m long will form. And **Trehualemu** (km 25) is also among the few places in Central Chile where fast lefts form tubes.

Places for Windsurfing

Below, we have first listed the most important windsurfing beaches from north to south, and then some of the windiest inland lakes of the Central Region.

Pichidangui

The beaches of this coastal resort located approx. 200 km northwest of Santiago offer ideal conditions for slalom/course, with 10 to 25 knot winds and somewhat warmer water temperatures. Good camping sites and reasonable cabañas starting from USD 10.00. In November 2001, the South American championships were held here. Access via the Panamericana.

Punta de Toro

Take Autopista del Sol to the oceanside resort Rocas de Santo Domingo 110 km west of Santiago that is very busy in the summer. At the remote Punta de Toro, approx. 20 km further south (access by fourwheel-drive via the beach) you will not feel anything of that zoo. Windsurfers will find big waves and wind with up to 30 knots. No infrastructure. Wave.

Diego Tirado

At La Sirena beach near Curanipe

La Boca

There is a 70 km paved road from Rocas de Santo Domingo past Pinochet's villa at Bucalemu, via the town of Rapel to the mouth (Spanish: *boca*) of the river of the same name. At this place, which is very popular with windsurfers, the wind blows side-on for a change and at a constant speed of about 25 to 30 knots. Camping possible. Wave, Slalom.

El Yeso reservoir: Windsurfing at 3,000 m

Matanzas

The sleepy fishing village of Matanzas is only a few kilometers south of La Boca. If you have fourwheel-drive, you can push about another two kilometers towards the north to 'Brisas de Matanzas' where 20 to 30 knot winds and an extraordinarily varied ocean fauna await you. Camping site (USD 5.00 per tent). Wave.

Three kilometers south of Matanzas is **Pupuyas** beach, which can also be reached only via the sandy beach. Wind side-on, 30 knots and above. No infrastructure. Wave.

Topocalma / Puertecillo

On these two remote beaches, simply the best waves of Central Chile break; 3.5 to 5 m high, several hundred meters long and absolutely perfect. Access and permit *see Beaches for Surfing, p. 180.* No infrastructure. Wave.

Pichilemu

The long waves of Pichilemu *(see Beaches for Surfing, p. 180)* will also satisfy windsurfers. Good selection of accommodations, camping sites, restaurants, and surfing providers. Wave.

Llico

This town near the place where Lago Vichuquén *(see next page)* empties into the Pacific lies 125 km west of Curicó; the last 50 kilometers are on unpaved roads. It is much quieter here than at Pichilemu, and the waves on the dark sandy beach are an insider tip among windsurfers. Strong winds (side-on) and choppy surf, ideal for jumping. Can be dangerous in directly onshore winds. Pretty hostería directly on the beach, small stores in town. Wave.

Curanipe

The pretty resort of Curanipe *(see Beaches for Surfing, p. 180)* is famous above all for La Sirena beach 10 kilometers to the south, where windsurfers can rent simple cabins across from the beach for USD 15.00. Wind side-off, Wave.

Embalse El Yeso

At an altitude of about 3000 m in the High Andes lies the bluish-green reservoir El Yeso like a jewel framed by brightly colored rock walls and glaciated peaks. This very sight makes a side trip into this tributary valley worthwhile. Strong winds and choppy waves make the long drawn-out reservoir a popular destination for windsurfers who crave speed. The gusty wind picks up around noon reaching up to 25 knots during the afternoon; 6-7 sq.m sail. The water is ice cold; take rubber boots and gloves!

Access from Santiago is via San José de Maipo. A few kilometers past the San Gabriel police station, a good gravel road turns left and heads up the valley along the reservoir to its northeastern end (about 75 km). You can pitch your tent at the flat, sandy bank; take a good sleeping bag! Slalom, freestyle.

Laguna Aculeo

This lagoon shoehorned between two low chains of hills southwest of Santiago is among the most popular weekend destinations for the capital's citizens. Consequently, it is very crowded in the summer – that is also true for windsurfers. Weak winds (10-20 knots) for beginners starting at 3 p. m., 8-10 sq.m sail. The water is pleasantly warm, but clouded. This is one of the few bodies of water where you can surf in your bathing suit!

Start from the town of Rangue on the southwest side of the lake. Two camping sites, surf gear rentals. Take Ruta 5 Sur to km 50, then turn west via Champa (65 km total). Course.

Lago Rapel

This multi-branch, 40 km long reservoir is also firmly in the hands of the people of Santiago. Only the steep southwestern and the northern bank have not been plastered with weekend cabins, watersport clubs, and bungalows. Moderate to strong winds in the afternoon, for 6 to 8 sq.m sails. Pleasant water temperature, in the summer, no wetsuit necessary during the day. A pain for surfers are the numerous powerboats.

From Santiago, take Ruta 78 (Autopista del Sol) to Melipilla (km 67), go through town to the road to Lago Rapel. After 127 km you will get to the eastern arm of the reservoir. A dirt road runs along its southern bank in a big semicircle, and back to the paved road along the southern arm of the lake. Several places for starting and camping sites. Slalom, course.

Lago Vichuquén

This 40 sq. km lake in the Coastal Cordillera used to be surrounded by virgin forests. Today, only eucalyptus and pine trees grow on its mostly steep banks. Around the lake, wealthy Chileans have built their summer homes, and so access is possible only in few places. Surfers enjoy the moderate, often very gusty winds (15 knots, 6-8 sq.m sail) well suited for slalom, and the option of shuttling to Llico beach located only a few km away *(see previous page)*.

Access from Curicó via Hualañe (75 km), then go 45 km on a good gravel road to the northern end of the lake (camping site). There is a road that goes all the way around the lake, and another camping site at Playa Paula on its southern end.

Laguna Aculeo near Santiago: An easy one for beginners

Rodrigo Fuenzalida

Diving
Exploring the Depth

Exploring the silent depths of the ocean has long been a dream with humans. And since the early 90's, an increasing number of recreational divers have been exploring the rough Pacific off the Central Coast – despite the Humboldt current which cools the waters down considerably. These areas cannot be compared to tropical waters. If you want to dive here, not only do you have to dress more warmly, but you also have to let go of the stereotypical ideas of coral reefs and brightly colored fish that will feed from your hand.

Chile's Pacific coast possesses a more rugged charm. Diving fans will find uncrowded waters, a large variety of submarine flora and fauna, as well as a number of spooky wrecks on the ocean floor. The waters of the Pacific with their distinct dark gray-green color have their very own appeal. The only color splotches in this surreal landscape are presented by schools of fish that swish by like silvery clouds, and reddish-colored crab, with some starfish interspersed for good measure. You might also want to pay special attention to the oceanfloor covered in algae and mollusks.

Permits

All diving is regulated by Dirección General del Territorio Marítimo, a department of the Navy (Armada). They issue their own diving permits, but inofficially, they also recognize the international CMAS and PADI licenses. However, any recognition is at the discretion of the navy inspectors, and you have no claim to it. To take part in a diving tour provided by an agency, you need to be licensed. Always sign in with the respective Harbormaster (Capitanía de Puerto) when you go diving. If you are found without license during inspections, your gear might be confiscated.

Best Season

Basically, you can dive year round. Water temperatures are most tolerable during the Summer months from December through March.

Access

Most diving grounds can be reached directly from the beaches. In some cases, piers or ramps are used as starting points. Occasionally, you will have to negotiate long and bumpy gravel roads. Many diving clubs and agencies offer boat trips to certain places, such as wrecks.

Conditions

Far from being "pacified", the Pacific Ocean is neither peaceful nor still. On the contrary, most part of the year, it is very rough. Even protected bays are exposed to strong surf that continues underwater, especially in the afternoons. Strong currents can drive divers against rocks or out to sea, and so on most beaches, it's best to dive in the morning.

Even in Summer, the low water temperatures (10 to 16 degrees Celsius) will necessitate a wetsuit (5 to 7 mm of neoprene). Visibility is rarely above 6 meters. In some places, diving conditions are also influenced by the tides, even though the differential is relatively small at 1 meter.

Don't even start looking for infrastructure specifically geared towards watersports, such as changing cabins or toilets on the beaches. Any camping on remote beaches, though possible, will be at your own risk, too.

Safety

If you have never gone diving in Chile before, you will absolutely need a locally knowledgeable diver as a guide. Unknown coastal areas can be full of invisible dangers: underwater reefs and cliffs, strong currents, sea urchins and sharp rocks on the beach, etc. There are no dangerous animals in Chilean waters, but it would not be smart to pick a fight with a sea lion. Otherwise, just follow all the safety rules divers are taught in their training classes. A word of warning especially for tourists, who want to get in a bit of snorkeling in a hurry: do not venture into unknown waters spontaneously.

Officially, diving under conditions that might require decompression, as well as in harbors and other waters reserved for sport and recreational use, is banned by the authorities.

In case of a diving emergency, contact the rescue service of the Navy by calling 137, or (32) 208 913 / 208 919 / 208 586. The

Five Golden Rules for Diving

△ Never go diving alone!

△ Hire a locally knowledgeable guide, and always leave information with a contact person at the beach.

△ Find out ahead of time about the weather forecast and conditions in the diving area.

△ Never dive deeper or longer than your level of training will allow.

△ For emergencies, carry a cell phone or a two-way radio.

only hyperbaric chambers are located at the Navy Hospital at Viña del Mar, Hospital Naval, Subida Alessandri s/n, ph. (32) 573 000, and at the hospital of Asociación Chilena de Seguridad, ACHS, in Santiago, Ramón Carnicer 201, Providencia, ph. (2) 685 30 00.

Equipment

All of the necessary gear, from goggles to wetsuits to bottles, can be rented from one of the numerous diving schools or agencies. In Santiago and Valparaíso, several stores specializing in diving gear offer accessories and parts *(see Addresses)*. Compressed air is readily available only in Santiago and Valparaíso.

Places for Diving

While the beaches in the Valparaíso area have been explored relatively thoroughly, there is a vast no-man's-land as far as diving is concerned, further south. No doubt, there will be worthwhile places for diving there, but they have not been described yet. Besides, it can be difficult to hunt down compressed air there. The following list provides some of the best-known places:

Pichidangui

This cute little coastal resort located 200 kilometers northwest of Santiago (take the Panamericana) is graced by good infrastructure for tourism. In the bay, the wreck of the freighter 'Indus 8' has found a resting place at 28 m, and there is also an underwater cave (14 to 24 m) where huge sponges have settled.

Los Molles

This fishing hamlet 10 km south of Pichidangui provides half a dozen very nice dives, trips to which are also offered by local agencies.

Zapallar bay: On the way to their underwater adventure

Zapallar

Even on sunny winter weekends, the clear waters of the protected bay at Zapallar, a coastal resort 175 km northwest of Santiago, attract a fair number of diving enthusiasts. A good starting point is right by the pier for the fishing boats, and you will soon be able to enjoy the flora and fauna down below that is bathed in a green light.

Valparaíso

While nothing recommends the bay of Valparaiso for diving near the beach due to the polluted waters of the harbor, there are attractions to be found such as the tugboat 'Caupolicán' that was sunk decades ago, at a depth of 24 m and the sailing ship 'Las Lositas' (14-22 m), which sank around 1800 and got its name from the numerous fragments of dishes and other stuff persistent divers can find here. While many other ships have perished here, they usually rest at much greater depths.

Laguna Verde

At the southern end of the long sandy beach at this small resort south of Valparaíso, divers will find interesting rock formations. Laguna Verde has its very own wreck, too, the Russian ship 'Eclíptica' (3-30 m) that sank in front of the Curaumilla lighthouse in 1973.

Quintay

The tug 'Falucho' rests at a manageable depth (15 m), with old harpoons, in front of the former whaling port Quintay (now a neat fishing port). Access by road via Ruta 68 – Quintay turn-off.

Algarrobo

At this popular beach resort located 115 km west of Santiago, you can dive with the penguins with some luck – at the rocky island across from San Pedro pier. A variety of fish, mussels and sponges live here in caves and cracks. Access by road via Ruta 68 – Algarrobo turn-off.

Punta de Tralca

Only few kilometers south of Algarrobo, Punta de Tralca offers a vast number of starfish colonies. At the point, beware of strong surf and currents.

On the Internet

www.directemar.cl
Official site of the Navy authorities, with all regulations about diving; in Spanish

www.gochile.cl/Activ/buceo.asp
Travel site with general information; in English

Augusto Olivares

**Paragliding
Like A Bird...**

7

188

Humankind's millenia-old dream of flying like a bird has finally come true. For decades now, daring people have been taking wing – with the wind in their faces, stomachs in knots, and their hearts beating; doing what many explorers have tried and failed to achieve for centuries, first with stiff kite-type devices, and later with huge parachutes. Meanwhile, the technology of the flying apparatus has been improved tremendously, and what used to be just 'hanggliding' at first has meanwhile turned into long cross country flights.

Because of its hot and sunny climate, Central Chile provides the ideal conditions for the forming of thermals on the Coastal and Main Cordillera slopes. From early Spring until well into the Fall, hang and paragliding enthusiasts can take off for a look at cities, mountains, and the ocean from a bird's eye view. Beginners especially appreciate the steep cliffs of the Coastal Cordillera that allow them to sail down to the beaches. Most launching sites close to the Andes, however, make more demands on paragliders' skills. In return, you will get to enjoy great views of the peaks, as well as an opportunity to keep going for more than 100 km.

Permits

In Chile, everything that travels by air is regulated by the Civil Aeronautics Administration (Dirección General de Aeronáutica Civil). They also issue the permits for Chilean paragliders, with the practical training being provided by accredited schools and the theoretical test being administered directly by DGAC. Paragliding schools must be members of Asociación Chilena del Vuelo Libre.

Foreigners who have a permit should bring it along if they want to fly in Chile, so that they can prove they are experienced. Licenses will be checked at launching points that are run by individuals or by the Asociación. There are, however, no rules about recognizing other countries' licenses.

Soaring pilots can contact a private soaring club *(see Addresses)*.

Five Golden Rules for Paragliding

△ Do not incur unnecessary risks!

△ When in doubt (unknown terrain, difficult conditions) don't start!

△ Recognize and respect your own limits.

△ Never fly alone; if possible, fly with another pilot or/and a contact person on the ground

△ Carry a two-way radio and/or a cell phone.

Best Season

December to March. From May to August, there are usually not enough wind or thermals for gliding.

Access

The search for good launching points knows no bounds, and experienced paragliders can let their imagination guide them. In many cases, however, access to hills will be blocked by fences and gates, and permission will have to be negotiated with owners or managers of the land. The standard spots introduced below are generally easy to get to. In some locations, private businesses charge a starting fee (per flight or day). Most of these places have favorable natural starting conditions, and very occasionally, they will even have ramps.

Conditions

The prevailing winds in Central Chile are from the southwest; and so most launching points are oriented towards that direction. While there are usually no thermals on the western slopes of the Coastal Cordillera due to the proximity of the sea - you will have to depend on wind alone -, gliders in the interior of the country can use both wind and thermals.

A rule of the thumb for paragliders: The coast is suitable for beginners, too, while the Andes are for advanced or expert gliders only. The degree of difficulty will change mainly with the time of day. On summer days (30 to 35 °C) the slopes heat up a lot during the day leading to the formation of strong thermals, up- and downdrafts, and turbulences. Consequently, the afternoon hours are for experienced pilots only. Less experienced gliders should not try their luck before 6 or 7 p.m.

Safety

The same rules hold as for all other high risk sports. And especially if it's your first time paragliding in Chile, you should gather thorough information beforehand and, if at all possible, go with a guide who knows the area and the sport. Some launching and landing spots are far from major cities, which makes an appropriate means of communication (two-way radio, cell phone) even more important. In emergencies, call the police at 133.

Equipment

Paragliding equipment is much easier to take on your trip to Chile than wings. The necessary equipment can also be rented from several providers, who also offer repairs and parts *(see Addresses)*. These places are usually run by the same expert pilots that offer classes and tandem flights.

Tandem Gliding

Even if you don't have a pilot's license, you can still see Chile from above. Most paragliding schools offer tandem gliding *(vuelos biplaza)*, with the customer getting into a tandem seat and taking off with an experienced instructor. Depending on the launching spot, prices vary from USD 25 to 50 *(see Addresses)*.

On the Internet

www.parapenteonline.cl
Very useful site of a Chilean paragliding instructor; in Spanish

http://planeadores.sofytec.cl
Site of the Club de Planeadores Santiago, information for soaring pilots; in Spanish

Launching Spots

The standard launching spots described below are equally suited for wings and parafoils. The bulk of our information is about the Santiago area and the Central Coast, while gliding areas further south are less frequented, such as the Pre-Cordillera near Rancagua, the coast near Matanzas, and the hot springs of Chillán. Those curious enough should find out more from paragliding enthusiasts in those places.

La Pirámide

This hill on the northeastern edge of Santiago with its view of a sea of buildings is one of the best places for classical style hang gliding, but it is also popular among experts for launching on cross country tours all the way to Los Andes (60 km to the north) or Rancagua (100 km to the south). They use the thermals on neighboring Cerro Manquehue to achieve the necessary altitude. Unfortunately, this launch pad was closed by the authorities recently due to an increasing number of conflicts with the airport in Vitacura. The Chilean Freeflight Association is hoping to get the closure repealed.

Alfredo Escobar

The La Pirámide launch pad near Santiago is controversial

Access via Vespucio Norte (Vitacura District), turn right after the bridge over the Mapocho and bear left towards Rotonda La Pirámide. A climb of approx. 350 m, no fees.

Santuario de la Naturaleza El Arrayán

The Nature Sanctuary of El Arrayán in the valley of the same name northeast of Las Condes is among the prettiest launch sites of the Central Region; for its views of Santiago on the one hand, and the High Andes on the other. Due to the somewhat difficult landing conditions in this narrow valley, this is not a site for beginners.

Access: Take Av. Las Condes all the way to the end (Plaza San Enrique), there, turn right onto Pastor Fernández. About 500 m past the bridge over the Mapocho river, Camino El Cajón veers off to the left (sign-posted) which will take you directly to the park entrance. Admission: USD 3.00, ask at the entrance for the key to a gate located further up the road, as well as for detailed information.

Farellones

This launching site at an altitude of about 2,600 m at the ski area of the same name offers flights over tree-less valleys of the High

For curious beginners: Tandem flying

Cuesta Barriga

Launch site in the Coastal Cordillera approximately 55 km west of Santiago. Given the difficult terrain, this is only a site for those who know the area, and advanced pilots. Ideal in Spring and Fall; in the Summer, the winds are too strong.

Take Ruta 68 (Santiago – Valparaíso), after the Lo Prado tunnel turn left in the valley (sign-posted) and follow the gravel road to its highest point. Ask for the key to the gate at the kiosk; free.

Andes, with views of Santiago lying below in its smog. In favorable conditions, you can launch from here in the Winter, too, and you can observe the skiers from above. Experts can get up to an altitude of about 4,000 meters. In the Summer, strong turbulences.

Acces via Av. Las Condes and the road to Farellones, approx. 60 km on a winding road west of Santiago. The launch site is located behind the Hotel Farellones by the Ski Club on the road to El Colorado. Free.

Batuco

Second only to La Pirámide as a classical place for wing and parafoil enthusiasts. The launching site is located on top of a low hill right in the middle of the Central Valley, 35 km north of Santiago. From here, you can only fly over the surrounding area. An ideal place for beginners, with stable thermals, your own ramp, and easy landing at the bottom of the hill. In the middle of Summer, it can be very windy here.

Take Ruta 5 Norte (Panamericana) to km 25, turn left to Batuco, go through town and head to the hill on Av. Italia (ask for the ceramics factories) north of there. You can drive all the way to the top, free.

Las Vizcachas

A good 'trampoline' for those who want to venture on a Cross Country north along the Pre-Cordillera and the eastern edge of the capital.

Access via Av. La Florida, past the race track (on the right) after you get to Cajón del Maipo, soon after that, turn left at La Obra (about 30 km from Santiago). Access controlled by private party, approx. USD 5.00 per flight.

Maitencillo / Cachagua

The homey beach town of Maitencillo, located about 160 km northwest of Santiago, is among the favorite destinations of coastal paragliders. From here, you can do flights along the 70 m cliffs to the north or the south, with landings on pretty beaches.

The privately owned launch site Aguas Blancas (parking, toilets, etc. available) is located about 3 km south of Maitencillo, fees (5 USD aprox.) per day.

There is another privately run place above the rocky coast on the road from Maitencillo to Cachagua.

Algarrobo

Flying in Mirasol, 5 km north of the beach resort of Algarrobo, is even easier than in Maitencillo. Its

Launch pad for beginners: At Algarrobo beach

altitude above the wide sandy beach is only 35 meters, making this an ideal place for beginners.

Access via Ruta 68 to Valparaíso, after Zapata tunnel turn left to Algarrobo (120 km from Santiago). Free.

Taking off from Cerro Batuco north of Santiago

In Between the Adventures
Relaxing

8

This title says it all: even the most ardent adventurer has to take a break every now and then. Here are a few tips for spending moments of passive and active relaxation after the hardships of hiking, climbing, biking or kayaking.

Thermal Spas and Hot Springs

There are several thousand hot springs bubbling up out of the ground along the entire length of the Chilean Andes. Only a small number of them are developed for tourism, while others are mere steaming mud holes, which doesn't take away from the spontaneous enjoyment of a rustic bath. Chapter 2 (Trekking) mentions some of the developed and the "wild" springs. If you want to really relax in between your adventures, you can choose from a range of accommodations from simple log cabins to luxury hotels.

El Corazón – Jahuel - Colina

Three thermal complexes with a rich tradition in beautiful surroundings, about 100 km (Corazón and Jahuel) and 44 km (Colina) respectively north of Santiago. The downside is that their springs only reach 20 to 26 °C, and some of the facilities are quite outdated. One of the spas that were modernized is Termas El Corazón, whose water in the big whirlpool is heated artificially; special spas and treatments; overnight stay from USD 65 p/p in a double, day ticket USD 10.

Photo: Casa Chueca resort on Río Lircay near Talca

194

Termas de Cauquenes

117 km south of Santiago in the Pre-Cordillera, you will find the stylish "thermal spa cathedral" of Cauquenes, one of Chile's oldest spa facilities. Individual baths (tub or jacuzzi), spring temperature 47 °C, good category hotel with haute cuisine by two first-class chefs; overnight stay: from USD 70 p/p with all meals; use of a tub USD 5 or 10 (jacuzzi).

Termas de Quinamávida/Panimávida

Two traditional spa facilities with fading charm in a rural environment 16 to 20 km east of Linares. Spring temperatures 24 and 32 °C, partially covered thermal pools, individual and mud baths. Special treatment, sauna; overnight stay from USD 50 p/p in a double with all meals, day use ticket USD 10.

Surrounded by forests: the Chillán spa hotels

Termas de Chillán

Largest and most luxurious thermal spa complex of the Central Region in the forests at Chillán volcano, 80 km east of the city of the same name. In Winter, also a ski center *(see next page)*. Spring temperatures up to 65 °C, at Hotel Pirigallo (3 stars) and the five-star Grand Hotel, a variety of pools, jacuzzis, steam and mud baths, sauna, medical treatments; also public thermal pools (only in the Summer months, admission about USD 6). Overnight stay: Pirigallo from USD 76 p/p in a double with all meals and access to the spa, Grand Hotel from USD 96.

See Addresses p. 227

On the Internet

www.termaschillan.cl

Spa facilities, Ski center, rates, reservations, etc.

Ski Areas

From mid-June until into October, skiers and snowboarders playing on the runs of the Central Region are virtually guaranteed snow. The ski centers near Santiago at more than 2,500 m have an excellent infrastructure with runs of all difficulties, lifts and hotels; but they are also expensive. Depending on the place and season, a day pass is about USD 20 to 35; renting an entire outfit and gear another USD 17 to 30. You have to add the cost of getting there, accommodations and meals. A complete week of skiing in an upper category hotel with all meals and ski passes will set you back about USD 700 to 950.

Only about an hour by car from Santiago, there are three ski areas at altitudes of 2,400 to 3,700 m: **El Colorado-Farellones, La Parva,** and **Valle Nevado**. Together, they boast 44 lifts, miles of runs, accommodations of different categories, discotheques, and restaurants. And it's not much further from Santiago to **Lagunillas**, a much more modest ski center in Cajón del Maipo (4 lifts, 13 runs). It's about three hours by car (149 km) from Santiago to **Portillo** (14 lifts), which is beautifully situated at an altitude of 3,000 m on the pass road to Mendoza/Argentina. The runs here end at the pretty Laguna del Inca.

The iced-over Laguna del Inca near Portillo

Far less frequented is the smaller, cheaper ski center of **Chapa Verde** in the Andes near Rancagua (5 lifts, 22 runs). Since the land is owned by the Codelco mining company, it can only be accessed by special bus from Rancagua (departs: Mon-Fri 9 a.m., Sat/Sun 8 a.m. from Av. Miguel Ramírez 665; returns: 5 p.m.).

The ski center at **Termas de Chillán** (80 km east of Chillán) allows you to connect snow with thermal baths *(see previous page)*. 9 lifts, 22 runs, fancy hotels right by the runs, and simpler accommodations lower down.

Information and reservations: see Addresses

Vineyards

Central Chile is famous for its top-notch wines that have drawn international acclaim over the last decade, even though winemaking has a long tradition here. It is especially worthwhile visiting the old vineyards with their adobe cellars and landscaped parks, even though most of them have changed their production methods to include modern technologies. Small vintners are the only ones to still make table wines *(Pipeño)* by traditional methods.

Many winemakers are within a half-day trip of Santiago, Curicó or Talca, and most of them offer guided tours that are often free, as well as winetasting. Some traditional-style Viñas lure their guests with their cellars full of tasty treasures and large estates, such as **Concha y Toro** in Pirque (25 km south of Santiago), **Cousiño Macul** in Peñalolén (meanwhile a suburb of Santiago), **Santa Rita** near Buin (50 km south of Stgo.) or

Undurraga near Talagante (35 km west of Stgo.) Further south, a competition between two "wine routes" (Ruta del Vino) has sprung up. These cooperatives of vineyards offer special tours for tourists around Santa Cruz, as well as Talca. In general, reservations by phone are recommended, especially for groups.

For more on wine, see Eats & Drinks, p. 203. Addresses of vineyards p. 229.

On the Internet

www.gochile.cl/eng/Guide/ChileSkiGuide/Chile-Ski-Guide.asp
Good overview of the Chilean ski areas; in English

www.chip.cl/tours/wine/background.htm
Information about Chilean wines and a number of wineries, with optional tour offer; in English

www.cnn.com/TRAVEL/DESTINATIONS/9705/chile.wine/index.html
CNN report on Chilean wines and wineries

www.chilewineroute.com
About the Maule Wine Road, with different options for tours; in English and Spanish

Oak is what gives Chilean reds their flavor

In Between the Adventures   8

Colonial Villages

While Santiago is buzzing with the hectic "modern" lifestyle between highrises and traffic jams, only miles from there time seems to have stood still in the rural areas. Sleepy villages with cobble-stone streets, tree-lined boulevards, and cheerfully painted adobe houses tell of by-gone times when the Spanish had settled the fertile Central Valley and made it the breadbasket and orchard of this colony. The picturesque charm of these places, their slow beat, and the reserved friendliness of their inhabitants will often only be appreciated at second glance. So, allow some time on your visit, keep your eyes open, and enjoy the little details: an old door here, a shaded patio there, or a rustic meal. Here are some of the most beautiful places between Santiago and Los Angeles:

Pirque

Beyond Puente Alto (20 km from the center of Santiago), Río Maipo puts a stop to the encroaching mass of the city, and in Pirque, on the other side of the river, what the Chileans call *campo*, the "country", starts. This is where the rich aristocrats used to reside in their summer houses and haciendas, and one of them, Melchor Concha y Toro, started growing vines in 1883. The Concha y Toro vineyard, today one of Chile's largest producers of wines, can be toured like parts of the park that was laid out at the same time *(see Addresses)*. Several rustic restaurants open their inviting doors for the tourist in and around Pirque, and in the Summer, a popular open air classical music festival is held here. Bus to Puente Alto, then use a Colectivo to Pirque.

Isla de Maipo

This small town southwest of Santiago also has its family-run vineyard (Santa Inés) with excellent wines. The quiet place with the unusual street plan owes its name to its location between two of the numerous branches of Río Maipo. On your way into town, you will drive over a local curiosity: a long, narrow railroad bridge whose tracks are sunk into the asphalt so that it can be used by cars, too. From Santiago, take Ruta 5 Sur to Buin, then turn west to Isla de Maipo (about 70 km). You can return via Talagante. Buses leave from Terminal San Borja in Santiago.

Vichuquén

This small town 110 km west of Curicó is one of the oldest settlements in the Central Region. Remnants of pre-Inca structures merge with the typical colonial buildings, cobble-stone streets and tile roofs. The Historical Museum displays artifacts that are thousands of years old. Buses leave from Curicó.

Villa Alegre - Yerbas Buenas

We mention these two colonial villages south of Talca as typical examples for many others like them in an area of old adobes with shaded porches, stately tree-lined boulevards, and dreamy squares reminiscent of times past. Among the things worth seeing: a small museum in Yerbas Buenas with its beautiful courtyard and a rustic tavern right around the corner. Buses leave from Talca and Linares.

Pomaire – Doñíhue – Chimbarongo - Quinchamalí

see Chapter 10 p. 207: Artisans' Villages

Typical adobe house at Vichuquén

Waterfalls

Of course, the most beautiful waterfalls are those that you hike to *(see Ch. 2)*. But these two spectacular falls in Central Chile are well worth a special day trip.

Salto del Maule

Proudly named "Ruta Internacional", this mostly gravelled road runs from Talca to the Andes towards Laguna del Maule and Pehuen-

Chile's largest waterfalls, Salto del Laja

che Pass. A few kilometers beyond the police station at La Mina (sign in here!) the road starts switchbacking up the mountain. In a place where the left drop-off widens into a flat spot (after about 150 km), a hardly visible trail leads to the left and the waterfalls, which are not visible from the road.

The first falls drop about 80 meters over basalt cliffs. About 30 minutes on foot further uphill, the second falls form a beautiful lagoon. Those who want to go for a short hike can follow the stream to a place where the volcanic ashes have formed strange sculptures.

Salto del Laja

Much easier to reach are the Río Laja falls that plunge into a deeply washed out gorge in the shape of a huge curtain about 100 meters wide. May to December are the best months for enjoying these miniature Niagara Falls as there is noticeably less water in the middle of Summer. Access via the Panamericana, 80 km south of Chillán, Salto del Laja exit. Several hotels und Camping sites.

The Maule Train

The last of the regular east-west passenger trains

The tracks between Talca and the coastal city of Constitución are some of the last ones in Chile to still see passenger trains run. The laid-back convoy consisting of an engine and a car keeps following Río Maule and sometimes stops in the middle of a field to let people get off and on. It reaches Constitución several times a day after 2.5 hours, where you can walk on the black lava beach with its high rock cliffs, or eat fresh fish in one of the small restaurants along the boardwalk.

On the Coast

Valparaíso - Viña

A fresh sea breeze characterizes the twin cities of **Valparaíso** and **Viña del Mar**. While the former looks busy and small-scale, the latter appears nouveau riche and trendy. A ride on the elevator *(ascensor)* up one of Valparaíso's many hills is not to be missed, as is a Marisco meal in a typical harbor restaurant at Caleta Membrillo. And the poet Neruda's spirit can still be felt in his whimsical house named La Sebastiana (Av. Alemana, Cerro Bellavista), as well as at his restored coastal refuge at **Isla Negra** near Algarrobo.

Beaches

Numerous beaches with good infrastucture stretch north of Viña del Mar, as well as south of there between Algarrobo and Cartagena; however, they tend to be crowded in the Summer. The picturesque fishing village of **Quintay** – quasi stuck to the cliffs - south of Valparaíso is worth a nice Sunday trip. No less attractive and far less crowded are the varied coasts of the Rancagua and Talca regions.

More information about specific beaches in Ch. 6 under Surfing and Windsurfing.

Putú Dunes

About 25 km north of Constitución, a widely unknown geographical rarity runs along the coast, a vast area of sahara-like sand dunes. Five kilometers after the last intersection towards Putú, a track turns off to the left. After few minutes, you will reach the edge of the dunes which seem to run north and south all the way towards the horizon – a great day tour.

Sea Lions

These animals that are slow on land but swift in the water can be seen all along the coast *(see p. 37)*. Especially impressive are the colonies living on huge rocks near the beach, such as at Loanco (between Constitución and Curanipe) and at Cobquecura (accessed from Chillán). Their powerful voices can be heard at quite a distance from the rocks in the crashing surf. With some luck, you can also see penguins.

Santiago

There is hardly a way past the capital for any Chile traveller, and without doubt, the city offers more than enough cultural attractions to fill several days with. The old center, the lively streets, its pretentious "Sanhattan", the city parks, amusement districts, museums, and theaters all provide a glimpse of Chile's past and presence, and plenty of more urban things to explore.

It would be beyond the scope of a book focusing on experiencing nature to try and describe Santiago's diverse offerings. For further information, please refer to specialized guide books, esp. the Lonely Planet Santiago Guide published in 2000. Information on current cultural events can be found in the newspapers and their Thursday and Friday supplements.

On the Internet

www.chiptravel.cl/region/santiago/valpo.htm
www.chiptravel.cl/region/santiago/santiago_index.htm
Important tourism-related addresses and operators in Valparaíso and Santiago; in English

The port city of Valparaíso, built on hills around the bay

Fernando Gómez

Eats & Drinks
Keeping Body and Soul Together

9

Chilean Cuisine
Hidden Pleasures

The country's soil and coastal waters produce an overwhelming variety of ingredients that make for an interesting offering. And yet, Chilean cuisine tends to be rather traditional and down-to-earth. Its pleasures are often hidden behind a menu modeled on European ones, and the few typical national specialties are more like homecooking than *haute cuisine*.

Fish and other Seafood

You will likely find the most Chilean specialties in restaurants serving fish and other seafood. The coast is not far anywhere, and so what's offered is fresh and of amazing variety. As for fish, **salmón** (salmon) and **trucha** (trout) lead the list - a dream prepared *a la mantequilla* (in butter) or *a la plancha* (grilled) - and cheap to boot, since salmon and trout are raised on farms in great numbers. But do not neglect to try "normal" fish: **congrio** (conger), which is also served in an excellent soup **(caldillo de congrio)** Pablo Neruda dedicated an appreciative poem to; **corvina** (seatrout), from whose raw white meat and onions the hors d'oeuvre **ceviche** is made; the simpler **merluza** (hake), the white **lenguado** (flounder), and the exquisite **albacora** (Albacore tuna). Popular ways of preparing fish are *al pil pil* (with garlic sauce) or *al vino blanco* (with a white wine sauce) besides the old stand-by *frito* (breaded and fried). Or add a few calories by ordering it *a la margarita* - in an irresistible white clam sauce.

The variety among other Chilean seafood is even more astounding; each region has its own specialty. Among Crustaceae in the Central region you will be offered mostly **jaiva** (crab) with its red claws. Among clams, **ostras** (oysters) and **ostiones** (scallops) are considered special delicacies, "slurped" raw with lemon. Others, such as **almejas**, **machas** and **choritos**, are boiled or steamed briefly and make a hearty **paila marina** (clam/fish soup). **Machas a la parmesana** are offered as an hors d'oeuvre, topped with melted cheese. Among the special treats are also **erizos** (sea urchins) rich in iodine, the soft

picorocos (barnacles) and the tender **locos**. The latter are so prized on the world market that they are meanwhile threatened by extinction.

Just Like at Mom's

The traditional cuisine of the Central valley is dominated by beef and chicken. **Parrillada**, a combination of various pieces of meat, beef and pork sausages is served directly on a small charcoal grill in many restaurants. Barbecues are an indispensable part of Chilean family gatherings and outings. The word **asado** signifies the meat as well as the occasion for the celebration. **Longaniza**, a spicy sausage, is served at these feasts, too. For an asado, **pebre** – an exceptionally hot sauce made from ají (Chile pepper), garlic and cilantro – or a variation thereof with fresh tomatoes (**chancho en piedra**) are de rigeur.

In gnarly restaurants you will find other home cooking specialties, such as **carne mechada** (stuffed beef brisket), **carne plateada** (meat boiled until very tender and "silver") or **escalopa**

Fernando Gómez

A must during the corn season: Pastel de choclo

9
Eats & Drinks

Expert hands making humitas

kaiser (schnitzel filled with cheese and ham). These dishes are usually served with mashed potatoes *(puré)*, rice *(arroz)* or fries *(papas fritas)*.

Among the classics is also what used to be "poor people's soup" - **cazuela** either *de vacuno* (from beef) or *de ave* (from chicken). This is a stew with potatoes, meat, corn, rice, onions, pumpkin, and peppers. Very tasty and filling is **pastel de choclo** (corn pudding), a sweet-and-sour combination made from grits, hamburger meat, chicken, eggs, raisins and olives that is topped with sugar and baked in an earthenware dish until golden. In the summer months you can enjoy **humitas**, grits wrapped in corn husks (similar to tamales).

Empanadas

Whether as an hors d'oeuvre, entree or as a snack, Chileans love their **empanadas** more than anything. These are yummy dough pockets that come in several sizes and variations: oven-baked *(al horno)* or deep-fried *(fritas)*, filled with a mix of meat, onion, egg and olives *(empanadas de pino)*, with cheese *(de queso)* or with clams *(de mariscos)*, to mention only the most popular ones. Patisseries also offer sweet versions (such as with apple or pear sauce).

Sandwiches & Completos

Before the respective chains blanketed Chile with North American fast food, the country already had a hamburger culture all of its own. These **sandwiches** are part of the standard menu in many simple restaurants, and they are far superior to the commercial fast food products if pre-

pared right. The most important varieties are: **Chacarero** (beef with green beans, tomatoes, green peppers and mayonnaise), **Barros Luco** (beef with cheese), **Barros Jarpa** (ham with cheese), **Ave** (chicken in a number of different variations, e.g., with *palta*). Guacamole is also a standard condiment besides mustard, ketchup and sauerkraut on the popular **completo**, a predecessor of the hot dog.

Fruit & Vegetables

The fields south and west of the capital, as well as the fertile valleys of the north produce a much broader range of fruit and vegetables than the standard side dish of **ensalada a la chilena** (salad from tomatoes and onions) would make you think. A stroll over one of the numerous street markets or Mercado Central in Santiago is sure to make your mouth water. In addition to numerous varieties of lettuce, cabbage, and legumes, there are **alcachofas** (artichokes) - surprisingly cheap when in season - served with a lemon-oil-mix or mayonnaise. Several kinds of avocados (called **palta** in Chile) are turned into tasty hors d'oeuvres.

Guayavas and papayas come from the desert oases, kiwis and cherimoyas from the fields around Santiago, as well as melons and strawberries, and in late Fall pomegranate, cactus and kaki fruit appear. All winter long, there will be piles and piles of oranges, apples and pears at the stalls. Dried peaches, soaked in their own juice and served with sprouted wheat kernels, form the basis for a yummy and nutritious drink that you can get from stalls in the streets in the summer: **mote con huesillos.**

Sweets

The Chileans are no slouches either when it comes to sweets. Before "industrial" cookies took over the store shelves, they already ate **alfajores** (filled cookies coated with chocolate or powdered sugar) and anything containing **manjar**, a sticky-sweet brown mix made from condensed milk and sugar. The German immigrants have contributed their fair share, as well as the name **kuchen** to this sweet culture, from bundt cake to Black Forest Torte **(torta selva negra)**.

Chilean Wine
French Roots

For lovers of good wine, Chile is a paradise. The vintners there have invested massively into modern technology over the last 15 years, diversified their production, gathered prizes at fairs, and conquered the international market. In Central Chile, due to the long, sunny summers, sediment-rich soils, and good irrigation, some of the (ungrafted) vines that were introduced from France in the 19th century still bear fruit. This is a haven for wine lovers - good wines are considerably cheaper than in Europe or North America.

The largest market share is held by the fashionable grapes such as Cabernet Sauvignon, Merlot, Chardonnay, and Sauvignon Blanc. Over the past few years, wineries have also been experimenting increasingly with varieties such as Syrah, Malbec, Pinot Noir, Sangiovese, Semillon, Riesling, and above all, Carmenère.

País

This grape that the conquistadores brought with them, is still the most frequently grown one in Chile. From these productive vines, simple reds are made for table wines.

Cabernet Sauvignon

The most important variety among the better reds comes from Bordeaux and grows in the Central Region between Río Aconcagua and Río Maule – still on the original vines (not grafted). The aromatic, fruity and tannin-rich wines are often improved through storage in oak barrels.

Merlot

Cabernet's "little brother" has been cultivated increasingly in recent years. It also comes from Bordeaux, and it produces lighter, less acidic and less complex reds.

Carmenère

Carmenère is originally from Bordeaux, where it was **the** grape for red wine before the Phylloxera plague hit in the middle of the 19th century. After that, this grape was not planted anywhere anymore – supposedly. About 15 years ago, enologists in Chile discovered that many of the Merlot vines imported from Europe were actually Carmenère. Today, they make for a promising production of varietal wines and cuvées. Carmenère has the potential for heavy-bodied, smooth wines, which Chile would like to use to make a name for itself.

The fine wines of the Central Region are popular worldwide

Sauvignon Blanc

The most important white grape also comes from Bordeaux and from the Loire river; it turns into an aromatic wine with strong character and strong acidity. Until a few years ago, it was made from the lesser Sauvignonasse vine. However, due to the boom in exports, most wineries have now planted young, unadulterated Sauvignon Blanc vines.

Chardonnay

This vine from Burgundy, a top favorite worldwide, did not come into fashion in Chile until the 90's. Especially in Valle Casablanca between Santiago and Valparaíso new plantings have been made. This fruity white with a hint of honey has less acidity than a Sauvignon Blanc and is considered the king of whites because of its complex character.

Vineyards see p. 196

Chicha

In the weeks during and after the wine harvest, **chicha** is celebrated every year. This young, hard grape cider (rarely made from other fruit) goes to one's head really fast and enjoys great popularity among Chileans. Besides empanadas, this naturally cloudy drink is an indispensable part of the celebrations for the national holidays in September.

Pisco
The National Schnaps

What would Chile be without its national drink? Pisco is among the symbols of Chilean patriotism like the Andes and the Pacific. It is mostly made from muscatel grapes, which thrive in the sunny desert valleys of northern Chile. The wine from these grapes is distilled – similar to cognac - in big copper tanks, then stored several months in oak or beech barrels, and finally brought to the different quality levels through adding various amounts of water. In the stores, you can buy: Selección (30 or 33 Vol%), Especial (35°), Reservado (40°) and Gran Pisco (43°). In recent years, stronger varieties have been offered, too (46° and even 50°).

While the 30° to 35° varieties are meant for making mixed drinks, pisco of 40° and higher is best enjoyed straight. The higher the alcohol content, the more aromatic and viscous the drink will get, and in the better brands, the aromatic taste should control the bite.

Chileans like their pisco best mixed with lemon, sugar, and beaten eggwhite: **Pisco sour** is the standard aperitif in restaurants of all kinds, and a favorite at private parties. In addition, pisco is also mixed with Coke, and used for creating a number of longdrinks.

Pisco Sour

△ Preparing Pisco sour is very easy: two parts pisco, one part fresh lemon juice (better: Pica limes), powdered sugar to taste, a little eggwhite. Mix with ice cubes until foamy, and serve in tall glasses.

On the Internet

www.nuevoanden.com/recetas.html
Lots of recipes for Chilean dishes; but only a few in English

www.winesofchile.com
Overview of Chilean wines and wineries; in English

Useful Information
Chilean ABC's

Accommodations

From fancy hotels to simple hostels, you will find a range of accommodations in all major cities and the vacation areas. In recent years, new hotels and bungalow complexes have been built in remote areas and in National Parks. The latter – so-called *cabañas* – are fully equipped small buildings incl. kitchenette, a cheaper alternative for families than hotels.

Hotels

The price-performance ratio can vary considerably among hotels *(hotel, hostería)*. There is no general classification system, and claims to so many stars do not say anything about the quality of a place. When making one's selection, it's always a good idea to look at size and location of a room, private bathroom *(baño privado)*, necessities (TV, phone), and service. Breakfast is usually included, but it's only worth mentioning when it's designated as *desayuno americano* or *buffet*. In high season (December to February), prices for medium and top hotels can be compared to European ones (starting at about USD 40.00 for a medium category single). Single rooms are usually not much cheaper than a double.

Hostels

Simple hostels *(residencial, hostal, hostería, casa de familia)* offer cheap accommodations, but you will have to make allowances when it comes to creature comforts. The closer to the bus station, the simpler the room, and the more questionable its cleanliness. There are very few youth hostels, and they are only open in mid-Summer (January/February).

Motels

Those travelling by car will find many motels along the Panamericana where guests usually stay in small bungalows. This discrete arrangement is not surprising given that these hotels are socially acceptable, sometimes quite fancy, locations for undisturbed sexual encounters, which often also function as normal hotels outside the big cities.

Reservations & Taxes
Room reservations are only necessary during high season and in tourist areas. Starting from medium category up, you can use a credit card for paying. International tourists need not pay value-added (sales) tax (18%) when paying in USD (cash or travellers' cheques), but this discount is not always applied automatically.

Long-term Housing
For longer stays in Santiago, the agency Contactchile offers housing alternatives with families or students. *See ad on page 215.*

Airport Shuttle

Santiago
Safe and comfortable vans run from door to door taking several people to the requested address for USD 5.00-7.00 each. This service can also be requested by phone for pick-ups from your Santiago address when leaving by plane: ph. 777 77 07. For two people, a taxi can be cheaper (negotiate the price beforehand). Airport buses run between the airport and Metro Los Héroes (about USD 1.50.)

Buses

City
If you want to use the *micros* (city buses), you should know your way around a bit. The most important stops are listed on the window. You will need exact change for the fare (about USD 0.50) dispensed by a machine or the driver. No passes.

Inter-Regional
Long distance buses run to all major and medium-sized cities offering three price ranges (Salón Cama - Ejecutivo/Semi Cama - Pullman/Turístico). For longer rides (usually at night) the more expensive sleeper (Salón Cama) is recommended since it offers more leg room, reclining seats, and better service on board. On long holi-

day weekends and when the vacation period starts and ends, prices will rise; so, get your tickets in plenty of time! On the main runs, there is a lot of competition, and it's worth comparing prices and levels of service while at the bus station or by phone (Yellow Pages under 'Buses Interurbanos'). An example for ticket prices: Santiago – Chillán (about 410 km) regular (Pullman) is about USD 6.00, in Ejecutivo it's USD 10.00, and in Salón Cama about USD16.00.

Regional
Smaller bus companies often make the runs within a region or to remote destinations, often with less comfortable vehicles. On short runs between neighboring towns there are also the cheap group taxis (usually yellow; *see Colectivos*).

Bus Terminals in Santiago

Terminal Alameda: directly by Universidad de Santiago Metro station; the companies "Tur-Bus" and "Pullman Bus" leave from here to all directions; to Viña/Valparaíso every 15 minutes.

Terminal Santiago (formerly, Terminal Sur): Alameda at Nicasio Retamales, 150 m west of Alameda terminal; all companies going to the coast and south.

Terminal Los Héroes: Tucapel Jiménez at Alameda, close to Los Héroes Metro stop; various companies going to the north.

Terminal San Borja (Terminal Norte): San Borja at Alameda, next to Estación Central: to the north and Greater Santiago.

Camping

Especially in some of the National Parks, tent camping is the only option. Most camping sites have only modest facilities; showers and hot water are an exception. In the tourist centers, privately run sites often offer more comfort, but sometimes only at a considerable price. Unregulated camping is legal in most National Parks, and it is usually not a problem in remote areas; however, one should try and ask the owner of the land for permission. Important: Leave no traces and take your trash. *See also p. 62.*

Citymaps

Simple maps are distributed at the tourist information centers and at travel agents'. More detailed ones can be purchased from kiosks and bookstores. The most current and complete map of Santiago is in the Yellow Pages of the phone directory.

Clothing

During the Chilean summer (November to March) you should be prepared for warm to hot, dry days and cool nights in Central Chile. Protect yourself adequately against the strong sun with a hat or cap, sun glasses and cream. For those who continue from here to the south, a warm sweater, a good rain coat and weatherproof shoes are essential. For tourists, the following would only apply for formal occasions (such as concerts, lunch/dinner invitations): Chileans emphasize conventional dress. If you don't want to raise eyebrows in the city, don't wear sandals and shorts. The same is true for too-revealing clothes for women who want to avoid unpleasant catcalls *(piropos)* from Chilean machos. *Hiking clothes see p. 61.*

Colectivos

These reasonably-priced group taxis run their fixed routes indicated on the signs on their roofs. They usually wait at the metro stations in Santiago, or at other central locations and leave when there is a minumum of riders. In other cities, they operate like buses. A colectivo can also be stopped anywhere along the way. At night, they will take you to a specific address for an additional fee, and as long as it is close to their route *(a domicilio)*.

Cost of Living

Contrary to other Latin American countries, Chile experiences no shortages, but it is relatively expensive. Consumer goods can be found at least in all major cities, but they are mostly imported and thus, more expensive than in industrialized countries (e.g., slide films). Food is offered in vast quantities, and it is of good quality and cheap, esp. fruit and vegetables. Tourism-related services are more expensive in Santiago and some tourism centers than in the rest of the country. Public transport, bus travel and simple restaurants are relatively cheap; e.g., a meal in a simple restaurant will set you back about 1000-2500 pesos or USD 1.50-3.75.

Crafts

Local crafts markets *(Ferias de Artesanía)* offer regional products made from wool, leather, clay, wood, baskets, silver or copper. A Chilean specialty are products made from or with lapis lazuli, a blue semi-precious stone occuring only in Afghanistan and Chile that is worked into artistic creations with silver and other metals (workshops/stores in Santiago's Bellavista section, sold on most crafts markets.)

MARKETS IN SANTIAGO

Santa Lucía
At Alameda and Carmen, right in the Center. Across from it, in a cave of Santa Lucía hill, a little hidden from view, the worthwhile Mapuche art market.

Bellavista
At Pío Nono and Santa María/Bellavista, standard goods, good prices. Pío Nono and Antonia López de Bello streets are filled with small stalls on Friday and Saturday night and all day Sunday.

Los Dominicos
Av. Nueva Apoquindo 9085, Las Condes, former Dominican monastery, good for a Sunday outing. Tasteful products, higher prices, good quality. Closed on Monday.

ARTISANS' VILLAGES

Pomaire
Lively potters' village halfway between the capital and the coast on Autopista del Sol (approx. 80 km from Santiago). Dark earthenware galore: rustic dishes, round jugs, cheerful figures at modest prices. Another specialty of Pomaire are the monster empanadas each weighing over a kilo. Buses leave from Terminal San Borja.

Doñihue

This village approx. 20 kilometers west of Rancagua is the secret capital of the huasos. This is where their fancy capes *(chamantos, mantas)*, cummerbunds and belts are woven and sold at steep prices. Buses leave from Rancagua.

Chimbarongo

Practically right on top of the Panamericana, the famous basket weavers of Chimbarongo sell their varied and cheap wares: containers of all kinds, dolls and decorations including living room furniture. 18 kilometers south of San Fernando.

Rari

Between the thermal spas of Quinamávida and Panimávida east of Linares, the modest burg of Rari has developed a rare tradition: items crafted from dyed horsehair, esp. small witch dolls.

Chillán

While Chillán is no village but a medium-sized city (and as such, not a must-see), it does have what may well be Chile's prettiest market: fruit, vegetables, crafts, and huasos hats – lots to choose from.

Quinchamalí

Potters' village 35 kilometers west of Chillán, a lot less hectic than Pomaire, but with at least equally attractive brown and black earthenware products. Buses leave from Chillán.

Customs and Manners

Basically, Chileans appreciate politeness and certain phrases, even though as a foreigner, you will enjoy a certain gringo/a bonus.

The **greetings** take some getting used to. Men shake hands with each other, while men and women as well as women among each other will blow a little kiss towards the right cheek, even among strangers, who can also add shaking hands to that. Same works for saying good-bye. What you should say is *Buenos días* (until Noon), *Buenas tardes* (Noon to approx. 8 p.m.), and *Buenas noches* (starting at approx. 8 p.m.), to take leave say *Hasta luego* or *Adiós*. When turning down an offer, always say *No, gracias*; just *Gracias* will usually be taken to mean consent *(Sí, gracias)*.

For **appointments** you usually have about 15 minutes "wiggle room". Long distance buses and planes are usually on time. **Little things** such as long hair and earrings in men, short skirts, unshaved legs and armpits in women, as well as insufficient deodorant are equally repulsive to the spiffy Chileans. At work, **dress** is formal, and in most offices, ties are required. However, people will quickly make the transition from the more formal address *(usted)* to the more casual *tú* with colleagues and acquaintances, except in very formal contexts, and especially young people (up to about 35 years of age) are not very likely to be addressed with *usted*. When in doubt, it is safer to stick with the more formal *(usted)*, especially with older people.

Chileans are very **hospitable** towards most foreigners. If possible, do not turn down invitations.

Driving

See also Rental Cars.

Santiago traffic is not for the faint of heart, or inexperienced drivers. If you decide to join the fray, drive defensively to deal with the aggressive Chilean way of driving, and do not expect any slack. It's important to plan any route you have to drive beforehand. Santiago's streets are confusing, poorly sign-posted, and strewn with potholes. On some of the major thoroughfares, the driving direction will change depending on rush hour traffic, and on days with smog warning levels Pre-emergencia or Emergencia even vehicles with catalytic converters can be banned from driving depending on their license plate numbers (announced in the media).

In town, the **speed limit** is 50 km/h, outside max. 100 km/h – and you wouldn't want to drive any faster anyway, given the state of most roads. Speeds are checked often, esp. on highways and freeways, punishment is harsh and involves a frequently tiresome bureaucratic procedure.

Gas (93, 95 or 97 octane) is about USD 0.60 per Liter, and it gets more expensive the further you get from the capital. On the major arterials leading out of Santiago as well as on some portions of the Panamericana, you have to pay **toll** at a station (approx. USD 3.00, double that on weekends.) The Panamericana is currently being expanded north and south of Santiago to turn it into a modern two-to-three-lane freeway with the addition of more toll stations.

Before you drive off into the unkown, it is a good idea to inquire about **road conditions**. Most secondary roads are not paved, and gravel roads of widely varying quality can deteriorate, especially from long rains. Less experienced drivers should be especially cautious on such roads. It is a good idea to carry a second spare tire for longer tours on gravel.

When **parking** the vehicle, make sure that nothing left is visible from the outside, esp. in cities. The informal and semi-formal parking lot attendants cannot always be trusted. Find secure parking for your car at night.

Important: Always carry car documents, passport, and driver's license with you! If you have questions or run into problems, turn to one of the numerous police stations (Carabineros, *see Police.*)

Electrical Appliances

The voltage is 220 V / 50 Hz, and appliances also need an adapter *(adaptador)* to plug into the Chilean sockets, which can be found in supermarkets or specialty stores.

Exit Visa

If you should leave via one of the small, non-networked border crossings to Argentina, e.g., on a tour of the Central Andes, you first need to obtain a Salvoconducto in one of the major cities from the Policía de Investigaciones to present with your Tourist Card at the border crossing.

Flight Confirmation

Most airlines require you to call and confirm in-country and international flights at least 48 hours before departure. It is also a good idea to call the airline about potential delays right before leaving for the airport. Phone numbers can be found in the Yellow Pages under 'Líneas Aéreas'.

Getting There

By Air
About a dozen European and North American airlines serve Santiago, some even daily. For flights from Europe the lower limit is around USD 600 and 900 roundtrip, depending on the season; direct flights from New York, Miami or Los Angeles start at USD 500 to 600. The Airpass from Lan Chile for in-country flights can only be booked through an agency abroad *(see In-country flights.)*

By Land
For travel from Peru, Bolivia or Argentina to Chile you can choose any of the border crossings. From May through September, inquire ahead of time about the road conditions for the Andean passes in Central and Southern Chile. Especially between Mendoza (Arg.) and Los Andes (Chile), you have to be prepared for snow drifts.

Tourist Card
Citizens of Australia, New Zealand, Great Britain, Canada, the USA, South Africa, as well as most EU countries do not need a visa, just their passport. Upon entry, they will receive a "Tarjeta de Turismo" (Tourist Card) which is valid for 90 days and has to be presented when leaving the country. Find a safe place for this inconspicuous piece of paper! If you do loose it, get a replacement in plenty of time before your departure (Policía Internacional in Santiago, General Borgoño 1052, or at a police station in one of the regions.) Those trying to leave without the card will most likely miss their flight or be kept waiting at the border for a long time.

Citizens of most African, Asian and formerly Soviet States will need a tourist visa that can be applied for at any Chilean Consulate.

Fees
Citizens of the USA, Canada, Australia and Mexico have to pay an entry fee when travelling through Santiago airport (not at any other point) that corresponds to the amount Chileans are

charged when travelling to the respective country: US citizens USD 61.00, Canadians USD 55.00, Australians USD 30.00, Mexicans USD 17.00.

Extension

The Tourist Card is easiest extended by leaving and re-entering the country (can be done on the same day.) Many foreigners use this loophole to extend their stay in Chile with this totally legal procedure that can theoretically be repeated virtually forever. However, there have been cases in which the border officials became suspicious the third or fourth time, started asking uncomfortable questions, and renewed the Tourist Card only for 30 days.

An official extension through a police station (without leaving the country) is only meant to be done once for another 90 days, and it has to be applied for one month before the card expires from the Extranjería in Santiago or any Regional capital. The price is USD 100.00; Santiago address: Teatinos 950, back of the building, close to Cal y Canto Metro station.

Luggage

Most airlines will now let you check two pieces of luggage at 32 kg each in addition to one piece of carry-on luggage – but do inquire beforehand to make sure! This means that you might be able to check a surfboard or a bike as your second piece. Taking them as additional luggage will cost about USD 70.00-90.00. Make sure to find out from your airline in plenty of time what requirements they might have for such items; e.g., bikes will generally need to be boxed, and you need to prepare for the required disassembly and assembly.

Customs Regulations

You can bring the following items into the country duty-free: unlimited amounts of cash, 400 cigarettes, 2 1/2 Liters of spirits, as well as all personal use items. Illegal are fresh food such as fruit, vegetables and milk products, as well as illegal drugs, and pornography. Plants and animals require a special permit from the health authorities, which has to be applied for in advance from any Chilean Consulate.

Guidebooks

From the travel books about Chile we recommend the Chile Handbook from Footprint Press which is updated every other year, or their South American Handbook published new every year. The Australian publisher Lonely Planet has also published several good guide books on Chile; most recently, the handy Santiago Guide. The Chilean travel guide Turistel which is updated annually has lots of detailed information (in Spanish) and good maps. It comes in three volumes plus road and camping maps, and can be bought from bookstores and kiosks.

Health

Diseases

In Chile there is no need to fear any specific health hazards. No special shots are necessary; there is no malaria or cholera. It is, however, advisable to update one's standard protection against typhoid, poliomyelitis, hepatitis, and tetanus. Beware of tap water, raw vegetables and fish or other seafood, raw eggs, and food offered in the streets. Wash and/or peel all fruit and vegetables carefully.

Dangers of the Outdoors

Besides the hazards of certain high risk sports there are two dangers to your health that lurk in comparatively tiny format: catching the hantavirus (see p. 62-63), and insect bites. In Chile, there are two poisonous spiders (see p. 47-48), and north of Talca, there is the vinchuca bug that can transmit the Chagas disease (see p. 49). There are no dangerous animals of prey or snakes. As for acute mountain sickness, see p. 65-66.

Medical Services

Medical treatment in private hospitals in Santiago and other major cities is comparable to top international levels. Before you leave for Chile, check with your existing health insurance on their coverage of international travel, or get additional insurance. All drugs are available, and most doctors speak English. Appropriate medical care can be more difficult to get in rural hospitals or at First Aid posts.

Holidays

New Year's Day (January 1), Good Friday, Easter Saturday and Sunday (varies), Labor Day (May 1), Iquique Naval Battle (May 21), Corpus Christi (June 22), St. Peter and Paul (June 29), Assumption of Mary (August 15), Day of National Reconciliation (first Monday in September), Fiestas Patrias (National Holiday, September 18), Army Day (September 19), Discovery of America (October 12), All Saints (November 1), Immaculate Conception (December 8), Christmas (December 25). A number of holidays are moved to a Monday to create a long weekend.

In-country Flights

Three private airlines - Lan Chile, Ladeco (which belongs to Lan Chile, too), and AeroContinente - serve all major cities of the country with modern fleets. Because of the enormous distances, flying is a fast and safe alternative for travel within Chile. Reservations through travel agents or directly with the airlines.

Roundtrip Ticket

Lan Chile offers a Chile roundtrip ticket (Lan Air Pass) that can only be purchased in connection with an international airline ticket to Chile and **before** the trip. The Airpass works with coupons (max. six per person) and is cheaper for passengers who fly to Chile with Lan (3 coupons USD 250, ea. additional one USD 60) than for the rest (3 coupons USD 350, ea. additional one USD 80). The coupons can be used within one month after the first internal flight, with some limitations on the routes. The individual flights can be booked in advance or on location, and they can be chosen freely, capacity permitting. The Airpass is definitely worthwhile for anyone who wants to fly more than twice within Chile.

Insurance

Before travelling to Chile, it's advisable to buy comprehensive coverage against loss of luggage and for international health insurance, as well as liability insurance. Private hospitals will recognize credit cards as a guarantee.

Mail

Chile's mail works well, if somewhat slow. The regular postage for a letter is 160 pesos in country, 230 to North America, and 260 overseas. The main post office on Plaza de Armas in Santiago is open Mon - Fri from 9 a.m. to 7 p.m., and Saturdays from 9 to Noon, and there are additional post offices in the suburbs. International mail is usually sent by airmail automatically *(vía aérea),* and it takes 4-8 days to Central Europe; which can be speeded up for a fee *(expreso)*. Important letters and packages should be sent by registered mail *(certificado)*. If you want to have someone send you mail to Chile, ask them to mark it 'Lista de Correos' (poste restante). The post offices will save this mail for 30 days. Nice postcards can be found at the Museo de Bellas Artes and the Museo Precolombino.

Media

Newspapers

The biggest daily with an extensive cultural section is the conservative, Pinochet-friendly *Mercurio*, one of the oldest newspapers of Latin America. The Mercurio Corporation also owns several other papers in Santiago and in the provinces. Other dailies are *La Tercera, El Metropolitano*, the evening paper *La Segunda* and the free papers *mtg* and *La Hora*. Current and independent information can be found in the online paper *El Mostrador* (www.elmostrador.cl). And a good overview of Chilean goings-on is provided by the English-language *News Review* which appears twice weekly.

Magazines

The market for magazines is dominated by gossip zines such as *Cosas* and *Caras*; political analyses are found in *Qué pasa* (liberal) and *Ercilla* (conservative). Biting satire, but also hard-hitting reporting is provided by the biweekly *The Clinic*.

International Press

International newspapers and magazines can be found – much more expensive – and with a delay of about two days at some kiosks, especially in the center of Santiago (Paseo Ahumada).

TV

Chilean TV is dominated by soccer, series and entertainment. The evening news are at 9 p.m. on most channels. Cable is standard in the better hotels, and more than 80 channels from all over the world are available.

Radio

Among FM stations, the fare is mostly music and entertainment; especially popular with young people: Rock&Pop (94.1) and Radio Zero (97.7). news at 93.3 (Cooperativa) and 100.9 (Chilena).

Metro

Santiago's fast, clean and safe Metro has no reason to hide compared to the undergrounds of the world, but so far, there are only three lines. The main line (1) runs modern French trains along the central east-west axis Alameda - Providencia - Apoquindo serving the center as well as the newer business districts of Providencia and Las Condes. At Los Héroes and Baquedano stops, you can change to one of the two lines connecting the southern parts of the city to the center. A single ticket is between 270 and 350 pesos (USD 0.40 – 0.55) depending on time of day; there are single and double tickets as well as strip tickets (boleto valor, USD 5.00) all of which include transfers.

Money

Currency

The official currency is the Chilean Peso (CLP), which uses the confusing symbol for USD ($). Over the last few years, the rate of inflation has sunk to 4%. The exchange rate has exploded following the Argentinian crisis in mid-2001; in November of 2001 it was about 1 USD = 700 CLP.

Spending Money

Take travellers' cheques and cash in US dollars (in a money belt, see Safety) and exchange money only in official places (**never** in the street) or banks (usually worse rates, and only open from 9-2.) Santiago has the best currency conversion rates; several exchange places are located on Agustinas between Ahumada and Bandera (open Mon-Fri 9-7, Sat morning), as well as near Manuel Montt, Pedro de Valdivia,

and Los Leones Metro stations. The AmEx office (Turismo Cocha) in El Bosque Norte 0440, Las Condes, Metro Tobalaba, Mon-Fri 9 a.m. – 7 p.m., is only worth the trip if you have large amounts in AmEx travellers cheques to convert. On the weekend, the larger hotels exchange money, too, but at a bad rate.

Cards

A good alternative is drawing cash (pesos) with your money or credit cards from automated tellers marked with the Cirrus, Plus or Maestro symbol in all major cities – know your PIN! You have to count of paying a fee (find out from your bank before you leave). You can use your regular credit cards to pay almost anywhere. Only major hotels and tourist agencies accept US dollars directly.

Police

In Chile, there are two police organizations, the uniformed police (Carabineros) and the plainclothes detectives (Policía de Investigaciones). The Carabineros are responsible for safety in the streets and enjoy a high level of trust among Chileans. It's important to always carry your papers with you in case you get stopped, in which case you would be asked for your ID (this is legal, if rare, in Chile). Never try to bribe a policeman!

Rental Cars

For renting a car, you have to be at least 21, present an international driver's license, and leave a blank payment slip with your credit card number as a guarantee. In addition to the major international agencies, there are often also local companies at the airports.

The rates are relatively high; but lower in Santiago than in the provinces. With smaller companies, you can try haggling; expect a discount for a long-term rental. A simple subcompact is between USD 25.00 and 40.00/day. The price should include free mileage (kilometraje libre), insurance (seguro), usually with deductible, and value-added tax (IVA). Also inquire about roadside assistance, parts service and liability in case of accident. It usually costs more to take a rental car across national borders, and it requires additional paperwork and insurance; not all rental companies offer this service.

For more on traffic, see Driving.

Safety

Compared to most Latin American countries, Chile is very safe for travelling. Exceptions, are, as everywhere, the slums and the centers of the big cities. Beware of (well-dressed) pickpockets who practice their swift tricks especially on buses, on the Metro, and in crowds on busy streets. Since as a foreigner you will stick out anyway, you should heed the following:

● Do not flaunt valuables, cameras, jewelry, etc.
● Leave larger amounts of cash, travellers' cheques, credit cards, airline tickets, passport, etc. in your hotel's safe, or carry them around your waist or on your chest in a special money belt/pouch.
● Always keep your eyes on your bags and luggage, clutch purses and daypacks in front of your body.
● Do not allow anyone to distract you (a popular ruse) in a crowd, e.g., when getting on and off the Metro or a bus.
● In cafés and restaurants, never hang your bag over the back of your chair, and never leave it unattended.
● Make a copy of your passport and keep it in a safe place (separate).

On the other hand, cases of robberies at gunpoint or muggings are rare. When in doubt, don't try to be a hero; hand over your money! It is better not to go for walks alone on Cerro San Cristóbal in Santiago, as well as on some of the hills of Valparaíso, and also avoid Cerro Santa Lucía in Santiago at night.

Leaving your luggage where you are staying is usually not a problem, even if they should not have a safe.

Police

When valuables are missing, go to the nearest police station, have a report filed (*dejar constancia*), and make a note of its number (for your insurance company).

Travelling Alone

Chile is safe even for those travelling alone, as long as they use common sense and safety rules. Women need to be resolute enough to get rid of unwanted attention. Chilean machos are usually only a nuisance when in a group, and verbally; otherwise, they are quite harmless. Never hitch-hike alone!

Shopping

Stores open between 9 and 10 a.m. and close around 8 p.m.; smaller stores observe a siesta between about 2 and 4 p.m. Department stores and super markets stay open longer in the evening (until 9, 10 or 11 p.m.), and they are also open on the weekend.

Over the past few years, numerous malls have sprouted all over the place. And the atmosphere alone is worth a visit to one of the typical fruit, vegetable and fish markets (e.g., Mercado Central in Santiago, Mercado de Chillán). In smaller stores, at market stalls and in the street it's OK to try and haggle a bit.

Taxis

Taking a taxi in Chile is safe and relatively cheap. The black cars with their yellow roofs can be hailed anywhere. In Santiago, there is a base price of 150 pesos (USD 0.25) plus from 60 to 80 pesos for each 200 m driven (or per minute when waiting). The rates are posted on the windscreen; the meter has to be where you can see it. For longer hauls or cross-country, you can negotiate a price beforehand. Tipping is not customary. You cannot rely on the drivers' sense of orientation, often they barely know their way around. The more you know about how to get to your destination, the better.

You can request a *radiotaxi* by phone to pick you up from your house (Yellow Pages under 'Taxi').

See also Colectivos, Airport shuttle.

Telephone Calls

The Chilean market for telephones has been vastly liberalized in recent years; several carriers compete with the still dominant, formerly state-owned company Telefónica CTC Chile.

Local Calls

From a regular phone line, approx. 25 pesos (USD 0.04) per minute between 8 p.m. and 8 a.m., and about 25% of that on weekends. Coin-operated phones charge at least 100 pesos (USD 0.15) per call (3 to 5 min), 200 pesos when calling a cell phone. For local calls, simply dial the respective phone number (no prefix).

In-country Calls

The rates for long distance calls are becoming more like those for local calls all the time. Dial the three-digit carrier code before the local prefix and phone number: carrier code + local prefix + phone number; e.g., Valparaíso via Bellsouth: 181+32 + phone number.

International Calls

The rates are confusing and change all the time, and there is no one place to find them all. You have to dial carrier-code + 0 + country code + prefix + phone number; e.g., Washington, D.C. via Telefónica: 188+01+202 + phone number. The cheapest rates to Europe and North America are around USD 0.25/minute, and quite a bit higher from a phone center (Centro de llamados).

Centros de llamados

Throughout the city centers, various phone companies maintain places from which calls can be made from the privacy of a booth, and faxes can be sent.

Phone Cards

A very handy item for travellers in Chile, prepaid phone cards named "Línea propia" from Telefónica allow calls to be made from and to any phone (local, long distance and mobile) without getting charged to that line. After dialling a specific number, the connection is made and the call is debited to the card (or to your virtual account) automatically. The rates are a bit more than those for regular phone lines, and the cards are available from kiosks, where you can also obtain cards for the public card phones.

Cell Phones

These have meanwhile become standard in Chile. The different calling plans are confusing, and coverage is mainly limited to the big cities and along the Panamericana. Foreigners without visa (i.e., most tourists) can only buy prepaid phones that are more expensive to use, and don't work for international calls (however, they can receive them.) There is hardly any difference between the two most important Prepago providers, Amistar (Telefónica) and Aló PCS (Entel). Watch for special offers with free minutes of airtime in exchange for some of the purchase price.

If you bring a compatible (GSM only) cell phone to Chile, it will only work if your provider offers roaming for the country (check before you leave).

Cell phone numbers all start with 09-; when dialling from another cell phone, omit this prefix. From abroad, dial 0056-9.

PLEASE NOTE: Starting in 2001 (after going to print) an eighth digit is supposed to be added in front of the 7-digit cell phone numbers. This change has not yet been integrated in this edition.

Important Phone Numbers	
△ Emergency	131
△ Fire	132
△ Police	133
△ Directory Assistance	103
△ Chile's Country Code	0056

Time Zone

UTC/GMT minus 4 hours. Daylight savings time in Chile starts on the second Sunday in October and ends on the second Sunday in March.

Tipping

In restaurants a tip of about 10% is expected; it is not included in the bill. It is customary to take all the change first and then leave a tip. Gas station and parking attendants also expect a tip of 100 to 200 pesos, but cab drivers are not tipped.

Tourist Information

The state-owned tourism agency Sernatur (Servicio Nacional de Turismo) maintains offices and information booths in all major cities and at the airports. The main office in Santiago is located at Av. Providencia 1550 (Metro Manuel Montt, Mon-Fri 9-5, Sat 9–1; ph. 236 14 16; Internet: www.sernatur.cl).

See Addresses, p. 228

Trains

Passenger trains, which have been pushed out of the market by the competition from buses and by a lack of timely investments for modernization, only run from Santiago south to Concepción (approx. 520 km) and Temuco (approx. 680 km) anymore. Compared to the bus, this train takes longer (approx. 12 hrs.); the original 1920's German sleeper coach, however, makes it a nostalgic trip back into the past. Leaves from Estación Central, Reservations: ph. (2) 376 85 00. There is fast and reliable light rail service once an hour between Santiago (Est. Central) and San Fernando.

see also Buses

Working in Chile

Foreign tourists are officially banned from working in Chile for money – unless their activity is entirely paid for from abroad (e.g., for artists, exchange teachers, etc.). A temporary work permit will only be issued in exceptional cases (from the Extranjería in Santiago or in the provinces), and it is usually restricted to international artists. However, there is a large, informal (grey) area in the Chilean labor market.

Chilenian & Chilenianisms
In the Jungle of Words

11

Those travelling in Chile should be able to communicate in Spanish. Most Chileans don't know too much English, even after years of English in school (which says more about the schools than about the Chileans). Especially in rural areas, English won't get you very far. You can make your trip more enjoyable by taking an intensive course beforehand or in-country, and by bringing a compact phrase book. This will help you make contact with the locals and allow you to ask for information in difficult situations.

This book does not wish to replace the intensive course or phrase book. Since even good students of Spanish find it quite challenging to understand the specific dialect and slang of Chileans, we will describe some of the most common national variants of Spanish, which Chileans call *castellano* (after its origin in Castilia).

Photo: Young Chileans' conversations are often Greek to foreigners

Pronunciation & Grammar

The Chileans are among the fast-talkers of the hispanic world. This wouldn't be too bad if they didn't also swallow parts of words that actually enhance comprehension – such as the final 's', which will leave you guessing as to singular or plural most of the time. So you might at first have a problem with dialogs such as, *"¿Cómo estas? – Maomeno noma."* (= 'mas o menos, no mas'; in English, 'so-so'). Other suffixes are shortened, too. Often, '-ado' will become '-ao' *(volao)*, '-ada' a stressed '-á' *(gallá)*, and 'para' a short 'pa' or 'para el' simply 'pal'.

As everywhere in South America, the Castilian *vosotros* with its corresponding conjugation is missing only to be replaced by *ustedes*, after which the verb is conjugated like after *ellos*.

Chilean slang presents an especially tricky feature: The verb endings for the second person in the plural ('-as', '-es') are replaced by '-ai' and '-ís', so *viajas* will become *viajai*, *sabes* - *sabís*. And consequently, *¿A dónde vai?* (Where are you going?), *¡No seai tonto!* (Don't be an idiot!), *¿Me podís dar fuego?* (Do you have a light?). Using these very informal expressions is strictly sanctioned in some circles, and since they sound strange coming from the mouth of a foreigner anyway, they are best left alone.

A popular means of emphasis that is used in many countries but seems especially popular in Chile is repeating words. This is also done to emphasize trueness or purity. So, in a restaurant, it's a good idea to order *café café* if you want the real thing instead of the ubiquitous instant coffee. And someone living in the very center of the city might say, *Yo vivo en el centro centro*.

The massive use of the diminutive suffixes '-ito' und '-ita' can also be found in other Latin American countries. They do not just mean 'little', as in *niñito* (little boy) or *mesita* (small table), but they have additional functions such as expressing endearment by using '-ito/ita' *(mamita)* or diminishing the urgency, directness or importance of a thing or an action. So, if someone says,

Espérese un momentito (Wait a moment) that doesn't mean at all that the moment will be short, but instead that the speaker wants to make waiting more palatable while possibly indirectly hinting that the moment may actually turn out to be quite long.

Chilean Slang

Chilean Spanish has a multitude of words and expressions that are only used inside the country, or only a few of the neighboring countries. Many go back to the influence of the Quechua and Mapudungun languages spoken by the native population of the area.

The following list can only present a selection of the most common words and expressions. For many of them, there are further related words (e.g., *copucha – copuchear - copuchento*). We have tried to limit this list to true Chileanisms and regionalisms that are hard or impossible to find in common dictionaries. Exceptions are very popular expressions *(a pata, tomar el pelo)* that can be heard more widely among speakers of Spanish.

In general, we would advise you not to use those words actively – it's too easy to put your foot in your mouth. Often, the meaning of a word can depend greatly on tone or context, and it's almost impossible to get those right without much practice. The favorite Chilean swearword, *huevón*, can be intended to sound like a put-down, buddy-buddy, or a term of endearment, depending on the situation.

The majority of words and expressions listed are only used in informal communication. Extremely vulgar expressions have additionally been marked *.

Many more Chilean expressions, phrases and proverbs can be found in an excellent booklet by John Brennan and Alvaro Taboada, *How to Survive in the Chilean Jungle* (Dolmen Ediciones), which is available from Chilean bookstores. The authors would like to thank John Brennan for graciously giving permission to use some of his translations.

A

achuntar	hit the nail on the head, guess
agarrar	*literally:* grip
agarrar onda	get into (the swing of things)
agarrar papa	be keen on sth.; *also:* take advantage of
agarrar para el fideo/hueveo*	pull one's leg
ahí	*literally:* there
¡No estoy ni ahí!	I don't give a rip, I don't care.
ahuevonado/a*, el/la	idiot *(see 'huevón')*
al lote	low key, casual
al tiro	immediately
apretado/a	stingy
apretar cachete*	beat it
arrugar*	bail/flake out
atado, el	problem, difficult situation; argument
atadoso/a	complicated *(people and things)*; quarrelsome
atinar	do the right thing; get it

B

bacán	great, terrific *(people and things)*
bajón, el	bummer, crisis
El está bajoneado.	He's bummed.
bomba, la	gas station
pasarlo bomba	see 'pasarlo chancho'
bueno	OK
Bueno, iya!	Alright!
bueno para...	do something very often, be good at something
El es bueno para la pelea.	He likes to argue/to fight

C

cabro/a, el/la	boy/girl; young man/woman; guy
cabro/a chico/a	little boy/girl, kid
cachar	understand *(from 'catch')*
¿Cachai?	Get it?
Me pegué la cachada.	I got it.
cachetón/a, el/la	show-off
cacho, el	problem, difficult situation

Espérate un cachito.	Just a second!
cachureo, el	stuff, junk
caerse el cassette	spill the beans
Se le cayó el cassette.	He tattled on sth. (confidential)
cagada*, la	misfortune, mishap; disaster *(see also, 'crema')*
El dejó la cagada.	He wrecked everything.
cagado/a*	stingy; very; "fucked"
Estoy cagada de calor.*	I'm [very] hot.
El está cagado.*	He's in a fix.
cagar*	screw somebody, screw up
La cagaste.*	You screwed up.
ni cagando*	not under any circumstances, no way, never
cahuín, el	mess *(caused by misunderstandings or scheming)*
caleta	quite a lot, very
caleta de veces	very often
callampa, la	slum
Esto vale callampa.	It isn't worth diddly squat.
cana, la	jail
caña, la	hangover *(see also, 'hacha')*
Ando con la caña.	I'm hung over.
capo, el	expert; clever guy
cara de raja* / careraja*	impudent, rude
cara de palo / carepalo	impudent, rude
carrete, el	bash, party
combo, el	wallop
Le pegué un combo.	I shot him one.
compadre, el	buddy
concha, la*	vagina *(literally:* shell)
concha de tu madre* / conchetumadre*	son of a bitch, asshole; *also: general expression of anger*
concho, el	leftover, dregs *(esp. in a bottle)*
condoro, el	mistake
Se mandó un condoro grande.	He messed up big time.

coñete	stingy
copete, el	alcoholic beverage, liquor
copucha, la	rumor, gossip
correr mano (a alguien)	feel somebody up *(sexually motivated)*
cortar	*literally:* cut (off)
cortar el queque	have the say, decide *(literally, divide the cake up)*
¡Córtala!	Cut it out! Quit!
creerse la muerte / la raja	be stuck-up
crema, la	mess *(literally: cream)*
Quedó la crema.	It was a disaster. *(see also, 'escoba')*
cuero	figure *(of a man/woman)*
Ella tiene buen cuero.	She looks great.
cuete, el	joint
cuico/a	snob, upper class person *(derogatory)*
culeado/a*	fucker *(big insult)*
culear*	fuck
culo, el	butt, ass *(see also, 'poto')*
curado/a	drunk

CH

chacotero/a, el/la	joker, person who tries to be funny
chamullo, el	fib, lie *(see also, chiva)*
chancho, el	*literally:* pig
irse al chancho	exaggerate
pasarlo chancho	have a good time, enjoy
chapa, la	(door)lock; code name
chape, el	head
enfermo del chape	crazy *(see also, 'mate')*
chato/a	full
Estoy chato.	I've had it.
chiva, la	white lie, excuse *(see also, 'chamullo')*
chocho/a	content, proud, happy
choreado/a	angry, upset
Estoy choreado.	I'm ticked off.
choro/a	cool, neat *(people or things)*
chueco/a	dishonest, false
chucha*	vagina; *also: general expression of anger, see 'chuta'*
mandar a la chucha*(a alguien)	tell someone to go to hell

¡Andate a la chucha!*	Go to hell!
chupar	drink; steal
¡Chuta!*	Shit! *Also, expression of surprise*

D

dar bola* / dar pelota* (a alguien)	take sb. seriously, pay attention to sb.
descueve, el	excellent, hot, great
despelote, el	mess
desubicado/a, el/la	clueless; *someone who flaunts social rules or behaves improperly*
¡dónde la viste!	You're kidding! *(expression of disbelief)*

E

embarrarla	mess something up
La embarraste con el Pepe.	You've really ticked off Pepe.
encachado/a	great, interesting *(people or things)*
ene	lots *(from math symbol 'n')*
enfermo/a de...	totally ... *(literally: sick)*
El está enfermo de enamorado.	He's totally in love.
engrupir	smoothtalk, talk someone into something (with lies)
escoba, la	disaster, mess *(literally: broom)*
Ella dejó la escoba.	She messed up royally. *(see also, 'crema')*
estar en otra	be disinterested
El está en otra.	His head is someplace else.

F

facha, la	looks, appearance *(see also, 'pinta')*
filo	get lost; over
firme, la	truth
fome	boring
fregado/a	difficult; exhausted
frito/a	stuck, done for *(literally: fried)*

gallo/a, el/la — guy *(man or woman)*
gamba, la — 100 pesos
ganso/a — stupid, naive, slow
¡No seai ganso! — Don't be such an idiot!
gil, el — idiot
grado uno/dos/tres — *The "bases" of sexual relations: First base = Kissing; Second base = Petting; Third base = Coitus*
gringo/a, el/la — (blond/e) foreigner *(see p. 15)*
grosso — great, sweet
guagua, la — baby
guata, la — belly
guatón/a — fatso

hacer dedo — hitch-hike
hacer el quite
(a alguien) — avoid someone
hacerse el leso — pretend
hacer tira — destroy
hacer tuto — *see, 'tuto'*
hacer una vaca — go in on (buying sth.) *(literally: vaca = cow)*
hacha, el — hangover *(alcohol-induced; literally: axe; see also, 'caña')*
hinchar — get on s.o.'s nerves
huevada*, la — *anything, usually unpleasant*
hueveo*, el — practical joke
huevear* — get on s.o.'s nerves
huevón/a*, el/la — *depending on tone and context, can be friendly ("buddy") to vicious ("Idiot"); often at end of sentence indicating familiarity*

inflar — boast, get on s.o.'s nerves; take sb. into account

jalar — do drugs *(usually cocaine)*
jodido/a* — complicated
Estoy jodido. — I'm in trouble.
junior, el — gofer *(in an office)*

lanza, el — pickpocket
lata, la — boredom
¡Qué lata! — What a shame!
lesera, la — garbage
lolo/a, el/la — teen-ager
luca, la — 1000 pesos

macanudo — super *(archaic)*
maestro chasquilla — *Handiman who repairs everything, but nothing right*
mandar a la chucha* — *see, 'chucha'*
mate, el — head
enfermo del mate — mentally ill
medio/a — great, huge *(literally: half)*
¡La media mina! — A hot chick!
meter la pata — *see, 'pata'*
micro, la — city bus
miedo — *literally: fear*
de miedo — excellent, great
mijito/a — Dear *(from: 'mi hijito/a' = my little son/daughter)*
milico, el — Military personnel *(derogatory)*
mino/a, el/la — man / woman *(with erotic connotations)*
mino rico — hot guy
monono/a — dolled-up, chic, cute
mortal — dressed to kill; great *(see, 'muerte')*
mostrar la hilacha — reveal one's real self *(negative)*
movida, la — move, robbery; illegal deal; party
muerte, la — to die for; great
La comida era la muerte! — The food was to die for!

nana, la — cleaning woman, nanny, cook *(usually all in one)*
nana puertas adentro — live-in maid

once, la — "elevenses", tea time
onda, la — attitude; mood; kind of person; style *(see also, 'agarrar onda')*

Ella es buena onda.	She's nice.
¡Qué mala onda el tipo!	That guy is being such an idiot!

paco, el	pig *(derogatory for: policeman)*
papa, la	baby food; simple and lucrative deal
parranda, la	boozing
pasarse	outdo oneself; help *(appreciative)*
¡Te pasaste!	Great job (thank you)! *(see also, 'siete')*
pasarse rollo/película	imagine sth., make sth. up; dream of sth. *(literally: roll a movie)*
pata, la	*literally:* foot, leg
a pata	on foot
a pata pelada	barefoot
meter la pata	put your foot in (your mouth), mess up
mala pata	bad luck
patota, la	group of friends, followers
patudo/a	impudent, rude
pega, la	job, position
pelambre, el	gossip
pelar (a alguien)	gossip about a person, badmouth a person
pelar cable	lose it, act crazy; be mentally ill
pelotudo/a*	idiot
penca	cheap, boring
pendejo/a, el/la	childish person
picada, la	cheap (but good) place to eat
picarse	be mad, upset
pichanga, la	pick-up soccer game
pichintún	a little bit
pila	a lot of
pilas, las	*literally:* batteries
¡Ponte las pilas!	Go for it! Try harder!
pilucho/a	(half) naked
pillar (a alguien)	catch someone
pillo/a	clever, sharp; rude
pinta, la	looks, appearance *(see also, 'facha')*
Ella tiene buena pinta.	She's goodlooking.

pintar monos	to show off, to act exaggeratedly *(in order to call attention to oneself)*
piola	perfect; satisfied, full *(from eating)*; quiet, relaxed
Quédate piola.	Stay calm.
pasar piola	not call attention to oneself
pito, el	joint
pituto, el	connection *(to receive special treatment or privileges)*
plop	*expression of surprise or perplexity (from the Chilean comic strip 'Condorito')*
¡Quedé plop!	I was speechless.
po	*emphasis; usually placed at the end of a sentence (from: 'pues')*
¡Ya po!	Get going already!
pololo/a, el/la	boyfriend / girlfriend
pololear	go steady, to have a serious relationship with someone
ponerle color	exaggerate, embellish
ponerle pino/empeño	make one's best effort with something
ponerse las pilas	see, 'pilas'
porfa	please *(abbreviation of 'por favor')*
por las puras	in vain, for nothing
porsiaca	just in case; by the way *(from: 'por si acaso')*
poto, el	butt, bottom *(see also, 'queque')*
pucha, puta*	oops!, shucks!; *sympathy or regret for a bad turn of events (e.g., 'Pucha, Ricardo!')*
pucho, el	cigarette
putear* (alguien)	bawl somebody out, insult, yell at someone

queque, el	butt *(funny)*
cortar el queque	see, 'cortar'

raja*	beat, very tired
la raja	amazing, excellent
rajado/a	very fast
rayado/a	crazy, insane

rasca	of bad quality, poorly made *(things)*; of bad taste or with lacking manners *(people)*
re-	very *(emphatic prefix)*
Ella es re-simpática.	She's totally nice.
regio/a	great, excellent *(upper-class slang)*
regalonear	pamper someone; pet
requete	very *(see also, 're')*
rico/a	sexy, attractive *(literally: delicious)*
rollo, el	difficult situation *(see also, 'pasarse rollo')*
Se metió en un rollo.	He's in a fix.
roto/a	clumsy or vulgar or low class person *(upper class slang)*

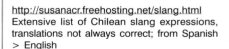

sacarse la mugre/ cresta	slave, work very hard
Me saqué la cresta.	I worked my fingers to the bone. *Also:* I took a beating. *(e.g. in an accident)*
Le sacaron la cresta.	They beat him up.
sepa Moya	Who knows!
siete, un	a 10; *expression of highest appreciation (from the Chilean school system, 7 = highest grade/ mark)*
Eres un siete.	Great job, thanks! *(see also, 'pasarse')*
siútico/a	stuck-up; in bad taste
sonar	fail, be very unsuccessful
Sonó nuestro plan.	Our plan failed / was nixed.
soplado/a	very fast; very simple; very clean
subirse por el chorro	(try to) take advantage of someone or something

taco, el	traffic jam
talla, la	joke
Le echamos una talla.	We pulled his leg.

tincar	guess, have a hunch; like
Me tinca que esto no va a funcionar.	I think that won't work.
¿Te tinca?	Do you like that? Do you agree?
tira, el	plainclothes policeman *(derogatory)*
tirar	*literally: throw, pull; also:* fuck
tirar a la chuña	be up for grabs, give away a lot of sth. *(e.g., money)*
tirar para arriba	overcome a difficult situation *(professional or social life, health)*
Está tirando p'arriba.	He's doing better.
tirar para la cola	bail/flake out
tiro al aire, un	loose cannon; unpredictable or aimless person
tomar el pelo (a alguien)	pull someone's leg
tuto, el	sleepiness *(cute)*
¿Vamos a hacer tuto?	Shall we go to sleep?
Todavía tengo tuto.	I'm still tired.

On the Internet

http://susanacr.freehosting.net/slang.html
Extensive list of Chilean slang expressions, translations not always correct; from Spanish > English

http://members.tripod.com/dichos/
Chilean Spanish Guide, an extensive glossary; Spanish > English

Addresses

Accommodation

Santiago

Residencial Santo Domingo, Santo Domingo 735, Stgo. Centro, Ph. (2) 639 67 33. Simple hostel in the center, US$ 7.00 p.p.

Hotel París, París 813, Stgo. Centro, Ph. (2) 664 09 21. The classic backpacker hostel in the center of Stgo., from US$ 10.00 p.p.

SCS Habitat, San Vicente 1798, Stgo. Centro, Ph. (2) 683 37 32, E-mail: scshabitat@yahoo.com. English speaking, great breakfast, good meeting point, 10 min. by bus from center, US$ 9.00 p.p.

Hostal Río Amazonas, Rosas 2234, Stgo. Centro, Ph.(2) 698 40 92, E-mail: amazona@entelchile.net, Web: www.altiro.com/amazonas. Colonial house close to the center, very friendly, double US$ 30.00

Hotel Monte Carlo, Victoria Subercaseaux 209, Stgo. Centro, Ph. (02) 633 55 77. Good location, modern rooms, friendly staff, double from US$ 40.00

Valparaíso

Casa Aventura, Pasaje Gálvez 11, Cerro Alegre, Ph. (32) 755 963, E-mail: casatur@ctcinternet.cl. Cosy place, English spoken, good information, excursions, US$ 9.00 p.p.

Villa Kunterbunt, Quebrada Verde 192, Playa Ancha, Ph. (32) 288 873. Laundry service, use of kitchen, US$ 10.00 p.p.

Viña del Mar

Residencial Blanchait, Av. Valparaíso 82-A, Ph. (32) 974 949. Friendly, clean, good service, from US$ 7.00 p.p.

Rancagua

Hotel Palace, Calvo 635, Ph. (72) 224 104. Simple, tiny rooms, near the railway station, double from US$ 15.00

Hotel España, San Martín 367, Ph. (72) 230 141. Old colonial building in the center, nice patio, double US$ 25.00

San Fernando

Imperio, Manuel Rodríguez 760, Ph. (72) 714 595. Hostel in the center, double from US$ 18.00

Curicó

Hotel Prat, Peña 427, Ph. (75) 311 069. Simple, clean, nice patio, 1 block from the plaza; from US$ 6.00 p.p.

El Capricho del Corazón, 35 km from Curicó (on the road to Hualañe), Ph. 09-753 46 96. Swiss-run guesthouse in the countryside, bed & breakfast US$ 12 .00 p.p.

Talca

Casa Chueca, Ph. (71) 197 00 96, 197 00 97, 09-837 14 40, E-mail: casachueca@hotmail.com, Web: www.trekkingchile.com. German/Austrian-run guesthouse 7 km outside Talca on Lircay River, bed & breakfast from US$ 10.00 p.p. *(see ad on last color page)*

Hospedaje Santa Margarita, near Pelarco, Ph. 09-3359051. Bed and breakfast in the countryside north of Talca, US$ 15.00 p.p.

Hotel Cordillera, 2 Sur 1360, Ph. (71) 221 817. Close to the center, good value, double from US$ 25.00

A

Addresses

Hotel Marcos Gamero, 1 Oriente 1070, Ph. (71) 223 100. Next to the main square, for those who seek more comfort, double US$ 50.00

Casas El Colorado, 46 km east of Talca, Ph. (71) 221 750. Close by Lake Colbún, colonial house, double from US$ 45.00

Constitución

Residencial Alameda, Av. Egaña 1120-A and Alameda 734, ph. (71) 671 896. Family-like, friendly, US$ 11.00 p.p.

Pelluhue (near Curanipe)

Casa Piedra, Ph. (73) 541 094. Nice location, close to the beach, US$ 10.00 p.p.

Cabañas Campomar, Ph. (73) 541 000, E-mail: campomar@ctcinternet.cl. Nice logcabins with ocean view, cabaña from US$ 30.00 (4 pers.)

Chillán

Hotel Claris, 18 de septiembre 357, Ph. (42) 221 980. 1 1/2 blocks from the plaza, clean, friendly, double from US$ 11.00

Complejo Turístico Rucahue, Las Trancas, 63 km from Chillán, Ph. (42) 239 863, Web: www.rucahuescalador.cl. Beautiful logcabins at the end of the paved road, US$ 50.00 (up to 7 pers.)

Youth Hostel Las Trancas, 63 km from Chillán, Ph. (42) 213 764. Nice rustic hostel with chimney room, from US$ 10.00 p.p.

Los Angeles

El Rincón, 16 km north of L.A., Ph. 09-4415019, E-mail: elrincon@cvmail.cl. German-run guesthouse in the country, bed & breakfast from US$ 10.00 *(see ad on p. 151)*.

Hotel Océano, Colo-Colo 327, Ph. (43) 342 432. Nice, clean, and close to the center, from US$ 10.00 p.p.

Andean Clubs

Santiago

Federación de Andinismo de Chile, Almirante Simpson 77, Providencia, Ph. (2) 222 08 88, Mon-Fri from 6 p.m., E-mail: contacto@feach.cl, Web: www.feach.cl

Club Aguila Azul, Almirante Simpson 3 of.102, Providencia, Ph. (2) 222 10 73, Meetings Wed 8 p.m., E-mail: caguilaazul@hotmail.com

Club Alemán Andino, Arrayán 2735, Providencia, Ph. (2) 232 43 38, Meetings Tue & Thu 8 p.m., E-mail: dav-chile@gruposyahoo.com

Club Wechupún, Almirante Simpson 77 p.3, Providencia, Web: www.wechupun.cl

Universidad de Chile / Rama de Montaña, E-mail: montanauch@hotmail.com, Web: www.montanauch.cl

Universidad Católica de Chile / Rama Montañis-mo, Web: www.makalu.cl

Universidad de Santiago (USACH) / Rama Andinismo, E-mail: ramausach@karakorum.cl, Web: www.karakorum.cl/rama

Valparaíso

Club Andino Valparaíso, Condell 1530, piso 4, of. 49, Ph. (32) 214 807, E-mail: andinovalparaiso@hotmail.com

Viña del Mar

Universidad Técnica F. Santa María / Club de Montaña, E-mail: patoji@elo.utfsm.cl, Web: www.defider.utfsm.cl/montana/

Rancagua

Club Andino Rancagua, Ph. (72) 292 78 (Luis Concha), E-mail: andinorancagua@hotmail.com, Web: www.geocities.com/andinorancagua

Talca

Universidad de Talca / Club de Escalada Deportiva, Web: www.geocities.com/e_deportiva/

Chillán

Club Andino Nevados de Chillán, Ph. (42) 226 266, E-mail: esca@entelchile.net, Web: http://habitantes.elsitio.com/nevados

Concepción

Universidad de Concepción / Rama Andinismo, Ph. (41) 204 482, E-mail: rauc@udec.cl, Web: www.udec.cl/rauc

Birdwatching

Unión de Ornitólogos de Chile (UNORCH), Av. Providencia 1108 of. 32, Santiago, Ph. (2) 236 81 78

Helmut Seeger, Cauquenes, Ph. (73) 512 274

Car Rental

Santiago

LyS, Miraflores 541, Stgo. Centro, Ph. (2) 633 76 00, E-Mail: rent@lys.cl

Seelmann, Las Encinas 3057, Ñuñoa, Ph. (2) 239 88 49, E-mail: seelmann@netline.cl

Costanera, Av. Andrés Bello 1255, Providencia, Ph. (2) 235 78 35, E-mail: costanera2000@yahoo.com

Avis, Ph. (toll free) 600-601 99 66, E-mail: reservas@avischile.cl

Chilean Embassies abroad

Australia

10 Culgoa Circuit, O'malley Act 2606, Canberra; Ph. (2) 628 624 30, E-mail: chilemb@embachileaustralia.com, Web: www.embachile-australia.com
Other consulates in Melbourne and Sidney

Canada

50 O'Connor Street, Suite 1413, Ottawa, Ontario K1P-6L2; Ph. (613) 235 44 02, E-mail: echileca@embachile-canada.com, Web: www.chile.ca
Other consulates in Montreal, Toronto and Vancouver

Great Britain

12 Devonshire Street, London W1G 7DS; Ph. (20) 758 063 92, E-mail: echileuk@echileuk.demon.co.uk

New Zealand

1-3 Willeston St., Willis Corroon House, 7th. Floor, P.O. Box 3861, Wellington; Ph. (4) 471 62 70, E-mail: echile@embchile.co.nz, Web: www.prochinz.co.nz

USA

1732 Massachusetts Avenue NW, Washington, D.C. 20036; Ph. (202) 785 17 46 or 530 41 14, E-mail : embassy@embassyofchile.org, Web: www.chile-usa.org.
Other consulates in: New York, Philadelphia, Miami, Chicago, Houston, San Francisco, Los Angeles, San Juan de Puerto Rico

Cybercafés

Santiago

Sonnets: Londres 43, of. 11 (Metro U. de Chile), Ph: (2) 664 47 25, E-mail: sonnets@operamail.com

Dazoca, Monjitas 448 (Metro Bellas Artes), Ph. (2) 633 93 77, E-mail: dazoca@yahoo.com

InternetCAFE, Av.Providencia 1370-A, 2nd floor (Metro Manuel Montt), Ph. (2) 264 98 66, E-mail: dazoca@yahoo.com

Phonet, General Holley 2312 (Metro Los Leones), Ph. (2) 335 61 06 , E-mail: cafephonet@hotmail.com

Cybercenter, General Holley 190 (Metro Los Leones), Ph. (2) 233 43 64 , E-mail: info@cybercenter.cl

Valparaíso

cerro.net, Papudo 526 (Cerro Concepción), Ph. (32) 252 694, E-mail: cerronet@hotmail.com

login.cl, Cóndell 1195, Ph. (32) 595 830, E-mail: login@login.cl

Viña del Mar

Phonet, Av. Valparaíso 651 loc 18-19 (Galeria Florida). Ph. (32) 692 105, E-mail: cafephonet@hotmail.com

ruevalparaiso, Av. Valparaiso 286, Ph. (32) 710 140, E-mail: 286@ruevalparaiso.zzn.com

Talca

Networks, 7 Oriente 1180, Ph. (71) 241 669, E-mail: networks@dnsmail.nworks.cl

Chillán

Gateway Informática, Libertad 360-B, Ph. (42) 238 855 , E-mail: gateway3@chilesat.net

Concepción

Cyber Café Concepción, Caupolicán 563, 2nd floor, Ph. (41) 253 992; also in: Portales 530 / Barros Arana 541 / Caupolicán 580

Environment

Comité Nacional pro Defensa de la Fauna y la Flora (CODEFF)
Santiago: Luis Uribe 2620, Ñuñoa, Ph. (2) 274 74 31, E-mail: secretaria@codeff.cl
Talca: Ph. (71) 223 893, E-mail: codeff.maule@terra.cl

Defensores del Bosque Chileno, Diagonal Oriente 1413, Ñuñoa, Santiago, Ph. (2) 204 19 14, E-mail: bosquech@entelchile.net

WWF, Temuco, David Tecklin, Ph. (45) 647 562, dtecklin@telsur.cl; Coordinator, Eco-Region Chilean Rainforests

Equipment Stores (Stgo.)

Trekking & Climbing

Al Sur, Calle Arzobispo 0637, Providencia, Ph. (2) 732 34 37, E-mail: alsur2000@yahoo.es; Climbing and trekking outfitter, international brands

Andesgear, www.andesgear.cl, Ph. 09-219 10 74, E-mail: consultas@andesgear.cl; Shop online for a vast selection of mountain climbing gear, with delivery service in Chile; in Spanish

Dako Sports, Av. Las Condes 9038, Las Condes, Ph. (2) 212 99 01; Trekking and climbing equipment

Doite, Av. Américo Vespucio 1670, Quilicura, Ph. (2) 603 78 73; Outlet of the Chilean manufacturer of camping and outdoor equipment

Hama, Compañía 1068, of. 1000, Stgo. Centro, Ph. (2) 671 36 61; Imported climbing accessories such as ropes, quickdraws, bolts, boots, etc.

Lippi, Av. Italia 1586, Ñuñoa, Ph. (2) 225 68 03; Clothing, backpacks, fleece, sleeping bags from their own production, reasonable prices

Lucci Montaña, Av. Providencia 2198 local 14 (Portal Lyon), Providencia, Ph. (2) 232 47 70; Technical mountaineering equipment

Patagonia, Helvecia 210, Las Condes, Ph. (2) 3351796, E-mail: patagoni@entelchile.net; Outdoor clothing of all kind, helpful

Mountain Biking

There are numerous bike shops in Santiago, and many of them do repairs and sell parts. When you encounter problems, we recommend you check the Yellow Pages under 'Bicicletas' for stores that carry your brand. Several big stores are concentrated along Avenida Vitacura, but the "bicycle street" San Diego (900 Block) in the southern center of the city is a better bet for cheap parts.

Surfing & Windsurfing

Hyperborea, Av. Cuarto Centenario 596, Las Condes, Ph. (2) 342 19 00

Nauti-Sport, Av. Las Condes 8606, Las Condes, Ph. (2) 211 43 78, E-mail: nautisport@entelchile.net

Windsurfing Chile, Las Carmelitas 30, Las Condes, Ph. (2) 211 19 59, E-mail: info@windsurfingchile.com *(see ad on p. 178)*

Diving

Christian Chappuzeau, Av. Francisco Bilbao 873, Providencia, Ph. (2) 204 36 61, E-mail: seawolfsub@entelchile.net

Cressi-sub, Av. Padre Hurtado 1549, Vitacura, Ph. (2) 201 37 66 *(see ad on p. 187)*

Scubapro, Av. Cristóbal Colón 5328, Las Condes, Ph. (2) 202 36 80

Paragliding

Genesis, Augusto Olivares, Ph. (2) 321 53 33, 09-537 54 41; International brands, repair service

Foreign Embassies in Santiago

Australia

Gertrudis Echeñique 420, Las Condes (Metro Alcántara); Ph. (2) 228 50 65

Canada

Nueva Tajamar 481 Torre Norte, piso 12, Las Condes (Metro Tobalaba); Ph. (2) 362 96 60

Great Britain

Av. El Bosque Norte 0125, Las Condes (Metro Tobalaba); Ph. (2) 370 41 00

New Zealand

El Golf 99 of. 703, Las Condes (Metro El Golf); Ph. (2) 290 98 02

USA

Av. Andrés Bello 2800, Las Condes (Metro Tobalaba); Ph. (2) 232 26 00

Indoor Climbing Wall

Climbing Planet, Av. Condell 703, Providencia (Metro Bustamante), Santiago; Ph. (2) 634 63 91, Web: www.climbingplanet.cl. Mon-Fri Noon - 10 p.m., Sat 10 a.m. – 8 p.m., Sun Noon – 8 p.m. 800 sq.m. of climbing walls, classes, equipment rentals; Prices: US$ 3.30 to 5.00 (5 hrs.), discounts for students

Minibus with Driver

Turismo Arpué, Stgo., Ph. (2) 211 71 65

Manzur Expediciones, Ph. (2) 643 56 51

Héctor Mondaca, Talca, Ph. (71) 245 334

Juan Pablo Salinas, Talca, Ph. 09-451 66 04

Mountain Guides
See also: Andean Clubs

Leonardo Cáceres, Talca; Ph. 09-892 36 25

Carlos Chacón, Talca; Ph. 09-639 59 76

Greensight, Parral, Ph. (73) 491 904, E-mail: greensight@latinmail.com

Ski Areas
See also p. 195

Portillo, Renato Sánchez 4270, Las Condes, Stgo., Ph. (2) 263-0606, Toll free from U.S. 800-829 5325; Hotel: Ph. (2) 243-3007, E-mail: info@skiportillo.com, Web: www.skiportillo.cl

La Parva, La Concepción 266, of. 301, Providencia, Stgo., Ph. (2), 264 14 66, E-mail: skilaparva@skilaparva.cl, Web: www.laparva.cl

Colorado-Farellones, Apoquindo 4900 (Edificio Omnium), Las Condes, Stgo., Ph. (2) 246 3344, E-mail: ski-colorado@ctcinternet.cl

Valle Nevado, Gertrudis Echeñique 441, Las Condes, Stgo., Ph. (2) 206 00 27, Web: www.vallenevado.cl

Lagunillas, Club Andino de Chile, Alameda 108 local 126, Stgo. Centro, Ph. (2) 638 04 97, E-mail: reservas@skilagunillas.cl, Web: www.lagunillas.cl

Chapa Verde, Rancagua, Ph. (72) 217 651, E-mail: chapaverde@entelchile.net, Web: www.chapaverde.cl

Termas de Chillán, Av. Providencia 2237, Loc. P-41, Providencia, Stgo., Ph. (2) 233 13 13; Chillán: Ph. (42) 223 887, E-mail: ventas@termaschillan.cl, Web: www.termaschillan.cl

Soaring Clubs

Club de Planeadores de Santiago, Av. Santa María 6100, Vitacura, Ph. (2) 218 41 09 or 218 81 71, Web: http://planeadores.sofytec.cl

Club Aéreo de Talca, Ph. (71) 233 266

Spanish Courses

Violeta Parra, Ernesto Pinto Lagarrigue 362-A, Bellavista, Stgo., Ph. (2) 229 82 46

Bellavista, Crucero Exeter 0325, Bellavista, Stgo., Ph. (2) 737 51 02, E-mail: fdo@cib.in.cl

Casa Chueca, Talca, *see Accommodation*

El Rincón, Los Angeles, *see Accommodation*

Thermal Spas
See also p. 194

Termas El Corazón, 100 km north of Stgo., Ph. (2) 236 36 36, (34) 482 852

Termas de Cauquenes, 35 km east of Rancagua, Ph. (2) 638 16 10, (72) 899 010

Termas de Quinamávida, 16 km east of Linares, Ph. (73) 213 887

Termas de Panimávida, 20 km east of Linares, Ph. (2) 639 39 11, (73) 211 743

Termas de Catillo, 26 km east of Parral, Ph. (73) 461 111. Nice setting with hikes in the surrounding area, from US$ 50.00 p.p. full board

Termas de Chillán *see Ski areas*

A

Addresses

Tour Operators

Agrotourism

Red Turismo Rural, Vilches, Ph. (71) 210 611. Camping, horseback riding and excursions.

Ecotours, Pelarco, Ph. (71) 197 12 30, 09-246 17 23. Meet local farmers and learn about their lives, customs, and products.

Diving

See Equipment Stores

Fly Fishing

Iván Castro, Talca, Ph. (71) 213431, E-mail: ficastro@chilesat.net

Viento Puelche, San Clemente, Ph. (71) 221 953, 09-324 66 68. Fly fishing and excursions in the Talca region.

Horseback Riding

Cascada Expediciones, Orrego Luco 040, Providencia, Stgo., Ph. (2) 234 22 74, Web: www.cascada-expediciones.com

La Ermita, Therese Matthews, Camino a Farellones km 11, Stgo., Ph. (2) 242 62 15, 09-221 78 81

Rutarriera, Radal Siete Tazas, Ph. (2) 554 91 39, 09-432 60 17, E-mail: rutarrie@netexpress.cl

Don Eladio, Reserva Nacional Vilches, Ph. 09-341 80 64

Hotel Melado, Reserva Nacional Los Bellotos, Ph. (2) 353 10 00

Mary Seppi, east from Linares, E-mail: mseppi@SCLSU.edu

Danilo "El Pollo" Contreras, Rari, Ph. 09-266 92 46

Kayaking / Rafting

KayaKing, Stgo., Ivo Simon, Ph. (2) 274 25 15, Web: www.kayak-chile.com *(see ad on p. 169)*

Turismo 7 Ríos, Talca, Ph. (71) 210 611, 09-795 03 72, E-mail: tour7rios@mixmail.com *(see ad on p. 169)*

Cascada Expediciones, *see Horseback Riding*

Motorcycle Rentals

Roland Spaarwater, Av. Ecuador 275, Chillán, Ph. (42) 231592, E-mail: ktm@ktmchile.cl, Web: www.ktmchile.cl

Mountain Biking

Pared Sur, Pablo Sepúlveda; Juan Esteban Montero 5497, Las Condes, Stgo.; Ph. (2) 207 35 25, E-mail: paredsur@paredsur.cl, Web: www.paredsur.cl *(see ad on p. 167)*

Nature & Adventure

Turismo Caminante, Talca, Ph. 09-837 14 40, (71) 197 00 97 or 197 00 96, E-mail: turismocaminante@hotmail.com, Web: www.trekkingchile.com *(see ad on p. 131)*.

Senderos Chile Expediciones, Los Angeles, Ph. (09) 714 39 58, (09) 833 38 35, E-mail: senderoschile@mixmail.com

Paragliding

Genesis, Stgo., Augusto Olivares, Ph. (2) 321 53 33, 09-5375441, E-mail: genparap@ parapenteonline.cl, Web: www.parapenteonline.cl

Andes Flying School, Fray Angélico 127, Las Condes, Stgo., Ph. (2) 201 16 71, E-mail: afschool@chilesat.net

Trekking

See Nature & Adventure

Windsurfing

Chile Adventours, Nicolás Catel, Stgo., Ph. 09-345 68 83, Web: www.chileadventours.com

Wine Tourism

Ruta del Vino Valle del Maule, San Javier, Ph. (73) 323 657, E-mail: wineroute@entelchile.net *(see ad on jacket flap)*

See also: *Vineyards*

Tourist Information (Sernatur)

See also: *Websites on Travel in Chile*

Santiago: Av. Providencia 1550, Providencia (Metro: Manuel Montt), Ph. (2) 731 83 36, 731 83 37, open Mon-Fri 9.30 a.m. to 8 p.m., Sat 9.30 a.m. to 6.30 p.m., E-mail: sernatur_stgo@entelchile.net; also at the International Airport

Viña del Mar: Av. Valparaíso 507 of. 305, Ph. (32) 882 285, E-mail: sernatur_valpso@entelchile.net

Rancagua: Germán Riesco 277, Ph. (72) 230413, E-mail: sernatur_rancag@entelchile.net

Talca: 1 Poniente 1281, Ph. (71) 233 669, E-mail: sernatur_talca@entelchile.net

Concepción: Aníbal Pinto 460, Ph. (41) 227 976, E-mail: sernatur_concep@entelchile.net

Vineyards

Note: Most vineyards require prior reservations by phone for tours.
See also p. 196

Ruta del Vino Valle del Maule, San Javier, Ph. (73) 323 657, E-mail: wineroute@entelchile.net; organizes tours and tastings in a dozen vineyards in the Maule region

Balduzzi, Av. Balmaceda 1189, San Javier (near Talca), Ph. (73) 32 21 38, E-mail: balduzzi@entelchile.net

Casa Donoso, near Talca, Ph. (71) 242 506, Web: www.casadonoso.cl

Calina, Camino Las Rastras km 7, near Talca, Ph. (71) 263 126

Concha y Toro, Virginia Subercaseaux 210, Pirque, Ph. (2) 821 70 69. Tours in English Mon-Fri 11.30 a.m. and 3 p.m., Sat. 11 a.m.

Cousiño Macul, Av. Quilín 7100, Stgo., Ph. (2) 284 10 11. Mon-Fri 11 a.m.

Errázuriz, Panquehue near San Felipe, Ph. (2) 203 66 88

Miguel Torres, Curicó, Panamericana km 195, Ph. (75) 310 455, Mon-Fri 9 a.m. to 12.30 p.m. and 2 to 5.30 p.m.

Santa Inés, Isla de Maipo, Ph. (2) 819 20 62, E-mail: vinoteca@demartino.cl, Mon-Fri: 10.30 a.m. to 1.30 p.m., 3 p.m. to 6.30 p.m., Sat. 10.30 a.m. to 1.30 p.m.

Santa Rita, Alto Jahuel, Buin. Ph. (2) 821 27 07.

Undurraga, Santa Ana (near Talagante), Camino a Melipilla km 34, Ph. (2) 817 23 08. Mon-Fri 9.30 a.m. to 4 p.m., Sat 10 a.m.

Websites on Travel in Chile

www.absolutechile.com
Hotels, transfers, tours, car rentals from a Santiago company; in English

http://away.com/chile/index.adp
The british travel portal with modest descriptions for Chile; in English

www.backpackersbest.cl
Selected places for backpackers in all of Chile, good value, with lots of details and prices; in English, German, and Spanish

www.backpackerschile.com
Backpacker accommodations between La Serena and Punta Arenas; in English

www.chile.com
Chile portal with modest information, not very user-friendly; very little in English

www.chile-hotels.com
500 hotels, car rentals companies, tours; general info and reservations; in English

www.chiptravel.cl
Good Chile portal, laid out by regions and topics; in English

www.gochile.cl
Most-visited tourism portal in Chile, good overview of the most important destinations and things to do; in English and Spanish

www.gorp.com/gorp/location/latamer/chile/top_twenty.htm
Top 20 adventure tours in Chile from the US outdoor portal, with commercial tours; in English

www.lonelyplanet.com/destinations/south_america/chile_and_easter_island/
General, but not very comprehensive, info on the country; in English

www.terramagica.com
Latin American travel portal with very good information about Chile; in English and Spanish

Index

PLEASE NOTE: All place names are listed in their Spanish version. Place names starting with an article in Spanish (El, La, Las, Los) can be found under their actual name; e.g., Las Chilcas will be found under ,C'. The same is true for rivers, mountains and volcanoes: Río Aconcagua goes under ,A'.

S = Sidebar

Index

Index

233

Index

Sources of Information Used

Albrecht, Volker et al.: Alpin-Lehrplan 9, Verlagsgesellschaft BLV 1983

Araya, Braulio / **Millie**, Guillermo: Guía de campo de las aves de Chile, Editorial Universitaria 1986

Calvin, William H.: Der Strom, der bergauf fließt, dtv 1997

Decker, Barbara und Robert: Vulkane, Spektrum Akademischer Verlag 1992

De la Vega, Santiago: Patagonia - Las leyes del bosque, Edición Contacto Silvestre, 1999

González-Ferrán, Oscar: Volcanes de Chile, Instituto Geográfico Militar 1994

Grau, Jürke / **Zizka**, Georg (eds.): Pflanzenwelt Chiles, Palmengarten Sonderheft 19, 1992

Hawking, Stephen W.: Die Suche nach der Urkraft des Universums, Rowohlt 1995

Hoffmann, Adriana: Flora silvestre de Chile, zona central / zona araucana, Ediciones Fundación Claudio Gay 1989 / 1997

Hoffmann, Adriana et al., Plantas Altoandinas en la Flora Silvestre de Chile, Ediciones Fundación Claudio Gay 1998

Hoffmann, Adriana et al.: Enciclopedia de los Bosques Chilenos, Colección Voces del Bosque, Defensores del Bosque Chileno 2000

La tierra en que vivimos, Editorial Antárctica 1983

Maran, Stephan P.: Astronomie für Dummies, MITP-Verlag 1999

Más Rutas, Trekking / Mountain Bike Chile 2000, Latitud 90 Limitada 1999

Natur Magazin, Dec. 1996

Oyarzún, Gastón: Chile - Los Andes, Editorial Kactus 1987

Plath, Oreste: Geografía del mito y la leyenda chilenos, Editorial Grijalbo 1994

Plath, Oreste: Folclor chileno, Editorial Grijalbo 1994

Raab, Peter: Naturlust, Verlag Herder 1996

Steffen, Dr. Hans: Patagonia Occidental, Edicion de la Universidad de Chile 1944

Spektrum der Wissenschaft, Dec. 1992

Stecker, Bernd: Ökotourismus, GTZ GmbH 1996

Trefil, James: Physik in der Berghütte, rororo 1997

Trekking- und Expeditionsmedizin, Gesellschaft für Alpin- und Höhenmedizin

Turistel, Turismo y Comunicaciones S.A. 1996 / 1997

Acknowledgements

Our special thanks go to our translator, **Teresa Reinhardt**, whose patient feedback and guidance on matters not only of fact, but also of intercultural sensitivity have made a substantial difference in the success of this book.

In their own special ways, our partners **Kathrein Splett** and **Rossana Vidal** proved indispensable. They supported us every step of the way with their advice and assistance.

We also owe big "Thank-you's" to **Rafael Parada**, whose creative mind, never-ending patience and countless hours of overtime produced the layout of this book, as well as to our drawing artists **Peter Splett** (cartoons) and **Leonardo Cáceres** (trail sketches).

A great number of people have contributed to this book by providing information or comments, permission to use illustrations, or marketing efforts. We would like to thank especially the following:

Rodrigo Barrionuevo
Mariano Bernal
Pablo Besser
Hannes Beth
John Brennan
Dr. Ariel Camousseight,
    Museo de Historia Natural
Julio Castiglione
Flor Concha, CITUC
Jaime Cordero, Dolmen Ediciones
Alfredo Escobar
Marcus Franken
Rodrigo Fuenzalida, Cressi-sub
Javier Garretón, Hiperboria
Fernando Gómez
Meike Grundmann, Cascada Expediciones
Patrick Hill
Adriana Hoffmann
Sven Olsson-Iriarte

José Pablo Jofré
Peter Krinner
Hugo Méndez
Paula Navarro, Museo de Historia Natural
Augusto Olivares, Escuela de Parapente
    Génesis
Johannes Reitter
Julio Saavedra
Peter Schmid Anwandter
Alexander Schneider
Claudio Seebach
Pablo Sepúlveda, Pared Sur
Horst und Ivo Simon
Martina Stich
Diego Tirado, Windsurfing Chile
Patricia Vera, Defensores del Bosque Chileno
Iván Witker
José Yáñez, Museo de Historia Natural

Maps & GPS Data

PLEASE NOTE: Maps shown in this book were submitted for government review and permission. They may differ from the description in the text and from maps published in other countries. For the recording of GPS data, the modern WGS 84 (World Geodetic System) with its degrees and minutes format for positions was used. The Chilean maps in this book, however, are based on the 1956 Canoa system resulting in major deviations in some cases. Our GPS data should not be transferred directly onto the maps; it is only meant for your orientation during the hike.

Data collection

For the purpose of improving and expanding this book, we would like to ask other outdoor enthusiasts for help. Please write to us with your suggestions, experiences, and GPS data – those following in your tracks will be grateful! E-mail us at turismocaminante@hotmail.com (Franz Schubert) or malte@contactchile.cl (Malte Sieber).

Descabezado Grande volcano at dawn

At the crater of Descabezado

Despalmado waterfalls on the way to Descabezado

Photo Gallery

Laguna Teno on the Peteroa – Azufre ascent

Boiling sulphuric acid in the crater of Peteroa

Franz Schubert

Arrieros never walk

Huasos have a lot of time

Malte Sieber

Nothofagus forest in the Fall

Matie Sieber

Tupungato volcano from the south-west

Crossing Azufre river on our way to Tupungato

On our way back from Cerro El Plomo

Pablo Sepúlveda

Matte Sieber

View of Melado Valley in the fall

Refreshing bath in Laguna Canelo

Franz Schubert

Malte Sieber

This is what keeps the Andes green

Mountain lagoon at the foot of San Pedro volcano

Franz Schubert

At the summit of Nevado de Chillán

On horseback in the forests near Termas de Chillán

The "elephant's legs" of Chilean palms in Ocoa

Edelweis

Tropaeolum

Espino

Chilco

Estrellita

Nassauvia

Avellano

Alstroemeria

Schizanthus

Chagual

Nastanthus

Quisco

A selection of Central Chile's flora

Franz Schubert / Malte Sieber

Franz Schubert

Occasionally, guanaco herds cross the border from Argentina

A very rare sight: the Andean deer huemul

Malte Sieber

The Chilean flamingo shows red and black in flight only

The hummingbird likes tasty blossoms

The Humboldt penguin has one stripe, his Magellanic cousin two

Don't mess with a fur seal!

Photo Gallery

Ice climbing at Cerro Negro

Pablo Sepúlveda

In the saddle near Quintay

Worth the effort: view of Cerro El Plomo

Pablo Sepúlveda

Rafting on Río Corel

Not recommended for beginners

Catching the tubes of the Pacific

At La Sirena beach near Curanipe

Diego Tirado

The Putú dunes near Constitución

At the rocky beach of Constitución

The bay of Valparaíso and Viña del Mar

Chile's most picturesque market in Chillán

Selling fresh fish at Caleta Duao